Research & Education Association

The Best Teachers' Test Preparation for the

PRAXIS II®
Elementary Education:
Content Knowledge (0014)

Shannon Grey, Ed.D.
Associate Professor
Princeton University, Princeton, N.J.

Anita Price Davis, Ed.D.
Professor Emerita
Converse College, Spartanburg, S.C.

Visit our Educator Support Center at:
www.REA.com/teacher

The competencies presented in this book were created and implemented by Educational Testing Service. For individual state requirements, consult your state education agency. For further information visit the PRAXIS website at www.ets.org.

PRAXIS II® and The PRAXIS Series™ are trademarks of ETS®.

Research & Education Association
61 Ethel Road West
Piscataway, New Jersey 08854
E-mail: info@rea.com

The Best Teachers' Test Preparation for the Praxis II® Elementary Education: Content Knowledge (0014)

Printed in the United States of America

Library of Congress Control Number 2008932815

ISBN-13: 978-0-7386-0400-8
ISBN-10: 0-7386-0400-3

 REA® is a registered trademark of Research & Education Association, Inc.

About Research & Education Association

Founded in 1959, Research & Education Association is dedicated to publishing the finest and most effective educational materials—including software, study guides, and test preps—for students in middle school, high school, college, graduate school, and beyond.

REA's Test Preparation series includes books and software for all academic levels in almost all disciplines. Research & Education Association publishes test preps for students who have not yet entered high school, as well as for high school students preparing to enter college. Students from countries around the world seeking to attend college in the United States will find the assistance they need in REA's publications. For college students seeking advanced degrees, REA publishes test preps for many major graduate school admission examinations in a wide variety of disciplines, including engineering, law, and medicine. Students at every level, in every field, with every ambition can find what they are looking for among REA's publications.

REA's practice tests are always based upon the most recently administered exams and include every type of question that you can expect on the actual exams.

REA's publications and educational materials are highly regarded and continually receive an unprecedented amount of praise from professionals, instructors, librarians, parents, and students. Our authors are as diverse as the fields represented in the books we publish. They are well-known in their respective disciplines and serve on the faculties of prestigious high schools, colleges, and universities throughout the United States and Canada.

Today, REA's wide-ranging catalog is a leading resource for teachers, students, and professionals.

We invite you to visit us at *www.rea.com* to find out how "REA is making the world smarter."

Acknowledgments

We would like to thank Larry Kling, Vice President, Editorial, for his editorial direction; Pam Weston, Vice President, Publishing, for setting the quality standards for production integrity and managing the publication to completion; Alice Leonard, Senior Editor, and Kathleen Casey, Senior Editor, for project management and preflight editorial review; Diane Goldschmidt, Senior Editor, for post-production quality assurance; Christine Saul, Senior Graphic Artist, for cover design; Rachel DiMatteo, Graphic Artist, for test design; and Jeff LoBalbo, Senior Graphic Artist, for post-production file mapping.

We also gratefully acknowledge Marianne L'Abbate for copyediting, Kathy Caratozzolo for typesetting, Ellen Gong for proofreading, and Terry Casey for indexing the manuscript.

About the Authors

Dr. Shannon Grey has had a successful career in education for over sixteen years. Dr. Grey graduated with honors with a B.S. in Early Childhood Development from New York University. She received her Master of Education degree from Rutgers, The State University of New Jersey's Graduate School of Education, with a specialization in Elementary Language Arts. Dr. Grey earned her Ed.D. from Rutgers in the area of Sociological and Philosophical Foundations of Education, specializing in Curriculum Theory and Development.

Dr. Grey taught elementary school for thirteen years in highly acclaimed public schools. During her time as a teacher she served as a mentor for novice educators, staff developer, and chairperson for several school-based and district-wide committees. Dr. Grey was also the co-creator of a summer institute aimed at instructing students in the areas of language arts and mathematics. As a faculty lecturer, she has taught classes in teacher education at Rutgers University. Currently Dr. Grey teaches and supervises student teachers for Princeton University's Program in Teacher Preparation.

Dr. Anita Price Davis is The Charles Dana Professor Emerita of Education and was the Director of Elementary Education at Converse College, Spartanburg, South Carolina. Dr. Davis earned her B.S. and M.A. from Appalachian State University and her doctorate from Duke University. She also received a postdoctoral fellowship to Ohio State University for two additional years of study.

Dr. Davis had worked more than 36 years at Converse College, where she served as the faculty advisor for Kappa Delta Epsilon, a national education honor organization. She also worked 5 years as a public school teacher.

Dr. Davis has received wide recognition for her work, including a letter of appreciation from the U.S. Department of the Interior, inclusion in Contemporary Authors, and a citation of appreciation from the Michigan Council of the Social Studies. She has authored/coauthored 23 funded grants for Converse College. She has served as a mentor and was a two-time President of the Spartanburg County Council of the International Reading Association. The state of South Carolina twice named her an outstanding educator, and she was twice a nominee for the CASE U.S. Professor of the Year.

Dr. Davis has authored, co-authored, and edited more than 80 books. She has written two college textbooks titled Reading Instruction Essentials and Children's Literature Essentials. Dr. Davis has published several history books and is also the author of more than 80 papers, book reviews, journal articles, and encyclopedia entries.

CONTENTS

CHAPTER 5
SCIENCE 169

PRACTICE TEST 1 189

PRACTICE TEST 2 235

INDEX 281

Introduction

ABOUT THIS BOOK

If you're looking to secure certification as an elementary teacher, you'll find that many states require the Praxis II: Elementary Education: Content Knowledge (0014) test. Think of this book as your toolkit to pass the test.

Deciding to pursue a teaching career already speaks volumes about you. You would not have gotten to this point without being highly motivated and able to synthesize considerable amounts of information.

But, of course, it's a different matter when you have to show what you know on a test. That's where we come in. We're here to help take the mystery and anxiety out of the process. We're here to equip you not only with the nuts and bolts, but, ultimately, the confidence to succeed alongside your peers across the United States.

We've put a lot of thinking into this, and the result is a book that pulls together all the critical information you need to know to pass the Praxis Elementary Education 0014 Test.

Let us help you fill in the blanks—literally and figuratively!—while providing you with the touchstones that will allow you to do your very best come test day and beyond.

In this guide, REA offers our customarily in-depth, up-to-date, objective coverage, with test-specific modules devoted to targeted review and realistic practice exams complete with the kind of detail that makes a difference when you're coming down the homestretch in your preparation. We also include a quick-view answer key and competency-categorized progress chart to enable you to pinpoint your strengths and weaknesses.

ABOUT THE PRAXIS SERIES

Praxis is the Educational Testing Service's (ETS) shorthand for Professional Assessments for Beginning Teachers. The Praxis Series is a group of teacher licensing tests that ETS developed in concert with states across the nation. There are three categories of tests in the series: Praxis I, Praxis II and Praxis III. Praxis I includes the paper-based Pre-Professional Skills Tests (PPST) and the Praxis I Computer-Based Tests (CBT). Both versions cover essentially the same subject matter. These exams measure reading, mathematics, and writing skills and are often a requirement for admission to a teacher education program. Praxis II embraces Subject Assessment/Specialty Area Tests, including the Praxis II Elementary Education series, of which the Praxis II 0014 exam is a part. The Praxis II examinations cover the subject matter that students typically study in teacher education courses such content as human growth and development, school curriculum, methods of teaching, and other professional development courses. In most teacher-training programs, students take these tests after having completed their classroom training, the course work, and practicum. Praxis III is different from the multiple-choice and essay tests typically used for assessment purposes. With this assessment, ETS-trained observers evaluate an instructor's performance in the classroom, using nationally validated criteria. The observers may videotape the lesson, and other teaching experts may critique the resulting tapes.

The Praxis II 0014 covers the content areas of reading and language arts, mathematics, science, and social studies. This study guide will deal with each of these broader content areas and, with the subareas such as is found in Social Studies.

Who Takes the Test?

Most people who take the Praxis II 0014 are seeking initial licensure. You should check with your state's education agency to determine which Praxis examination(s) you should take; the ETS Praxis website (*www.ets.org/praxis/*) and registration bulletin may also help you determine the test(s) you need to take for certification. You should also consult your education program for its own test requirements. Remember that colleges and universities often require Praxis examinations for entry into programs, for graduation, and for the completion of a teacher certification program. These requirements may differ from the baseline requirements the state has for teacher certification. You will need to meet both sets of requirements.

When Should I Take the Test?

The Praxis II 0014 is a test for those who have completed or almost completed their teacher education programs. Each state establishes its own requirements for certification; some states specify the passing of other tests. Some states may require the test for initial certification; other states may require the test for beginning teachers during their first months on the job. Generally, each college and university establishes its own requirements for program admission and for graduation. Some colleges and universities require certain tests for graduation and/or for completion of a teacher education program. Check with your college and the state teacher certification agency for details.

When and Where Can I Take the Test?

ETS offers the Praxis 0014 seven times a year at a number of locations across the nation. The usual testing day is Saturday, but examinees may request an administration on an alternate day if a conflict—such as a religious obligation—exists.

How Do I Get More Information on the ETS Praxis Exams?

To receive information on upcoming administrations of the Praxis II 0014 test or any other test consult the ETS registration bulletin or website.

Contact ETS at:

Educational Testing Service
Teaching and Learning Division
P.O. Box 6051
Princeton, NJ 08541-6051
Phone: (609) 771-7395
Website: *www.ets.org/praxis*
E-mail: *praxis@ets.org*

Special accommodations are available for candidates who are visually impaired, hearing impaired, physically disabled, or specific learning disabled. For questions concerning disability services, contact:

ETS Disability Services: (609) 771-7780
TTY only: (609) 771-7714

Provisions are also available for examinees whose primary language is not English. The ETS registration bulletin and website include directions for those requesting such accommodations.

You can also consult ETS with regard to available test sites; reporting test scores; requesting changes in tests, centers, and dates of test; purchasing additional score reports; retaking tests; and other basic facts.

Is there a registration fee?

To take a Praxis examination, you must pay a registration fee, which is payable by check, money order, or with American Express, Discover, MasterCard, or Visa credit cards. In certain cases, ETS offers fee waivers. The registration bulletin and Web site give qualifications for receiving this benefit and describe the application process. Cash is not accepted for payment.

Can I retake the Test?

Some states, institutions, and associations limit the number of times you can retest. Contact your state or licensing authority to confirm their retest policies.

HOW TO USE THIS BOOK

What do I study first?

Read over REA's subject reviews and suggestions for test taking. Studying the reviews thoroughly will reinforce the basic skills you will need to do well on the exam. Make sure to do the practice questions in this book so that you will be familiar with the format and procedures involved with taking the actual test.

When should I start studying?

It is never too early to start studying; the earlier you begin, the more time you will have to sharpen your skills. Do not procrastinate! Cramming is not an effective way to study because it does not allow you the time needed to learn the test material.

FORMAT OF THE TEST

The Praxis II 0014 is a two-hour exam composed of 120 multiple-choice questions.

Content Categories	Approximate Number of Questions	Approximate Percentage of Examination
I. Language Arts	30	25%
II. Mathematics	30	25%
III. Social Studies	30	25%
IV. Science	30	25%

The multiple-choice questions assess a beginning teacher's knowledge of certain job-related skills and knowledge. Four choices are available on each multiple-choice question; the options bear the letters A through D. The exam uses four types of multiple-choice questions:

1. The Roman Numeral Multiple-Choice Question

2. The "Which of the Following?" Multiple-Choice Question

3. The "Complete the Statement" Multiple-Choice Question

4. The Multiple-Choice Question with Qualifiers

The following sections describe each type of question and suggested strategies.

Roman Numeral Multiple-Choice Questions

Perhaps the most difficult of the types of multiple-choice questions is the Roman numeral question because it allows for more than one correct answer. **Strategy:** Assess each answer before looking at the Roman numeral choices. Consider the following Roman numeral multiple-choice question designed to test science content:

The drop in temperature that occurs when sugar is added to coffee is the result of

    I.   sugar passing from a solid to a liquid state.

    II.   sugar absorbing calories from the water

    III. heat becoming latent when it was sensible

    (A) I only

    (B) I and II only

    (C) I, II and III

    (D) I and III only

In reviewing the questions, you should note that you may choose two or three answers by selecting (B), (C), or (D), while it is possible to choose only one answer by choosing answer (A).

The correct answer is (C) because it includes three correct statements. The sugar does pass from a solid to a liquid state (I), the sugar does absorb calories from the water (II), and the heat does become latent when it is sensible (III). Since I, II, and III are all causes of the drop of temperature when sugar is added to coffee, *all three* must be included when choosing an answer.

"Which of the Following?" Multiple-Choice Questions

In a "Which of the Following?" question, one of the answers is correct among the various choices.

Strategy: Form a sentence by replacing the first part of the question with each of the answer choices in turn, and then determine which of the resulting sentences is correct. Consider the following example:

Which of the following geological processes displaces solids as a result of gravity ?

(A) Weathering

(B) Soil erosion

(C) Glacial activity

(D) Volcanic activity

Using the suggested technique, one would read:

(A) Weathering is the geological process that displaces solids as a result of gravity.

(B) Soil erosion is the geological process that displaces solids as a result of gravity.

(C) Glacial activity is the geological process that displaces solids as a result of gravity.

(D) Volcanic activity is the geological process that displaces solids as a result of gravity.

The correct answer is (B). *Volcanic* activity is the only process by which material is from inside the Earth is brought to the surface, and it is not by force of gravity. The other processes (A) and (C) are the means of wearing down of the Earth's surface.

Not all "Which of the Following?" multiple-choice questions are as straightforward and simple as the previous example. Consider the following multiple-choice question.

An experiment is planned to test the effect of microwave radiation on the success of seed germination. One hundred corn seeds will be divided into four sets of 25 each. Seeds in Group 1 will be microwaved for 1 minute, seeds in Group 2 for 2 minutes, and seeds in Group 3 for 10 minutes. Seeds in Group 4 will not be placed in the microwave. Each group of seeds will be soaked overnight and placed between the folds of water-saturated newspaper. During the measurement of seed and root length, students note that many of the roots are not growing straight. Efforts to straighten the roots manually for measurement are only minimally successful as the roots are fragile and susceptible to breakage.

Which of the following approaches is consistent with the stated hypothesis?

(A) At the end of the experiment, straighten the roots and measure them.

(B) Use a string as a flexible measuring instrument for curved roots.

(C) Record the mass instead of length as an indicator of growth.

(D) Record only the number of seeds that have sprouted, regardless of length.

The answer to the question is (D). The hypothesis is to evaluate seed germination as a function of microwave irradiation. Recording the overall growth or length of the seed root, while interesting, is not the stated hypothesis. Choice (C) would be a good approach if the hypothesis were to relate seed growth to some variable, as it would more accurately reflect the growth of thicker or multiple roots in a way that root length might not measure.

Strategy: Underline key information as you read the question. For instance, as you read the previous question, you might underline or highlight the sentence: "An experiment is planned to test the effect of microwave radiation on the success of seed germination." This sentence will remind you of the stated hypothesis of the experiment and will prevent your having to read the entire question again. The highlighting will thus save you time; saving time is helpful when you must answer 110 questions in two hours.

Complete the Statement Multiple-Choice Questions

The "Complete the Statement" multiple-choice question consists of an incomplete statement for which you must select the answer choice that will complete the statement correctly. Here is an example:

A circular region rotated 360° around its diameter as an axis generates a

    (A) cube.
    (B) cylinder.
    (C) cone.
    (D) sphere.

The correct answer is (D), a sphere, which results when a circle is rotated 360°.

Multiple-Choice Questions with Qualifiers

Some of the multiple-choice questions may contain qualifiers—words like *not, least,* and *except*. These added words make the test questions more difficult because rather than having to choose the best answer, as is usually the case, you now must actually select the opposite. **Strategy:** Circle the qualifier. It is easy to forget to select the negative; circling the qualifier in the question stem is a flag. This will serve as a reminder as you are reading the question and especially if you must re-read or check the answer at a later time. Now consider this question with a qualifier:

Which of the following is NOT characteristic of Italian Renaissance humanism?

(A) Its foundation is in the study of the classics.
(B) Intellectual life was its focus.
(C) It was noticeable in the artistic accomplishments of the period.
(D) It was based on learning and understanding about what it means to be human.

You are looking for the *exception* in this question, so you want to compare each answer choice to the question to find which answer is *not* representative of Italian Renaissance humanism. Humanism is NOT learning and understanding, nor is it the study of being human, so (D) is the correct answer. Humanism was an intellectual movement based on the study of the classics. And, artistic accomplishments of the period did reflect the characteristics of the Renaissance.

You should spend approximately one minute on each multiple-choice question on each of the practice tests—and on the real exams, of course. The reviews in this book will help you sharpen the basic skills needed to approach the exam and offer you strategies for attacking the questions. By using the reviews in conjunction with the practice tests, you will better prepare yourself for the actual tests.

You have learned through your course work and your practical experience in schools most of what you need to know to answer the questions on the test. In your education classes, you gained the expertise to make important decisions about situations you will face as a teacher; in your content courses, you should have acquired the knowledge you will need to teach specific content. The reviews in this book will help you fit the information you have acquired into its specific testable category. Reviewing your class notes and textbooks along with systematic use of this book will give you an excellent springboard for passing the Praxis II 0014.

SCORING THE TEST

The number of raw points awarded on the Praxis II 0014 is based on the number of correct answers given. Most Praxis examinations vary by edition, which means that each test has several variations that contain different questions. The different questions are intended to measure the same general types of knowledge or skills. However, there is no way to guarantee that the questions on all editions of the test will have the same degree of difficulty. To avoid penalizing test takers who answer more difficult questions, the initial scores are adjusted for difficulty by using a statistical process known as equating. To avoid confusion between the *adjusted* and *unadjusted scores*, ETS reports the *adjusted scores* on a score scale that makes them clearly different from the *unadjusted scores*. *Unadjusted scores* or "raw scores" are simply the number of questions answered correctly. *Adjusted scores*, which are equated to the scale ETS uses for reporting the scores are called "scaled scores." For each edition of a Praxis test, a "raw-to-scale conversion table" is used to translate raw to scaled scores. The easier the questions are on a test edition, the more questions must be answered correctly to earn a given scaled score.

The college or university in which you are enrolled may set passing scores for the completion of your teacher education program and for graduation. Be sure to check the requirements in the catalogues or bulletins. You will also want to talk with your advisor. The passing scores for the Praxis II tests vary from state to state. To find out which of the Praxis II tests your state requires and what your state's set passing score is, contact your state's education department directly.

Score Reporting

When Will I Receive My Examinee Score Report and in What Form Will It Be?

ETS mails test-score reports six weeks after the test date. There is an exception for computer-based tests and for the Praxis I examinations. Score reports will list your current score and the highest score you have earned on each test you have taken over the last 10 years.

Along with your score report, ETS will provide you with a booklet that offers details on your scores. For each test date, you may request that ETS send a copy of your scores to as many as three score recipients, provided that each institution or agency is eligible to receive the scores.

STUDYING FOR THE PRAXIS II 0014

It is critical to your success that you study effectively. Throughout this guide you will find *Praxis Pointers* that will give you tips for successful test taking. The following are a few tips to help get you going:

- Choose a time and place for studying that works best for you. Some people set aside a certain number of hours every morning to study; others may choose to study at night before retiring. Only you know what is most effective for you.

- Use your time wisely and be consistent. Work out a study routine and stick to it; don't let your personal schedule interfere. Remember, seven weeks of studying, is a modest investment to put you on your chosen path.

- Don't cram the night before the test. You may have heard many amazing tales about effective cramming, but don't kid yourself: most of them are false, and the rest are about exceptional people who, by definition, aren't like most of us.

- When you take the practice tests, try to make your testing conditions as much like the actual test as possible. Turn off your television, radio, and telephone. Sit down at a quiet table free from distraction.

- As you complete the practice test, score your test and thoroughly review the explanations to the questions you answered incorrectly.

- Take notes on material you will want to go over again or research further.

- Keep track of your scores. By doing so, you will be able to gauge your progress and discover your strengths and weaknesses. You should carefully study the material relevant to your areas of difficulty. This will build your test-taking skills and your confidence!

Study Schedule

The following study course schedule allows for thorough preparation to pass the Praxis II 0014. This is a suggested seven-week course of study. However, you can condense this schedule if you are in a time crunch or expand it if you have more time. You may decide to use your weekends for study and preparation and go about your other business during the week. You may even want to record information and listen to your mp3 player or tape as you travel in your car. However you decide to study, be sure to adhere to the structured schedule you devise.

WEEK	ACTIVITY
1	After reading the first chapter to understand the format and content of this exam, take the first practice test. Our score chart will indicate your strengths and weaknesses. Make sure you simulate real exam conditions when you take the test. Afterward, score it and review the explanations for questions you answered incorrectly.
2	Review the explanations for the questions you missed, and review the appropriate chapter sections. Useful study techniques include highlighting key terms and information, taking notes as you review each section, and putting new terms and information on note cards to help retain the information.
3 and 4	Reread all your note cards, refresh your understanding of the exam's subareas and related skills, review your college textbooks, and read over notes you took in your college classes. This is also the time to consider any other supplementary materials suggested by your counselor or your state education agency.
5	Begin to condense your notes and findings. A structured list of important facts and concepts, based on your note cards, college textbook, course notes, and this book's review chapters will help you thoroughly review for the test. Review the answers and explanations for any questions you missed on the practice test.
6	Have someone quiz you using the note cards you created. Take the second practice test, adhering to the time limits and simulated test-day conditions.
7	Review your areas of weakness using all your study materials. This is a good time to retake the practice tests, if time allows.

THE DAY OF THE TEST

Before the Test

- Dress comfortably in layers. You do not want to be distracted by being too hot or too cold while you are taking the test.

- Check your registration ticket to verify your arrival time.

- Plan to arrive at the test center early. This will allow you to collect your thoughts and relax before the test; your early arrival will also spare you the anguish that comes with being late.

- Make sure to bring your admission ticket with you and two forms of identification, one of which must contain a recent photograph, your name, and your signature (e.g., a driver's license). You will not gain entry to the test center without proper identification.

- Bring several sharpened No. 2 pencils with erasers for the multiple-choice section; pens if you are taking another test that might have essay or constructed-response questions. You will not want to waste time searching for a replacement pencil or pen if you break a pencil point or run out of ink when you are trying to complete your test. The proctor will not provide pencils or pens at the test center.

- Wear a watch to the test center so you can apportion your testing time wisely. You may not, however, wear one that makes noise or that will otherwise disturb the other test takers.

- Leave all dictionaries, textbooks, notebooks, calculators, briefcases, and packages at home. You may not take these items into the test center.

- Do not eat or drink too much before the test. The proctor will not allow you to make up time you miss if you have to take a bathroom break. You will not be allowed to take materials with you, and you must secure permission before leaving the room.

During the Test

- Pace yourself. ETS administers the Praxis II 0014 in one two-hour sitting with no breaks.

- Follow all of the rules and instructions that the test proctor gives you. Proctors will enforce these procedures to maintain test security. If you do not abide by the regulations, the proctor may dismiss you from the test and notify ETS to cancel your score.

- Listen closely as the test instructor provides the directions for completing the test. Follow the directions carefully.

- Be sure to mark only one answer per multiple-choice question, erase all unwanted answers and marks completely, and fill in the answers darkly and neatly. There is no penalty for guessing at an answer, do not leave any answer ovals blank. Remember: a blank oval is just scored as wrong, but a guessed answer has a chance of being right!

Take the test! Do your best! Afterward, make notes about the multiple-choice questions you remember. You may not share this information with others, but you may find that the information proves useful on other exams that you take. Relax! Wait for that passing score to arrive.

Language Arts

LANGUAGE ARTS INSTRUCTION

The language arts include all the subjects related to communication. The school curriculum often gives most attention to reading, writing, literature, and spelling; listening and speaking are other essential parts of the language arts curriculum. A balanced language arts curriculum addresses each topic. Ideally, reading, writing, spelling, listening, speaking, and even literature are integrated into other content areas.

Stages of Learning to Read

Like Clay (1966), Martha Combs (2006) recognizes the first stage in literacy as the emerging stage but also notes two other stages of development in literacy. Combs's three stages are:

Emerging literacy stage: Children in this stage are making the transition from speaking to writing and reading—with support from others. Reading might involve predictable books; these books will be at the children's frustration reading level initially, but as the children practice, the books are at the instructional level of the children—and eventually at their independent level. Shared reading and interactive writings, which the children compose and the teachers record, provide practice and build confidence.

Developing stage: Children in the developing stage are becoming more independent in their reading, their writing and, their speaking. These children are usually on a middle-first- to late-second-grade level. Their texts should include many decodable words—these are words that follow a regular pattern and have a predictable sound: *man*, *tip*, *me*. The children can practice their decoding skills as they read and gain confidence; they are progressing with their handwriting skills and are becoming more independent in spelling words they need in writing.

Transitional reading stage: Children who are transitional readers usually have an instructional reading level of second grade or beyond. Ideally, these children should spend much of their time with independent-level and instructional-level materials. Their instructors are still there to help them, but the children are able to refine their old skills and practice new skills.

Literacy: What Is the First Stage in the Scope and Sequence of Learning to Read?

Marie M. Clay (1966) coined the term *emergent literacy* in her unpublished 1966 doctoral dissertation, "Emergent Reading Behavior" (University of Auckland, New Zealand). She defined *emergent literacy* as the stage during which children begin to receive formal instruction in reading and writing and the point at which educators and adults expect them to begin developing an understanding of print.

Today, educators use the term to describe the gradual development of literacy behavior, or the stage in which students begin learning about print. Educators usually associate emergent literacy with children from birth to about age five. During the emergent literacy period, children gain an understanding of print as a means of conveying information. It is essential that they develop an interest in reading and writing in this stage (Tompkins 2006).

Some educators suggest that reading readiness or emergent literacy is a **transitional period**, during which a child changes from a nonreader to a beginning reader; others suggest that reading readiness/emergent literacy is a stage (Clay 1979). The Southern Regional Education Board's Health and Human Services Commission (SREB 1994) cautions that children go through emergent literacy at individual rates.

Some **transmission educators** suggest that if a child is not ready to read, the teacher should get the child ready. Others declare that the teacher should not begin formal reading instruction until the child is ready. Most reading readiness advocates take the position that there are certain crucial factors that a teacher or parent should consider in deciding if a child is ready to read (Davis 2004).

Identifying Concepts of Print

An important part of emergent literacy is the skill of identifying print concepts, which involves being able to identify the parts of a book, indicating the directionality of print, and recognizing the connection between spoken and written words.

Parts of Books

Clay (1985) developed a formal procedure for sampling a child's reading vocabulary and determining the extent of a child's print-related concepts. For instance, her assessment checks whether a child can find the title of a book, show where to start reading the book, and locate the last page or end of the book. These components, considered essential before children can begin to read, may differ from those typically considered essential, such as discriminating between sounds and finding likenesses and differences in print (Finn 1990; Davis 2004). A teacher or parent might hand a book to a child, with the back of the book facing the child and in a horizontal position. The adult would then ask questions such as "Where is the name of the book?" "Where does the story start?" "If the book has the words *the end*, where might I find those words?" (Davis 2004).

PRAXIS Pointer

Read all of the answers for the multiple-choice questions. You may think you have found the correct response but do not assume it is. Read through each choice to be sure that you are not making a mistake by jumping to conclusions.

Directionality of Print

Another part of the skill of identifying concepts of print is being able to indicate the directionality of print. The reader in American society must start at the left side of the page and read to the right. This skill is not an in-born skill but rather one acquired through observation or through direct instruction. Some societies do not write from left to right. For instance, in ancient Greek society, writing followed the same pattern as a person would use when plowing: the reader would start at the top of the page and read to the right until the end of the line, turn, drop down a line, read that line to the left, turn, drop down a line, read that line to the right, and so on. Other languages, such as Hebrew, require the reader to begin at the right and read to the left. Japanese writing is generally vertical (Davis 2004).

To teach left-to-right direction, the teacher can place strips of masking tape on the child's desk, study center, or table area. One strip goes where the left side of the book or writing paper would be and one strip where the right side of the book or writing paper would be. The child colors the left side green and the right side red. The teacher helps the child use this device as a clue to remember on which side to begin reading or writing and reminds the child that *green* means "go" and *red* means "stop." Ideally, the teacher should use similar strips on the chalkboard or poster paper to model writing from left to right (Davis 2004).

Children can also remember on which side to begin reading by holding up their hands with their thumbs parallel to the floor. The left hand makes the shape of the letter *L*, for "left," the side on which to begin reading; the right hand does not make the *L* shape. Another way a teacher can help children who are having trouble distinguishing left from right, or on which side to begin reading and writing, is to point to sentences while reading from a big book or writing on the board; observing the teacher do this can help children master print directionality. Books that are 18 × 12 inches or larger are designed for this purpose and are effective with groups of children. Teachers or parents can also model directionality by passing their hands or fingers under the words or sentences as they read aloud. In fact, reading aloud is an essential activity in the school and at home throughout the school years (Davis 2004).

Teachers can use games such as Simon Says or songs such as "The Hokey Pokey" to give children practice in the skills of distinguishing left from right. In another instructional game, each child holds a paper plate as if it were a steering wheel, and the teacher calls out directions such as "Turn the wheel to the left" and "Turn your car to the right." As the children "drive" their cars, the teacher observes whether they are turning the wheel in the correct direction (Davis 2004).

Voice-to-Print Match

Being able to recognize the connection between the spoken word and the written word is important to developing reading and writing skills. During the emergent literacy period, children should begin to understand that the printed word is just speech written down. Shared reading (discussed in more detail in the next section, "Identifying Strategies for Developing Concepts of Print") can help children gain this understanding. As the adult reads aloud, the children join in with words, phrases, repetitions, and sentences they recognize. They begin to make the connection between the printed word and the spoken word and between phonemes and graphemes. **Phonemes** are the speech sounds; **graphemes** are the written symbols for the speech sounds. These voice-to-print relationships are important to reading (Davis 2004).

Identifying Strategies for Developing Concepts of Print

Emergent literacy research cautions that in preschool and kindergarten programs, teachers should avoid isolated, abstract instruction and tedious drills. Teachers should avoid programs that tend to ignore and repeat what the children already know. Programs that focus on skills and ignore experiences often place little importance on reading as a pleasurable activity and ignore early writing—important components of whole language (Noyce and Christie 1989).

Phonological Awareness

Increased phonological awareness occurs as children learn to associate the roughly 44 speech sounds in the English language with their visual representation. Children learn to pronounce these 44 sounds as they begin to talk. Because the English language has only 26 letters, it obviously is not a phonetic language; that is, there is no one-to-one correspondence between letters and sounds. The 26 letters are combined in many different ways to reproduce the needed sounds.

When they try to write, children in the early grades create **invented spellings** by applying their understanding of spelling rules. As children progress through the grades, their spellings usually become more conventional.

J. R. Gentry (1981) identifies the stages that students go through in their spelling development. These stages are particularly evident in the writing of students in a whole language classroom. The stages include the **precommunication stage**, when the student randomly uses letters; the **prephonetic stage**, when the student begins to use some letters correctly; the **phonetic stage**, when the student spells the words the way that they sound; the **transitional stage**, during which the student uses both correct spelling and phonetic spelling; and the **correct spelling stage**, when the student spells words correctly (Davis 2004).

Phonics

The most commonly used method of teaching reading in the United States, from colonial times through the 1920s, was the phonics method. Other reading methods—the sight word method, modified alphabet approach, and the whole language approach, for example—came into being after the 1920s. However, phonics is still an important part of reading instruction in the United States.

The phonics method of teaching reading emphasizes the association between the grapheme (the written symbol) and the phoneme (the speech sound). The phonics method attempts to relate spelling rules to the process.

William Holmes McGuffey and Rudolf Flesch were proponents of the phonics method. McGuffey produced his series of reading books in 1836. The readers used phonics while teaching morals to students; it was a cultural force, not just a reading textbook. By 1920, sales of McGuffey readers had reached 122 million. In 1955, Flesch wrote *Why Johnny Can't Read—And What You Can Do About It* to warn parents that the reason many children could not read was that the schools were not using the phonics approach.

Phonics is, of course, a skills-based approach. There are several **advantages of the phonics method** that are readily apparent. One important advantage of the phonics method is that it gives children tools for decoding, or figuring out, how to read and pronounce words that they do not know immediately. Because the phonics approach involves phoneme–grapheme associations, auditory learners—those who learn best through the sense of sound—often prefer to read using phonics. Auditory learners can usually hear a sound and associate it easily with its

PRAXIS Pointer

Be prepared. Don't waste time on "beat-the-test" strategies. Organize a study schedule and keep to it to avoid test anxiety.

printed symbol. Using phonics with auditory learners is an evident advantage. A third advantage of this method with its emphasis on sound–symbol relationships is that phonics readers can often transfer their skills to spelling. Spelling involves associating sounds with letters; it is the opposite of phonics, which associates symbols with sounds. A final advantage is that phonics readers are often good spellers (Davis 2004).

At its January 1997 meeting, the board of directors of the International Reading Association (IRA) passed a position statement titled "The Role of Phonics in Reading Instruction." The key assertions were that phonics is an important aspect in beginning reading instruction, primary teachers value and teach phonics, and effective phonics is integrated into the total language arts program ("IRA Takes a Stand on Phonics," 1997). There are, however, **disadvantages to the phonics method**. A major disadvantage of phonics is that visual learners may not read well by this method. A second disadvantage of the method is that the rules do not hold true all the time. In his now-classic study, Theodore Clymer (1963) reports that he found few phonics generalizations that held true in more than 50 percent of the cases in the primary grades. Four years later, however, Mildred Hart Bailey (1967) found in her study of phonics rules that 27 of the 45 generalizations identified by Clymer held true in 75 percent of the words appearing most often in reading materials for grades 1 through 6.

A third disadvantage of the phonics method is that some students are confused when they learn a phonics rule and then encounter frequent exceptions; inconsistencies pose a problem for them. Some educators, though not all, note a fourth disadvantage to the phonics method: they believe that there is no basis for the view that there are subskills, such as phonics, that students need to read; they see the skills as mythical (Davis 2004).

To help children learn phonics, many teachers find certain techniques for teaching the method helpful. Students should have opportunities to practice the phonics rules and generalizations in context; instructors should make every effort to illustrate the transfer of the phonics rules and generalizations to everyday materials and to other subjects. Analytic phonics (using phonics in context with actual materials), as opposed to synthetic phonics (phonics taught in isolation from meaningful books and materials, often using worksheets), seems to be the more helpful technique. Teachers can introduce a phonics rule or generalization as it appears, but such an incidental approach does not ensure that all students meet and practice the most frequently encountered phonics rules. A structured, systematic, sequential program of phonics helps ensure that readers have at their disposal an arsenal of skills to decode new words and spell the words correctly. Such a plan of presenting the rules and regulations of phonics can help eliminate gaps in students' word-attack skills (Davis 2004).

Marie Carbo (1993), nationally known for her work with reading styles, recognizes the importance of making available phonics instruction in any reading program. She particularly warns, "a good whole language program does include phonics." In *Becoming a Nation of Readers*, the Commission on Reading (1986) stresses that phonics is an essential strategy for beginning reading. Teachers should use a systematic approach and present the skills in meaningful sentences, passages, and materials, not just as words in isolation.

A word of caution for teachers of phonics is that in the beginning, students may read slowly. When students begin to commit high-frequency words to memory, however, reading speed and, in turn, comprehension will increase (Davis 2004). The young child begins recognizing letters and their sounds. These skills will help the child with reading and spelling. Another technique that will help the child in attacking unknown words is analyzing the structure of the words, or structural analysis (Davis 2004).

Developmentally Appropriate Classrooms, Materials, and Curriculum

The SREB (1994) states that the classroom, materials, and curriculum should be developmentally appropriate. **Developmentally appropriate** is a concept with two dimensions: individual appropriateness and age appropriateness. **Individual appropriateness** recognizes that each child is unique. Ideally, schools and teachers respect and accommodate individual differences, which include growth, interest, and styles. **Age appropriateness** implies that there are sequences of growth and change during the first nine years that a teacher must consider when developing the classroom environment and experiences. In general, the age-appropriate skills considered necessary for reading—during the reading readiness period and beyond—are visual discrimination, auditory discrimination, and left-to-right direction (Davis 2004).

Seven Types of Traditional Literature

There are seven types of traditional fiction: parables, fables, fairy tales, folktales, noodlehead tales, myths, and legends. Each has certain characteristics that set it apart from the others.

Parables

A **parable** is a story that is realistic and has a moral. The story is **didactic**: it teaches a lesson. Unlike the fable, the parable can be, but is not necessarily, true. The biblical figure Jesus often taught with parables. One of his best known parables is "The Prodigal Son" (Luke 16:11–32 New Revised Standard Edition); others include "The Good Samaritan" (Luke 10:30–36 New Revised Standard Edition), "The Lost Coin" (Luke 15:8–11 New Revised Standard Edition), and "The Parable of the Seeds on Rich and Fallow Ground" (Mark 4:3–8; Luke 8:5–8 New Revised Standard Edition).

Fables

A **fable** is a nonrealistic story with a moral. The fable often has animals as main characters. **Aesop**, a Greek slave supposedly born around 600 B.C.E., is often credited with having developed the fable; however, whether he actually did so—or ever actually existed—is debatable. Charlotte Huck, the noted children's literature authority and the author of *Children's Literature in the Elementary School* (1968), states that fables were actually in Greek literature as early as 800 B.C.E. (362–64). "The Fox and the Crane," "The Fox and the Crow," and "The Fox and the Grapes" are among the best-known fables. Some scholars use the classification **beast tale** for fables in which animals behave as humans. Translators changed Aesop's Fables from Greek to Latin and to English. William Caxton published these fables in England in 1484. It was some time after the publication of these fables that the Grimm Brothers (1800s) and Charles Perrault (1697) secured the preservation in writing of these fables by publishing them.

Fairy Tales

Fairy tales have the element of magic; they do not necessarily have fairies in them. They often have a certain pattern and may present an "ideal" to the listener or the reader. For instance, fairy tales such as "Cinderella," "Snow White," and "Rapunzel" convey a message about the "proper" woman. According to these tales, the ideal woman is beautiful, kind, and long-suffering; she waits for her prince to come and to save her from any disappointment or disaster that may occur.

Charles Perrault first recorded the French fairy tales in the 1600s; they are still in print. It was not until the 1800s that the Grimm Brothers recorded German fairy tales, Joseph Jacobs recorded British fairy tales, Peter Asbjørnsen and Jørgen Moe recorded

Scandinavian fairy tales, and Aleksandr Nikolayevich Afanasev recorded Russian fairy tales. All these tales are in current editions in English or the language of origin.

Sometimes, writers, such as Nathaniel Hawthorne, use the term **wonder tales** to refer to these fairy tales with their magical elements. The characters of witches, wizards, talking beasts, and other magical animals often possess and demonstrate these magical elements. The use of the **magic three** is another frequent feature of the fairy tale; for instance, the stories often involve three wishes, three attempts at achieving a goal, and three siblings. Another characteristic of a fairy tale is that the listener or reader knows that goodwill always wins out over evil. A youngster may find frightening witches, wicked ogres, and evil forces, but in the end the protagonist will ". . . live happily ever after." Stereotyping is another characteristic of the fairy tale. As soon as the storyteller or the reader says the word *stepmother*, for instance, the listener knows that the woman is wicked. Likewise, mere mention of the setting as being in the *woods* conveys a message of fear, impending doom, and evil. The word *prince* causes one to envision a young, handsome man on a white horse. The *princess* is usually the youngest in the family, beautiful, soft-spoken, kind, inactive, and waiting for her prince to come. Such demure fairy-tale female characters stand in direct contrast to the assertive female characters of folktales.

Folktales

Folktales are in the language of the people. The stories do not necessarily have a moral. In fact, entertainment is often the main purpose of folktales. In the 1600s and 1700s, early residents of the Appalachian Mountains, for instance, took many of the fairy tales of England, Scotland, and Ireland with them to the "new" country. The fairy tale "Cinderella" became "Ashpet" in the Appalachians (Chase 1948, 119). The quiet, passive Cinderella became the hard-working, smart, active Ashpet, a character more like the mountain women who had to work and assist their men. "The Bremen Town Musicians" (Grimm, 301–04) became "Jack and the Robbers" in another mountain tale (Chase 1943, 40–6).

Noodlehead Tales

Another example of the humorous folktales are the noodlehead tales. The **noodlehead tales** are tales that have a character or characters whom the listener can outsmart. The listener often finds these stories particularly humorous because the characters in these stories make the listener feel superior. "Epaminondas" is an example of noodlehead tale.

The humor in all types of folktales may be coarse, and the diction is often that of the particular group of people who originated the tales. Richard Chase collected many of the Appalachian folktales and recorded them. He transcribed the tales on paper and told them in personal appearances, on records, and on tapes for the public. He was always careful to use the mountain dialect. His *Jack Tales* (1943) and *Grandfather Tales* (1948) are among his best-known works

Likewise, other cultures around the world have their own unique folktales and fairy tales. For instance, Perrault's French tale of "Cinderella" is "Tattercoats" in Jacobs's collection (1959); in this British version, the prince falls in love with a dirty, ragged girl—not a beautiful, well-dressed figure at the ball. The Norwegian tale *East o' the Sun and West o' the Moon* (Asbjørnsen and Moe 1946) tells the story of Cinderlad, not Cinderella. The Jewish folktale of *Zlateh the Goat* (Singer 1966; illustrated by Maurice Sendak) tells of the survival of a young boy and his goat in a snowstorm.

Myths

Myths are stories to explain things that the teller does not understand. Greeks and Romans used myths and their associated heroes and heroines to explain thunder, fire, and the "movements" of the sun. Norse myths, too, explain phenomena—especially those associated with the frost, snow, and the cold climate of the north. Likewise, Native American myths explain such phenomena as why the rabbit does not have a tail and why the constellations exist. (Some of these Native American myths have derived the name *legend* instead of the correct name of *myth*.) Another name for these explanations is **pourquoi tales**. Most cultures have their own myths.

Legends

Legends are stories—usually exaggerated—about real people, places, and things. George Washington, for instance, was a real person. However, all the stories about him are not true. Because there were no silver dollars minted during the American Revolution, it would have been impossible for him to have tossed a silver dollar across the Potomac. Paul Bunyan may actually have been a logger or lumberjack; it is doubtful that he owned a blue ox or had a pancake griddle large enough that his cook could tie hams on his feet and skate on it. The careful reader of literature realizes that though legends are generally part of traditional literature, they continue to spring up with modern figures, animals, and places as their central elements.

FIGURATIVE LANGUAGE

What Are Some Examples of Figurative Language that Students Can Look for in Literature and Use in Their Own Writing?

One criterion for evaluating juvenile fiction is the writing style of the author. A writer can employ many devices to enhance the flow of the words, to make the writing more appealing, and to clarify the meaning. Figurative language is one such device.

Figurative language includes the use of similes, metaphors, and personification; it is a way of adding information and description to the writing and of encouraging the reader to think about the text. All the details are not "spoon-fed" to the reader.

A **simile** is a comparison between two unlike things that uses *like*, *than*, or *as*. For example, in the memoir *October Sky*, Homer describes Jake Mosby, the new junior engineer, by saying, "He's got more money than Carter's got little liver pills" (Hickam 1998, 145). Homer overhears a secretary tell some other women that "he looks just like Henry Fonda" (146). Homer's mother notes that on one occasion Jake is "drunk as Cooter Brown" (146). This figurative language brings imagery to the mind of the reader, requires the reader to think, and adds information to the description.

A **metaphor** is a comparison in which one thing is likened to some other, very dissimilar thing. For example, the character Jake in *October Sky* calls the *McDowell County Banner* "a grocery-store rag" (Hickam 1998, 154). Homer calls the rocket fuel "rocket candy" because of its sweetish odor (181). He also refers to a cord as "a thick electrical umbilical" (199).

Personification is the attribution of human characteristics or behaviors to animals, ideas, inanimate objects, and so on. For instance, Hickam writes that the "big golden moon hovered overhead" (1998, 53). Later he writes that "a shuttle car darted in, its crab-like arms sweeping up the coal thrown out" (199).

Reading Strategies

Looking at strategies used by proficient readers helps teachers make skillful choices of activities to maximize student learning in subject area instruction. Anne Goudvis and Stephanie Harvey (2000) offer the following list:

Activating prior knowledge: Readers pay more attention when they relate to the text. Readers naturally bring their prior knowledge and experience to reading, but they comprehend better when they think about the connections they make among the text, their lives, and the larger world.

Predicting or asking questions: Questioning is the strategy that keeps readers engaged. When readers ask questions, even before they read, they clarify understanding and forge ahead to make meaning. Asking questions is at the heart of thoughtful reading.

Visualizing: Active readers create visual images based on the words they read in the text. These created pictures enhance their understanding.

Drawing inferences: Inferring is when the readers take what they know, garner clues from the text, and think ahead to make a judgment, discern a theme, or speculate about what is to come.

Determining important ideas: Thoughtful readers grasp essential ideas and important information when reading. Readers must differentiate between less important ideas and key ideas that are central to the meaning of the text.

Synthesizing information: Synthesizing involves combining new information with existing knowledge to form an original idea or interpretation. Reviewing, sorting, and sifting important information can lead to new insights that change the way readers think.

Repairing understanding: If confusion disrupts meaning, readers need to stop and clarify their understanding. Readers may use a variety of strategies to enhance comprehension when meaning goes awry.

Confirming: As students read and after they read, they can confirm the predictions they originally made. There is no wrong answer. One can confirm negatively or positively. Determining whether a prediction is correct is a goal.

Using parts of a book: Students should use book parts—such as charts, diagrams, indexes, and the table of contents—to improve their understanding of the reading content.

Reflecting: An important strategy is for students to think about, or reflect on, what they have just read. Reflection can be simply thinking, or it can be more formal, such as a discussion or writing in a journal.

While providing instruction in a subject area, the teacher needs to determine if the reading material is at the students' level of reading mastery. If not, the teacher needs to make accommodations either in the material itself or in the manner of presentation.

Checking for Understanding

Teachers need to be explicit about teaching students to be aware, to check for understanding, and to use reading comprehension strategies to make meaning. To monitor and repair students' understanding, teachers should explicitly teach them to do the following (Goudvis and Harvey 2000):

- Track their thinking through coding with sticky notes, writing, or discussion.

- Notice when they lose focus.

- Stop and go back to clarify thinking.

- Reread to enhance understanding.

- Read ahead to clarify meaning.

- Identify and articulate what is confusing or puzzling about the text.

- Recognize that all of their questions have value. (There is no such thing as a stupid question.)

- Develop the disposition to question the text or author.

- Think critically about the text and be willing to disagree with its information or logic.

- Match the problem with the strategy that will best solve it.

Depending on the situation, instructors may use these strategies across the curriculum in any subject area. In addition, the effective teacher can use graphic organizers such as these:

Double-entry journals: The student enters direct quotes from the text (with page number) in the left column and enters "thinking options"—such as "This is important because . . . ," "I am confused because . . . ," "I think this means . . ."—in the right column.

Venn diagrams: Venn diagrams consist of two overlapping circles in which the student compares two items or concepts by placing specific criteria or critical attributes for one in the left circle, for the other in the right circle, and attributes or characteristics that are shared by the two in the overlapping section shared by the two circles.

Webs or maps: The student charts a concept or section of text in a graphic outline. The web or map begins with the title or concept often written in the middle of the page and branches out in web fashion; students note specific bits of information on the branches or strings of the web. Arrows or lines in other formats can make connections from one bit of information to another. The map or web helps the student to think about the reading passage and illustrate its structure; with the map or web, the student is able to make a passage more concrete and develop a visual representation of the book or reading section (Davis 2004).

Mapping and Webbing

Story mapping or webbing helps students think about a reading passage and its structure. Some typical devices in good narrative fiction and that might be useful on a story map include setting, stylistic devices, characters, and plot. A class reading Wilson Rawls's *Where the Red Fern Grows* (1961/1976) created the story map shown here:

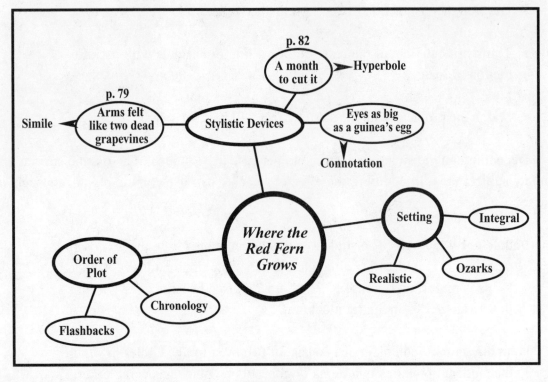

Story Map

Study Plans

The teacher can acquaint students with several plans to help them read content materials. Many of these plans already exist, and the teacher and the students can simply select the plan(s) that works best for them with various subjects. Students may use **mnemonic devices**, or memory-related devices, to help them remember the steps in reading a chapter effectively. Students often use plans like the following SQ3R plan when reading text in content areas:

Survey: Before reading a passage or an entire section of the text, the student should look over the assigned page or chapter and consider some questions. Are there illustrations, charts, or diagrams? What are some of the chapter headings? Are some words in bold type?

Question: The student may wish to devise some questions that the chapter will probably answer. If an assigned chapter has questions at the end, the student can look over the questions before reading the chapter; the questions serve as a guide to the text.

Read: The student now reads the passage to answer the questions at the end of the chapter or to answer the questions that the student developed before reading the chapter.

Recite: The student attempts to answer orally or in writing the student-developed questions or the questions at the end of the chapter.

Review: The student reviews the material to double-check the answers given in writing or orally at the previous step.

MODES OF WRITING

For years, educators believed that reading preceded writing in the development of literacy. This belief has recently changed.

Stages in Writing Development

Emerging literacy research indicates that learning to write is an important part in a child's learning to read. As children begin to name letters and read print, they also begin to write letters and words. Writing development seems to occur at about the same time as reading development—not afterward, as traditional reading readiness assumed. Whole language seeks to integrate the language arts rather than sequencing them. Just as change has marked educators' beliefs about reading instruction and the way that reading develops, change has also marked the methods and philosophies behind the teaching of writing in the schools.

Children seem to progress through certain stages in their writing. Although many authorities have examined the stages in writing development, Alexander Luria presents the most thoroughly elaborated model (Klein 1985; Davis 2004). He cautions, however, that the stages are not entirely a function of age. Luria explains that it is not uncommon to find children from three to six years old who are the same age but are two to three stages apart in their writing. He also notes that children do not advance systematically through the stages. At times, a child may regress or zigzag. At other times, the child may appear to remain at one level without progression or regression. Here is a summary of Luria's stages in writing:

Stage 1: The undifferentiated stage from ages three to five is a period that Luria defines as a prewriting or preinstrumental period. The child does not distinguish between marks written on a page. The marks (writing) seem merely random to the child and do not help the child recall information.

Stage 2: The differentiated stage from about age four is when the child intentionally builds a relationship between sounds and written expression. For instance, the child represents short words or short phrases with shorter marks and longer words, phrases, or sentences with longer marks. The child might use dark marks to help remember a sentence such as "The sky was dark." Making such marks is an example of mnemonics, or associating symbols with information.

Stage 3: The pictographic stage from ages four to six is the period that Robert Klein (1985, 66) says is "the most important stage in the development of the child's perception of writing-as-a-conceptual-act."

The Writing Process

Teachers in the early 1970s were very concerned with spelling and punctuation in students' papers. The teacher did all the "correcting" and watched carefully for grammatical, spelling, and punctuation errors. In the late 1970s, writing "experts" denounced students' compositions as being too dull. The schools began to foster creative writing and encouraged teachers to provide opportunities for creative writing each week. However, many teachers began to view the creative writing as lacking in structure. **Process writing** has since become the fashionable term in writing. With process writing, students engage in several activities (Noyce and Christie 1989):

Prewriting stage: During the first stage in the writing process, the students begin to collect information for the writing that they will do.

Composing or writing stage: The classroom resembles a laboratory. Students may consult with one another and use various books and materials to construct their papers. At this stage, the student-writers do not worry about spelling and mechanics. This is the drafting stage. Some students use invented spelling as they try to apply their understanding of spelling rules. The students may later edit and revise the words, but on first writing their drafts, they can simply record the word quickly and go on to the next word in the sentence.

Revising stage: Writers polish and improve their compositions.

Editing/evaluating/postwriting stage: Students read and correct their own writing and the works of others. The teacher does not have to do all the evaluating. Students use the dictionary, their thesaurus, their peers, and even the spell-check program on the classroom computers.

Rewriting stage: After their self-evaluations and after their classmates and teachers share praise and constructive criticisms, including spelling and punctuation corrections, the students rewrite their compositions.

In some classes, the students publish their own works and even have an **author's chair** from which the writers can tell some things about themselves, discuss their writing process, and read their compositions aloud (Noyce and Christie 1989). This is often called the **publishing stage**. Writing that is published in the classroom can be as informal as a final draft handwritten by a student or as formal as a book bound by a school's publishing center. Teachers do not necessarily have their students take each piece of writing to the publishing stage. According to research, the most effective writing process includes at least the prewriting, composing, revising, and editing/evaluating/postwriting stages (Bennett 1987).

Types of Writing

Writing serves many different functions. The main functions, however, are to narrate, to describe, to explain, and to persuade. Students need to be aware of each of these types of literature. In any event, the four categories are neither exhaustive nor mutually exclusive.

The narrative is a story or an account of an incident or a series of incidents. The narrative may be nonfiction—autobiographical, for example—or fiction.

The purpose of **descriptive** writing is to provide information about a person, place, or thing. Descriptive writing can be fiction or nonfiction. E. B. White uses description when he relates what the barn is like in *Charlotte's Web* (1952); the book itself, however, is fiction. Realtors use descriptive writing when they advertise a house in a local newspaper; the general public expects the descriptions of events in the local paper to be factual.

The purpose of **expository** writing is to explain and clarify ideas. Students are probably most familiar with this type of writing. While the expository essay may have narrative elements, the storytelling or recounting aspect is minor and subservient to that of the explanation element. Expository writing is typical of many textbooks; for instance, the writing in a textbook on how to operate a computer would likely be expository.

PRAXIS Pointer

Mark up your test book. Crossing out answer choice(s) you know are inappropriate will save you time.

The purpose of **persuasive** writing is to convince the reader of something. Persuasive writing fills current magazines and newspapers and permeates the World Wide Web. The writer may be trying to push a political candidate, to convince someone to vote for a zoning ordinance, or even to promote a diet plan. Persuasive writing usually presents a point; provides evidence, which may be factual or anecdotal; and supports the point. The structure may be very formal, with counterpositions and counterarguments. Whatever the organizational pattern, the writer's intent is to persuade readers of the validity of some claim. Nearly all essays have some element of persuasion.

Authors choose their form of writing not necessarily just to tell a story but to present an idea. Whether writers choose the narrative, descriptive, expository, or persuasive format, they have something on their minds that they want to convey to their readers. When readers analyze writing, they often seek first to determine its form. There are other types of writing, of course. For instance, **speculative** writing is so named because, as the Latin root suggests, it looks at ideas and explores them rather than merely explaining them, as expository writing does. The speculative essay is often meditative; it often makes one or more points, and the thesis may not be as obvious or clear-cut as that in an expository essay. The writer deals with ideas in an associative manner and plays with ideas in a looser structure than the writer might do in an expository format. This "flow" may even produce intercalary paragraphs, which present alternately a narrative of sorts and thoughtful responses to the recounted events.

Modes of Writing for a Variety of Occasions, Purposes, and Audiences

The writer must consider the audience, the occasion, and the purpose when choosing the writing mode. The writer's responsibility is to write clearly, honestly, and cleanly for the reader's sake; the **audience** is very important. After all, writing would be pointless without readers. Why write? Why add evidence, organize your ideas, or correct bad grammar? The reason to do any of these things is that someone out there—an audience—needs to understand what you mean to say. The teacher can designate an audience for students' writing. Knowing who will read their work, students can modify their writing to suit the intended readers. For instance, a fourth-grade teacher might suggest that the class take their compositions about a favorite animal to second graders and allow the younger children to read or listen to the works. The writers will realize that they need to use manuscript—not cursive—writing, to employ simple vocabulary, and to omit complex sentences when they write for their young audience.

The **occasion** helps to determine the elements of the writing. The language should fit the occasion; particular words may have certain effects: evoke sympathy or raise questions about an opposing point of view, for instance. The students and teacher might try to determine the likely effect on an audience of a writer's choice of a particular word or words.

The **purpose** helps to determine the format (narrative, expository, descriptive, persuasive) and the language of the writer. The students, for instance, might consider the appropriateness of written material for a specific purpose: a business letter, a communication with residents of a retirement center, or a thank-you note to parents. The teacher and students might try to identify persuasive techniques used by a writer in a passage.

In selecting the mode of writing and the content, the writer might ask the following:

- What would the audience need to know to believe me or to accept my position? (Imagine someone you know [visualize her or him] listening to you declare your position or opinion and then saying, "Oh yeah? Prove it!")

- What evidence do I need to prove my idea to this skeptic?

- With what might the audience disagree?

- What common knowledge does the audience share with me?

- What information do I need to share with the audience?

The teacher might wish to have the students practice selecting the mode and the language by adapting forms, organizational strategies, and styles for different audiences and purposes.

SPEECH

Conventions of Standard American English

The way you speak can vary depending on whom you are speaking to—just as what you wear can vary depending on whom you are going to see. More commonly, language varies according to geographic region, ethnic group, social class, and educational level. The language usually used in U.S. schools is Standard American English. This formal language (dialect) is the language in texts, newspapers, magazines, and the news programs on television.

There are other forms of the English language beside Standard American English. Some variations are the forms spoken in Appalachia, in urban ghettos, and by Mexican Americans, particularly in the Southwest. In all these variations, the syntax, phonology, and semantics differ from Standard American English. When instructing students who do not speak the standard dialect, teachers should not try to replace the culture or the language with Standard American English; the goal of school is to add Standard American English to students' language registers (Tompkins 2006). The teacher may talk at this time about alternative ways to say what the students do not say in Standard American English.

Elementary-age children, in particular, need direct instruction to develop proper speaking habits. This includes using an appropriate tone and volume of voice depending on the audience and situation. Students should be provided with opportunities to express their thoughts, share their writing, or discuss content in small- and large-group settings. The teacher should model desired speaking behaviors, in addition to informing students of expectations and norms. Young children should practice making eye contact while speaking with others. Along with speaking skills, students should be encouraged to develop strong listening skills. This includes looking at the speaker, listening quietly, and responding in a positive manner. Speaking and listening skills are integral aspects of language arts instruction.

REFERENCES

Aesop. *The Fables of Aesop: Selected, Told Anew, and Their Social History Traced by Joseph Jacobs*. New York: Macmillan, 1950.

Afanasev, Aleksandr Nikolayevich. *Russian Fairy Tales*. Translated by Norbert Guterman. New York: Pantheon, 1975.

Alcott, Louisa Mae. *Little Women*. Boston: Little, Brown, 1968. First published 1868 by Roberts Brothers, Boston.

Asbjørnsen, Peter, and Jørgen Moe. *East o' the Sun and West o' the Moon*. Evanston, IL: Row, Peterson, 1946.

Bailey, Mildred Hart. "The Utility of Phonic Generalizations in Grades One Through Six." *Reading Teacher* 20:5 (February 1967): 413–18.

Banks, Lynne Reid. *The Indian in the Cupboard*. Garden City, NY: Doubleday, 1980.

Barry, Leasha M., Betty J. Bennett, Lois Christensen, Aliciia Mendoza, Enrique Ortiz, Migdalia Pagan, Sally Robison, and Otilia Salmón. *The Best Teachers' Test Preparation for the FTCE: General Knowledge*. Piscataway, NJ: Research and Education Association, 2005.

Beim, Lorraine, and Jerrold Beim. *Two is a Team*. New York: Harcourt, Brace, 1945.

Bloom, Benjamin, Max D. Engelhart, Edward J. Furst, Walker H. Hill, and David R. Krathwohl. *Taxonomy of Educational Objectives: The Classification of Educational Goals. Handbook I: Cognitive Domain*. New York: Longmans, Green, 1956.

Bonham, Frank. *Durango Street*. New York: Dell, 1975. First published 1965 by Dutton, New York.

Bryant, Sara Cone. *Epaminondas and His Auntie*. Boston: Houghton, 1938.

Byars, Betsy. *The Summer of the Swans*. New York: Viking Press, 1970.

Capote, Truman. *Complete Stories of Truman Capote*. New York: Random House, 2004.

Carbo, Marie. "Reading Styles and Whole Language." *Schools of Thought II*. Video. Bloomington, IN: Phi Delta Kappa, 1993.

———. "Teaching Reading with Talking Books" *Reading Teacher* 32:3 (December 1978): 267–73.

Chase, Richard. *Jack Tales*. New York: Houghton Mifflin, 1943.

———. *Grandfather Tales*. New York: Houghton Mifflin, 1948.

Clay, M. M. "Emergent Reading Behavior." PhD diss., University of Auckland, New Zealand, 1966.

———. *Reading: The Patterning of Complex Behavior*. Auckland, New Zealand: Heinemann Educational Books, 1979.

Cleaver, Vera, and Bill Cleaver. *Where the Lilies Bloom*. New York: Lippincott, 1969.

Clymer, Theodore. "The Utility of Phonic Generalizations in the Primary Grades." *The Reading Teacher* 16 (January 1963): 252–58.

Combs, Martha. *Readers and Writers in Primary Grades: A Balanced and Integrated Approach*. Upper Saddle River, NJ: Pearson, 2006.

Commission on Reading. *Becoming a Nation of Readers*. Washington, DC: U.S. Department of Education, September 1986.

Coerr, Eleanor. *Sadako and the Thousand Paper Cranes*. New York: Putnam, 1977.

Cook, Jimmie E., and Gregory J. Nolan. "Treating Auditory Perception Problems: The NIM Helps." *Academic Therapy* 15:4 (March 1980): 473–81.

Cormier, Robert. *The Chocolate War*. New York: Dell, 1977. First published 1974 by Pantheon, New York.

Dahl, Roald. *Charlie and the Chocolate Factory*. New York: Knopf, 1972. First published 1964 by Knopf, New York.

Davis, Anita P. *Children's Literature Essentials*. Boston: American Press, 2000.

Davis, Anita P., and Ed Y. Hall. *Harriet Quimby: First Lady of the Air (An Activity Book for Children)*. Spartanburg, SC: Honoribus Press, 1993.

———. *Harriet Quimby: First lady of the Air (An Intermediate Biography)*. Spartanburg, SC: Honoribus Press, 1998.

Davis, Anita P., and Thomas R. McDaniel. "Essential Vocabulary Words." *Reading Teacher.* 52:3. (November 1998): 308–9.

Davis, Anita P., and Katharine Preston. *Discoveries.* Hillsborough, ID: Butte Publications, 1996.

Davis, Anita Price. *Reading Instruction Essentials.* 3rd ed. Boston: American Press, 2004.

De Angeli, Marguerite. *Bright April.* Garden City, NY: Doubleday, 1946.

Defoe, Daniel. *Robinson Crusoe.* Boston: Houghton Mifflin, 1972. First published 1719 by W. Taylor Publishers, London.

Dodge, Mary Mapes. *Hans Brinker.* New York: Grosset and Dunlap, 1963. First published 1912 by Thomas Nelson, London.

Dolch, Edward William. "Dolch Sight Word List." Champaign, IL: Garrard Press, 1960.

Finn, Patrick J. *Helping Children Learn to Read.* New York: Longman, 1990.

Flesch, Rudolf. *Why Johnny Can't Read—And What You Can Do About It.* New York: Harper and Row, 1955.

Fry, Edward. "Fry's Readability Graph: Clarifications, Validity and Extension to Level 17." *Journal of Reading* 21:3 (December 1977): 242–52.

———. "The New Instant Word Lists." *Reading Teacher* 34:3 (December 1980): 264–89.

Garis, Howard. *Uncle Wiggly's Adventures.* New York: Platt and Munk, 1915. First published 1912 by R. F. Fenno, New York.

Gentry, J. R. "Learning to Spell Developmentally." *Reading Teacher* 34:4 (January 1981): 378–81.

Gipson, Fred. *Old Yeller.* New York: Harper, 1956.

Golding, William. *Lord of the Flies.* New York: Perigee, 1954.

Goudvis, Anne, and Stephanie Harvey. *Strategies That Work.* Portland, ME: Stenhouse Publishers, 2000.

Grimm, Jacob, and Wilhelm Grimm. *Grimm's Fairy Tales*. Chicago: Follett, 1968.

Gunning, Thomas G. *Creating Reading Instruction for All Children*. Boston: Allyn and Bacon, 1996.

Heckleman, R. G. "A Neurological-Impress Method of Remedial-reading Instruction." *Academic Therapy* IV (Summer 1969): 277–82.

Henry, Marguerite. *Brighty of the Grand Canyon*. New York: Scholastic, 1967. First published 1953 by Rand McNally and Company, Chicago.

Hesse, Karen. *Out of the Dust*. New York: Scholastic, 1999. First published 1997 by Scholastic, New York.

Hickam, Homer H., Jr. *October Sky*. New York: Dell, 1999. First published 1998 as *Rocket Boys* by Delacorte, New York.

Hinton, S. E. *The Outsiders*. New York: Dell, 1983. First published 1967 by Viking, New York.

Hollingsworth, Paul. "An Experimental Approach to the Impress Method of Teaching Reading." *Reading Teacher* 31 (March 1978): 624–26.

Huck, Charlotte S., and Doris Young Kuhn. *Children's Literature in the Elementary School*. New York: Holt, Rinehart and Winston, 1968. First published 1961 by Holt, Rinehart and Winston.

"IRA Takes a Stand on Phonics." (Vol. 14:5) *Reading Today* (April/May 1997): 1–4.

Jackson, Jesse. *Call Me Charley*. New York: Harper, 1945.

Jacobs, Joseph. *Favorite Fairy Tales Told in England*. Boston: Little, Brown, 1959.

Karlin, Robert. *Teaching Elementary Reading*. New York: Harcourt Brace Jovanovich, 1971.

Keats, Ezra Jack. *The Snowy Day*. New York: Viking Press, 1962.

Kellogg, Steven. *Paul Bunyan*. New York: Morrow, 1986. First published 1925 by James Stevens, Knopf Publishers, New York.

Klein, Marvin L. *The Development of Writing in Children Pre-K through Grade 8*. Englewood Cliffs, NJ: Prentice Hall 1985.

Knight, Eric. *Lassie Come Home*. New York: Scholastic, 1966. First published 1940 by John C. Winston, Philadelphia.

Konigsburg, E. L. *From the Mixed-up Files of Mrs. Basil E. Frankweiler*. New York: Atheneum, 1967.

Lee, Harper. *To Kill a Mockingbird*. New York: Warner Books, 1982. First published 1960 by J. B. Lippincott, Philadelphia.

Lewis, C. S. *The Lion, the Witch, and the Wardrobe*. New York: Macmillan, 1988. First published 1950 by Geoffrey Bles, London.

Mager, Robert F. *Preparing Instructional Objectives*. Palo Alto, CA: Fearon Publishers, 1962.

Marzano, Robert J., and Daisy E. Arredondo. *Tactics for Thinking*. Aurora, CO: Mid-Continent Regional Education Laboratories, 1986.

Michaelis, John U., and Jesus Garcia. *Social Studies for Children: A Guide to Basic Instruction*. Boston: Allyn and Bacon, 1996.

Miles, Miska. *Mississippi Possum*. Boston: Little, Brown, 1965.

Montgomery, L. M. *Anne of Green Gables*. New York: Farrar, Straus, and Giroux, 1935. First published 1908 by L. C. Page and Company, Boston.

Mowat, Farley. *Never Cry Wolf*. Toronto: Bantam Books, 1984. First published 1963 McClelland and Stewart Limited, Toronto.

Norton, Mary. *The Borrowers*. New York: Harcourt, Brace, 1953.

Noyce, Ruth M., and James F. Christie. *Integrating Reading and Writing Instruction in Grades K–8*. Boston: Allyn and Bacon, 1989.

Peck, Robert Newton. *Soup*. New York: Knopf, 1974.

Perrault, Charles, et al. *Favorite Fairy Tales Told in France: Retold from Charles Perrault and Other French Storytellers*, edited by Virginia Haviland. Boston: Little, Brown, 1959. (These stories have been translated and retold from the following French sources:

- "The Twelve Dancing Princesses," from *Contes Du Roi Cambrinus* by Charles Deulin (Paris, E. Dentu, Editeur, Libraire de la Société des Gens de Lettres, 1874).

- "Puss in Boots" and "The Sleeping Beauty in the Wood," from *Histoires Ou Contest Du Temps Passé* by Charles Perrault (1697).

- "Drakestail," from *Affenschwanz Et Cetera. Variantes Orales De Contes Populaires Français Et Étrangers* compiled by Charles Marelle (2nd e. Westermann, 1888).

- "Beauty and the Beast" by Mme. Le Prince de Beaumong in *Contes De Fées Tirés De C. Perrault, De Mmes. D'Aulnoy Et Le Prince De Beaumont* (Paris, Libraire Hachette & Cie, 1875).

Peterson, Jeanne Whitehouse. *I Have a Sister—My Sister Is Deaf.* New York: Harper and Row, 1977.

Rawlings, Marjorie Kinnan. *The Yearling.* New York: Scribner, 1938.

Rawls, Wilson. *Where the Red Fern Grows.* New York: Bantam, 1976. First published 1961 by Doubleday, Garden City, New York.

———. *Summer of the Monkeys.* New York: Dell, 1977.

Richardson, Judy S., and Raymond F. Morgan. *Reading to Learn in the Content Areas.* Belmont, CA: Wadsworth, 1990.

Routman, Regie. *Conversations: Strategies for Teaching, Learning, and Evaluation.* Portsmouth, NH: Heinemann, 2000.

Routman, Regie. *Invitations: Changing Teachers and Learners.* Portsmouth, NH: Heinemann, 1994.

Routman, Regie. *Writing Essentials.* Portsmouth, NH: Heinemann, 2005.

Sanders, Dori. *Clover.* New York: Fawcett Columbine, 1991.

Shotwell, Louisa Rossiter. *Roosevelt Grady.* Cleveland: World, 1963.

Shreve, Susan. *The Flunking of Joshua T. Bates.* New York: Knopf, 1984.

Singer, Isaac Bashevis. *Zlateh the Goat and Other Stories.* New York: Harper, 1966.

Southern Regional Education Board Health and Human Services Commission. *Getting Schools Ready for Children: The Other Side of the Readiness Goal.* Atlanta, GA: Southern Regional Education Board, 1994.

Spinelli, Jerry. *Maniac Magee.* Boston: Little, Brown, 1990.

Spyri, Johanna. *Heidi*. New York: Messner, 1982. First published 1885 by Cupples, Upham and Company, Boston, Massachusetts. (Translation by Louise Brooks.).

SREB. *See* Southern Regional Education Board.

Steinbeck, John. *The Grapes of Wrath*, New York: Viking, 1939.

Steptoe, Javaka, ed. *In Daddy's Arms I am Tall: African Americans Celebrating Fathers*. New York: Lee and Low Books, 1997.

Steptoe, John. *Stevie*. New York: Harper and Row, 1969.

Stevenson, Robert Louis. *Treasure Island*. New York: Scribner, 1981. First published 1883 by Cassell Publishers, London.

Swift, Jonathan. *Gulliver's Travels*. Garden City, NY: Doubleday, 1945. First published about 1726 by the fictional publisher Richard Sympson.

Taylor, Mildred D. *Roll of Thunder, Hear My Cry*. New York: Dial Press, 1976.

Tompkins, Gail E. *Literacy for the 21st Century: A Balanced Approach*. 4th ed. Upper Saddle River, NJ: Pearson, 2006.

Trelease, Jim. *The Read-Aloud Handbook*. New York: Penguin Books, 1985.

Tsuchiya, Yukio. *Faithful Elephants: A True Story of Animals, People, and War*. Boston: Houghton Mifflin, 1988.

Twain, Mark. *The Adventures of Tom Sawyer*. New York: Morrow, 1989. First published 1876 by American Publishers, Hartford, Connecticut.

————. *Tom Sawyer and Huckleberry Finn*. New York: Knopf, 1991.

"Using a Neurological Impress Activity." No author. *www.sil.org/lingualinks/ literacyprogram/usinganeurologicalimpressactiv.htm*.

Vacca, Richard T., and Jo Anne L. Vacca. *Content Area Reading*. 3rd ed. Glenview, IL: Scott, Foresman, 1989.

Ward, Lynd. *The Biggest Bear*. New York: Houghton Mifflin, 1952.

White, E. B. *Charlotte's Web*. New York: Harper and Row, 1952.

Wilder, Laura Ingalls. *Little House in the Big Woods*. New York: Harper, 1953.

Wyss, Johann. *Swiss Family Robinson*. New York: Sharon, 1981. First published 1818 in English in London by M. J. Godwin and Company, as translated from German of M. Wiss of 1812 and published in Zürich..

Yarbrough, Camille. *Cornrows*. New York: Coward, McCann, and Geoghegan, 1979.

Yashima, Taro. *Crow Boy*. New York: Viking Press, 1955.

CHAPTER

Mathematics

3

SCOPE AND SEQUENCE OF SKILLS

The main topics (scope) in elementary mathematics and the sequence (order) in which the school introduces the topics is essentially the same in all states. The table on the next page details these main topics and their introduction order.

Sets and Number Concepts

A basic mathematical concept is that of **set**. A set is a collection of things, real or imagined, related or unrelated. Students may manipulate the objects within the set in various ways.

Classifying Objects in a Set

Classification allows the students to sort materials according to some specific criteria. A child who is not yet able to count, for example, might sort objects by whether the objects are soft or hard, by whether a magnet will attract them, or by other attributes.

Ordering objects in a set. Students may **order** the objects or arrange them in size from smallest to largest or from largest to smallest.

Table 3-1. Scope and Sequence of Skills

Grade Level	Numbers, Order, Values	Addition, Subtraction	Ratios, Measurement, Decimals	Fractions, Comparisons	Equations, Colors, Geometry	Multiplication, Division	Graph, Estimation, Solving
Kindergarten	Count by 1s and 10s to 100 Count by 2s and 5s Write numbers to 10 Write families to 100 Use values of 10s and 1s place	Add single digits with no regrouping	Use dime, nickel, penny, and dollar Tell time on hour and half hour Name days of week and seasons Identify cup and quart Read inches	Recognize ½, ⅓, and ¼ Compare longer, shorter, taller, etc.	Recognize primary and secondary colors and black Recognize square, circle, and triangle Use *up, down, top,* and *next*		Identify what comes next Read pictographs and simple bar graphs
1	Count by 1s, 2s, 5s, and 10s Use place values of 1s, 10s, and 100s	Write and give addition facts from 1 to 18 Add with regrouping in 1s place Subtract without regrouping	Name months and days Tell time on quarter hour Use nickel, dime, and quarter Identify pint and pound	Recognize ½, ⅓, ¼, ⅕, ⅙, ⅛	Recognize circle, square, oval, diamond, triangle, and cube		Read bar graphs Identify height and length Round numbers using a number line
2	Identify even and odd numbers Use tally marks Use and explain the value of 1,000s place Determine greater than, less than, equal to Identify what comes before and after Use Roman numerals	Add with carrying in 1s, 10s, and 100s place Perform horizontal addition Solve word problems	Name months and their abbreviations Tell time on five minutes Perform operations with money, including $5, $10, and $20 bills Read a Fahrenheit thermometer Identify liquid and dry measures	Compare two numbers Read fraction words Identify fractional parts of groups and sets	Determine area, perimeter, and volume Recognize pyramid, pentagon, and hexagon	Use multiplication facts from 0 to 10	Round numbers, height, and time Read grids and line graphs

(Continued)

Table 3-1. (Continued from previous page)

Grade Level	Numbers, Order, Values	Addition, Subtraction	Ratios, Measurement, Decimals	Fractions, Comparisons	Equations, Colors, Geometry	Multiplication, Division	Graph, Estimation, Solving
3	Read word numbers to 1 million Show expanded numbers Explain the properties of 1 and 0 Use the terms *odd, tally marks, greater than* Be able to tell what comes before, what comes after Use the 1000s place Use Roman numerals	Use sum, estimating, borrowing, word problems Demonstrate carrying or regrouping in the 1s, 10s, and 100s place Use horizontal addition Solve word problems	Use Fahrenheit and Celsius temperature measurements Use tenths Add and subtract dollars and cents Be able to use months and their abbreviations Tell time with accuracy to five minutes Perform operations with money Recognize five, ten and twenty dollar bills Use both liquid and dry measures	Identify fractional parts of whole and sets Rename fractions Compare numbers using greater than, less than, and equal signs Use fraction words Demonstrate the use of fractional parts of groups Use sets to illustrate fractions and illustrate fractions with sets	Compute the volume of cube Recognize rays, angles, congruent shapes, and prisms Compute area and perimeter of volume, pyramid, pentagon, hexagon	Use division facts from 1 to 10 Calculate 1- and 2-digit quotients with and without remainders Use multiplication facts 0 to 10	Continue work with graphs and grids Round numbers to the 10,000 place Tell time accurately to the minute
4	Use values to 100 billion Use and recognize prime and composite Determine factors Give ordinal and cardinal numbers	Give addition properties Add and subtract numbers up to 6 digits Subtract with regrouping Subtract money	Use the terms AM and PM Explain the term *century* Compute time in various time zones Use the prefixes *milli-, centi-, deci-, deca-, hecto-, kilo* Convert fractions to decimals Perform operations on decimals and ratios Use equal ratios	Recognize fractional parts of whole and name them correctly Give word fractions Provide equivalent fractions Add and subtract fractions with like and unlike denominators	Recognize shapes and solids Use the terms *obtuse, vertex, ray, diameter, radius* Perform operations on equations	Calculate averages Use aeros in the quotient correctly Multiply 2- to 3-digit numbers	Compare and coordinate graphs

(Continued)

Table 3-1. *(Continued from previous page)*

Grade Level	Numbers, Order, Values	Addition, Subtration	Ratios, Measurement, Decimals	Fractions, Comparisons	Equations, Colors, Geometry	Multiplication, Division	Graph, Estimation, Solving
5	Determine prime factors Use factor trees Use exponents Equal, not equal	Apply addition properties and facts Apply addition operation with 2 to 6 digits Determine missing addends Work with equations Subtract Estimate	Use standard and metric measure Count change Solve problems with ratios and percentages Figure amount of sales tax Determine discounts	Find least common multiples Solve problems with unlike denominators Perform operations on mixed numerals Rename numbers Reduce fractions to lowest terms	Use a compass and a protractor Solve measurement problems using surface area Perform operations on fractions Recognize and use chords Classify polygons	Calculate mean, mode, and median Problem solve by choosing the proper operation Figure probability with one-variable problems Demonstrate ability to apply calculator math	Multiply 3-digit numbers Calculate averages with remainders Divide money Estimate quotients Determine division and multiplication properties
6	Round to 10s, 100s, and 1000s place Use scientific notation Use the correct order of operations Use integers Calculate square roots	Continue addition and subtraction Continue to work with equations	Cross products Divide and multiply by 10, 100, 1000 Determine equal ratios Use cross products to solve for *n*	Determine reciprocals Divide by fractions Perform operations on fractions Divide by whole and mixed numbers	Construct a right and equilateral triangle, and a parallelogram and square Bisect an angle	Choose the proper operation Find patterns Set up budgets Apply some business math, such as figuring interest and balancing a check book.	Divide using 4-digit divisors Estimate quotients Supply missing factors

Patterning objects in a set. Students may try arranging the objects in a set to duplicate **a pattern that they observe**. The students may, for instance, try to replicate a color pattern with beads: red, yellow, red, yellow, and so on. Later, they may try to replicate a number pattern using magnetic numbers; the pattern may be 2, 4, 6, etc. They may even match the correct number of pennies to the magnetic number for another type of patterning. Making a pattern of geometric shapes would be another example, for instance, square, circle, triangle, square, circle, triangle, etc.

Comparing objects in a set. Students may **compare** objects in a set to objects in another set as a help in preparing for number skills. Is there a chair for each toy bear? Does each child in the set of children in the classroom have a carton of milk? Does each carton of milk have a straw for the child to use? Later, the students will compare each object in a set with a counting number; this will give the total number of objects in the set.

Students may try pairing objects with the numbers that they have memorized through rote, this is **oral counting**. After classifying objects, a student may try counting the objects in the groups. For example, if the teacher asks, "How many objects were soft?" the answer is a number that tells how many, and the student will have to count to find the answer.

Number. Number is a concept or idea that indicates how many. Children may memorize the counting numbers from 1 to 10 and be able to count by rote before they start school. Many times, however, there is little understanding in the beginning of what a number is. After the students have some idea of the value of the numbers, they may arrange the numbers from largest to smallest or smallest to largest. Students may try counting by pairing the objects with a number on the number line; this will give a visual comparison. The set {1, 2, 3, 4, . . . } can represent counting numbers. Study the following number line. Notice that the counting numbers start with 1 and that 0 is not in the set of counting numbers.

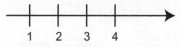

Whole numbers are the counting numbers plus 0: {0, 1, 2, 3, . . . }. Study the following number line. Notice that 0 is part of the set of whole numbers.

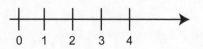

A **number** is a concept; a **numeral** is a symbol used to represent a number. The students must be able to read and to write the numerals. This skill is an important part of a student's early mathematical development. An important part of mathematical learning and of language arts learning is being able to read and to represent the numbers in words: *one*, *two*, *three*, and so on. Students may also try another way of counting: **skip counting**. They may start with 1 and count only the odd numbers: 3, 5, 7, 9, and so on. **Odd numbers** are those that cannot be evenly divided by 2. Students may also try skip counting with another beginning point; for instance, they may start with 2 and count only the even numbers: 2, 4, 6, 8, 10, and so on. **Even numbers** are those that one can evenly divide by 2.

Base-10 Numeration System and Place Value

Our numeration system uses the Hindu-Arabic numerals (0, 1, 2, 3, 4, 5, 6, 7, 8, 9) to represent numbers. Our numeration system follows a **base-10 place-value** scheme. As we move to the left in any number, each place value is 10 times the place value to the right. Similarly, as we move to the right, each place value is one-tenth the place value to the left. For example, in the number 543, the value of the place that the 5 is in (100s) is 10 times the value of the place that the 4 occupies (10s). The place value of the 3 is one-tenth the place value of the 4.

Expanded notation can show the value of each number in its place. Using the same number 543, the values are $(5 \times [10 \times 10]) + (4 \times [10 \times 1]) + (3 \times 1)$. **Exponential notation** can show the value of each number. Using the same number 543, the exponential values are $(5 \times 10^2) + (4 \times 10^1) + (3 \times 10^0)$.

THE FOUR BASIC OPERATIONS

Operations indicate what one is to do with numbers. There are four main operations: addition, subtraction, multiplication, and division. Multiplication is repeated addition. Division is repeated subtraction.

Addition is an operation that, when performed on numbers of disjoint sets (sets with different members), results in a **sum**. One can show addition on a number line by counting forward. Addition is also a **binary operation**, meaning it combines only two numbers at a time to produce a third, unique number. Adding two whole numbers always results in a whole number. The **algorithm** of addition is the form in which we write and solve an addition example. Familiar short forms are

2 (addend) + 3 (addend) = 5 (sum) and

$$
\begin{array}{r}
2 \text{ (addend)} \\
+\ 3 \text{ (addend)} \\
\hline
5 \text{ (sum)}
\end{array}
$$

The operation of **subtraction** is the **inverse** of addition: what addition does, subtraction undoes. Like addition, subtraction is a binary operation; that is, we work on only two numbers at a time. The result is a third, unique number called the **difference**. Given two whole numbers, subtracting the smaller number from the larger one results in a whole number. However, subtraction of whole numbers does not result in a whole number if the larger whole number is subtracted from the smaller one. The algorithm of subtraction is the form in which we write and solve a subtraction example. Familiar short forms are

5 − 3 = 2 and

$$
\begin{array}{r}
5 \text{ (minuend)} \\
-\ 3 \text{ (subtrahend)} \\
\hline
2 \text{ (difference)}
\end{array}
$$

Addition problems with a missing addend are solved with the operation of subtraction, for example, ___ (addend) + 3 (addend) = 5 (sum).

Multiplication, like addition and subtraction, is a binary operation. The result of the operation of multiplication is the **product**. The product of multiplying two whole numbers is always a whole number.

The operation of **division** has the same inverse relation to multiplication as subtraction has to addition: what multiplication does, division undoes. For example, multiplying 4 by 9 results in a product of 36; dividing 36 by 9 "gives back" a **quotient** of 4. Teaching division should parallel teaching multiplication.

Modeling the Operations

There are four ways to model the operations:

1. Concrete method. With the concrete method, the teacher allows the students to use real objects. The students can represent a set and take away objects from it (subtraction), or they can combine two sets with no common objects (addition).

2. Semiconcrete method. With the semiconcrete method, the students work with visual representations (pictures) instead of actual objects.

3. Semiabstract method. With the semiabstract method, the students work with one symbol (tally marks, x's, y's, etc.) to represent objects; instead of actual objects, pictures, or abstract (numerical) representations, the students use one symbol. The semiabstract method can be used to represent, for instance, a multiplication problem. If there are three rabbits and if each rabbit eats four carrots each day, how many carrots will the rabbits eat in one day?

        Rabbit 1   ////

        Rabbit 2   ////

        Rabbit 3   ////

4. Abstract method. With the abstract method, the student matches the elements of a given group with abstract numbers. To represent three rabbits eating four carrots daily using the abstract method, the student would set up the problem as 3×4.

Regrouping in Addition and Subtraction

Regrouping in addition, a process that teachers and students once called *carrying*, is evident in addition problems, such $16 + 7$ and $26 + 6$. To begin working with students on this process, the teacher would ideally drop back to the concrete level. For example, to work on the problem $16 + 7$, the teacher would have the students make one bundle of 10 straws and lay 6 straws to the side; when the students see 7 straws added to the 6 straws, they realize that they need to make another bundle of 10 straws. When they make that second bundle, they have the answer: two groups of 10 and 3 extra straws, or 23.

Regrouping in subtraction, a process that teachers and students once called *borrowing*, is evident in problems such as 23 – 7. The students can readily see that they cannot subtract the big number 7 from the small number 3; to accomplish this process, the students again can use concrete objects to begin the process. With two bundles of 10 straws and one group of 3 straws on the table, the students should count out 7 straws; when the students see that they cannot subtract 7 from 3, they can unbundle one packet of 10 straws and place the 10 straws with the 3 straws. The students can pull 7 straws from the 13; 6 straws will be left along with one bundle of 10—the answer: 16.

Modeling Multiplication

As noted earlier, pairs of operations that "undo" each other are **inverse**. Multiplication and division are inverse, or they "undo" one another.

An **array** can model a multiplication problem. The first number in a multiplication problem is the vertical number in an array; the second number is the horizontal number. The following is the array for $2 \times 3 = 6$.

x	x	x
x	x	x

Multiplication Properties and Algorithms

The **multiples** of any whole number are the results of multiplying that whole number by the counting numbers. For example, the multiples of 7 are 7, 14, 21, 28, and so on. Every whole number has an infinite number of multiples.

Terms related to multiplication and key properties of the multiplication operation include the following:

Multiplicative identity property of 1. Any number multiplied by 1 remains the same, for instance, $34 \times 1 = 34$. The number 1 is called the **multiplicative identity**.

Property of reciprocals. The product of any number (except 0) multiplied by its reciprocal is 1. The **reciprocal** of a number is 1 divided by that number. Remember that dividing by 0 has no meaning; avoid dividing by 0 when computing or solving equations and inequalities.

Commutative property for addition and multiplication. The order of adding addends or multiplying factors does not determine the sum or product. For example, 6 × 9 gives the same product as 9 × 6. Division and subtraction are not commutative.

Associative property for addition and multiplication. Associating, or grouping, three or more addends or factors in a different way does not change the sum or product. For example, (3 + 7) + 5 results in the same sum as 3 + (7 + 5). Division and subtraction are not associative.

Distributive property of multiplication over addition. A number multiplied by the sum of two other numbers can be handed out, or distributed, to both numbers, multiplied by each of them separately, and the products added together. For example, multiplying 6 by 47 gives the same result as multiplying 6 by 40, multiplying 6 by 7, and then adding the products. That is, 6 × 47 = (6 × 40) + (6 × 7). The definition of the distributive property of multiplication over addition can be stated simply: the product of a number and a sum can be expressed as a sum of two products. The simple notation form of the distributive property is

$$a(b + c) = (a \times b) + (a \times c).$$

Another major concept in multiplication is **regrouping**, or carrying. The term *regrouping* indicates the renaming of a number from one place value to another. The short algorithm we are most familiar with does not show the steps that illustrate the regrouping. Students must be able to use the multiplication facts, multiply by 0, and apply regrouping to solve problems such as 268 × 26.

Special Properties of 0 and 1

The **natural numbers** include the set of counting numbers (1, 2, 3, 4, 5, . . .) and the set of whole numbers (0, 1, 2, 3, 4, 5, . . .). The natural number 0 has special mathematical significance with respect to the operation of addition. The number 0 added to any natural number yields a sum that is the same as the other natural number; 0 is, therefore, the **additive identity**, or the **identity element of addition**.

Because multiplication is repeated addition, 0 holds a special property with both multiplication and addition. The **multiplication property of 0** states that when a factor is multiplied by 0, then the product is 0. The **identity element of multiplication** is 1; the identity element of multiplication means that any factor multiplied by 1

◄ *PRAXIS Pointer*

Read the question before studying graphs, maps or tables. Then read the graph with the question in mind.

gives that factor. Zero is not an identity element for subtraction or for division. Subtraction does not have an identity element. Even though $4 - 0 = 4$, it is not true that $0 - 4 = 4$. Division by 0 is not possible, so 0 is not an identity element for division.

Factors, Primes, Composites, and Multiples

Factors are any of the numbers or symbols in mathematics that, when multiplied together, form a product. For example, the whole-number factors of 12 are 1, 2, 3, 4, 6, and 12. A number with only two whole-number factors—1 and the number itself—is a **prime number**. The first few primes are 2, 3, 5, 7, 11, 13, and 17. Most other whole numbers are **composite numbers** because they are *composed* of several whole-number factors. The number 1 is neither prime nor composite; it has only one whole-number factor: 1.

As noted earlier, the **multiples** of any whole number are the results of multiplying that whole number by the counting numbers. For example, the multiples of 7 are 7, 14, 21, 28, and so on. Every whole number has an infinite number of multiples.

Modeling Division

Division, the inverse of multiplication, can be represented in two ways: measurement and partition. With **measurement division**, the students know how many in each group (set) but do not know how many sets. Here is an example: A homeowner has a group of 400 pennies. He plans to give each trick-or-treater five pennies. How many trick-or-treaters can receive a treat before the homeowner has to turn out the porch light? In this case, the students know the number of pennies (measurement) each child will receive; they need to find the number of children.

In **partitive division**, students know the number of groups (sets), but they do not know the number of objects in each set. Here is an example: There is a plate of eight cookies on the table. There are four children at the table. How many cookies does each child get if they divide the cookies evenly? The question asks the students to determine how many are in each group.

No properties of division—commutative, associative, and so on—hold true at all times. Division is the most difficult of the algorithms for students to use. Division begins at the left, rather than at the right. Also, to solve a division problem, students must not only divide but subtract and multiply as well. Students must use estimation with the trial quotients; sometimes it takes several trials before the trial is successful.

Rational Numbers, Fractions, Decimals, and Percents

Rational numbers are all the numbers that can be expressed as the quotient of two integers; **integers** are counting numbers, the opposite of counting numbers, and zero. Rational numbers can be expressed as fractions, percents, or decimals.

Common **fractions** are in the form a/b, where a and b are whole numbers. Integers can be expressed as fractions, but not all fractions can be expressed as integers. For example, the number 4 can be expressed as 4/1. However, the fraction 1/4 cannot be expressed as an integer, or as a whole number. There are more fractions than whole numbers; between every integer is a fraction. Between the fraction and the whole number is another fraction; between the fraction and the other fraction is another fraction, and so on. Negative and positive fractions are not integers unless they are equivalent to whole numbers or their negative counterparts.

Decimal numbers are fractions written in special notation. For instance, 0.25 can be thought of as the fraction 1/4. All decimal numbers are actually fractions. When expressed as decimals, some fractions terminate and some do not. For instance, 0.315 is a terminating decimal; 0.0575757 . . . is a repeating (nonterminating) decimal. All fractions, however, can be written as decimals. There are more decimals than integers. Fractions, decimal numbers, and percents are different ways of representing values. It is useful to be able to convert from one to the other. The following paragraphs provide some conversion tips.

The practical method for changing a fraction into a decimal is by **dividing the numerator by the denominator**. For example, 1/4 becomes 0.25 when 1 is divided by 4, as follows:

$$4\overline{)1.00}^{\,.25}$$

Naturally, this can be done longhand or with a calculator. (If the fraction includes a whole number, as in 23/5, the whole number is not included in the division.) The decimal number may terminate or repeat. Converting a simple fraction to a decimal number never results in an irrational number. **Irrational numbers** are all the real numbers that are not rational; irrational numbers include $\sqrt{2}$, $\sqrt{3}$, pi, etc. **Rational numbers** are all numbers that can be expressed as the quotient of two integers. (A number cannot be expressed with 0 in the denominator.) **Real numbers** are all the numbers that can be represented by points on the number line. The set of real numbers includes all the rational numbers (positive numbers, negative numbers, and 0) and all the irrational numbers ($\sqrt{2}$, $\sqrt{3}$, pi, etc.). To convert a nonrepeating (terminating) decimal number to a fraction in lowest terms, write the decimal as a fraction with the denominator a power of 10, and then reduce to lowest terms. For example, 0.125 can be written as 125/1,000, which reduces to 1/8. Any decimal number can be converted to a **percent** by shifting the decimal point two places to the right and adding the percent symbol (%). For instance, 0.135 becomes 13.5%. (If the number before the percent symbol is a whole number, there is no need to show the decimal point.)

A percent can be converted to a decimal number by shifting the decimal point two places to the left and dropping the percent symbol. For example, 98% becomes 0.98 as a decimal.

A percent can be converted to a fraction by putting the percent (without the percent symbol) over 100 and then reducing. In this way, 20% can be shown as $^{20}/_{100}$, which reduces to 1/5.

Ratio, Percents, Proportion

Ratio notation is an alternative method for showing fractions. For example, 2/5 can be expressed as "the ratio of 2 to 5." The use of ratio notation emphasizes the relationship of one number to another. To show ratios, one may use numbers with a colon between them; 2:5 is the same ratio as 2 to 5 and 2/5.

To illustrate the equivalencies and conversions just described, consider the fraction 19/20. As a decimal, it is 0.95. As a percent, it is 95%. As a ratio, it is 19 to 20, or 19:20.

Proportion is an equation of two equivalent ratios. For example, $2/5 = N/10$ asks the problem solver to supply the missing numerator to make the two fractions equivalent.

Function Machine

Teachers often use the function machine to encourage the students to find the missing addend, the missing factor, the missing operation, and so on. The function machine can also be used as an introduction to algebra.

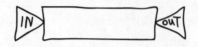

If one inserts the number 4 into the 3 times function machine pictured in the figure, the output would be 12.

The following function machine is a subtraction machine. If the output is 12 and the input is 15, what is the value of the function machine?

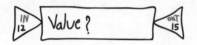

The function machine above is, of course, a +3 function machine.

INFORMAL GEOMETRY AND MEASUREMENT

Types of Angles and Pairs

An **angle** consists of all the points in two noncollinear rays that have the same vertex. More simply, an angle is commonly thought of as two arrows joined at their bases; the point at which they join is called the **vertex**. Two angles are **adjacent** if they share a common vertex, they share only one side, and one angle does not lie in the interior of the other.

Angles are usually measured in **degrees** (°). A circle has a measure of 360°; a half circle, 180°; a quarter circle, 90°, and so forth. If the sum of the measures of two angles is 90°, the two angles are **complementary**. If the sum of the measures of the two angles is 180°, the two angles are **supplementary**. If two lines intersect, they form two pairs of **vertical angles**.

If a third line intersects two intersecting lines at the same point of intersection, the third intersecting line is called a **transversal**. In the following drawing, *t* is the transversal.

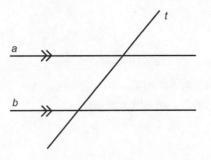

Two lines crossed by a transversal form eight angles. The four angles that lie between the two lines are called **interior angles**. The interior angles that lie on the same side of the transversal are called **consecutive interior angles**. The interior angles that lie on opposite sides of the transversal are called **alternate interior angles**. In the previous figure, angles *A* and *D* are alternate interior angles, as are angles *B* and *C*.

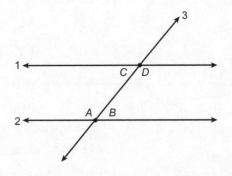

Consider the drawing shown on the next page. The four angles that lie outside the two lines are the **exterior angles**. Exterior angles that lie on the same side of the transversal are the **consecutive exterior angles**, and those that lie on opposite sides of the transversal are the **alternate exterior angles**. Angles *A* and *D* are alternate exterior angles; they have the same degree measurement. Angles *B* and *C* are also alternate exterior angles. An interior angle and an exterior angle that have different vertices and have sides on the same side of the transversal are the **corresponding angles**.

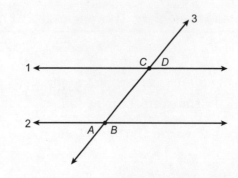

If the measures of two angles are the same, the angles are **congruent**. An angle with a measure of 90° is a **right angle**. An angle measuring less than 90° is an **acute angle**. An angle measuring more than 90° is an **obtuse angle**.

Lines and Planes

If lines have a point or points in common, they are said to **intersect**. Lines are **perpendicular** if they contain the sides of a right angle. Lines are **parallel** if they do not intersect.

Through any two points, there is exactly one straight **line**; straight lines are one-dimensional. A **plane** is two-dimensional (think of a surface without elevations or depressions). These concepts form the foundation of other important geometric terms and ideas.

The Pythagorean Theorem

Triangles have various properties. One is that the sum of the measures of the three angles of any triangle is 180°. If students know the measures of two angles, they can deduce the third using first addition and then subtraction. The **Pythagorean theorem** states that in any right triangle with legs (shorter sides) a and b and a hypotenuse (longest side) c, the sum of the squares of the sides equals the square of the hypotenuse. In algebraic notation, the Pythagorean theorem is given as $a^2 + b^2 = c^2$.

PRAXIS Pointer

Work quickly and steadily. You have two hours to complete the test. Avoid focusing on any one problem too long. Taking the practice tests in this book will help you learn to budget your precious time.

Basic Characteristics of Geometric Shapes

Point

Students in the elementary grades typically solve problems involving two- and three-dimensional geometric figures (for example, perimeter and area problems, volume and surface-area problems). A fundamental concept of geometry is the notion of a point. A **point** is a specific location, taking up no space, having no area, and frequently represented by a dot. A point is considered one dimensional. Through any two points, there is exactly one straight line; straight lines are one dimensional.

Plane

A **plane** is two dimensional (think of a surface without elevations or depressions). That definition forms the foundation for other important geometric terms and ideas. The **perimeter** of a two-dimensional (flat) shape or object is the distance around the object. **Volume** refers to how much space is inside a three-dimensional, closed container. **Area** is a measure that expresses the size of a plane region; it is expressed in square units. It is useful to think of volume as how many cubic units fit into a solid. If the container is a rectangular solid, the volume is the product of width times length times height. If all six faces (sides) of a rectangular solid are squares, the object is a cube.

Polygon

A **polygon** is a simple closed curve formed by the union of three or more straight sides; a **regular polygon** is one whose angles are equal in measure. Every polygon that is not regular is irregular.

In an *n*-sided regular polygon, the sides are all the same length (**congruent**) and are symmetrically placed about a common center (that is, the polygon is both equiangular and equilateral). Only certain regular polygons can be constructed using the classical Greek tools of the compass and straightedge.

The terms *equilateral triangle* and *square* refer to regular polygons with three and four sides, respectively. The words for polygons with more than five sides (for example, *pentagon, hexagon, heptagon,* etc.) can refer to either regular or nonregular polygons, although the terms generally refer to regular polygons unless otherwise specified.

Regular Rectangle

A **regular rectangle** is a quadrilateral (four-sided figure) in which sides opposite each other are both of equal length and parallel. A square is the special case of a regular rectangle whose angles are equal (90°) and all sides are of equal length and parallel. If each side of a regular rectangle is of length s, the area (A) and perimeter (P) is given as follows:

$$A = s^2 \text{ (square)}$$

$$A = l \times w \text{ (quadrilateral)}$$

$$P = 4s \text{ (square)}$$

$$P = l + l + w + w \text{ (or } 2l + 2w) \text{ (quadrilateral)}$$

Regular Triangle

The area of a triangle is the product of half its base multiplied by its height. Using either the Pythagorean theorem or trigonometric functions, one can assign each side a length of b and can describe the height of a **regular triangle** (an equilateral triangle) in terms of the length of its sides. The length is equal to b multiplied by the square root of 3/4, so that the area and perimeter are as follows:

$$A = b^2 \sqrt{3/4}$$

$$P = 3b$$

Polygons in a Plane

In a plane, three-sided polygons are *triangles*, four-sided polygons are *quadrilaterals*, five-sided polygons are *pentagons*, six-sided polygons are *hexagons*, and eight-sided polygons are *octagons*. (Note that not all quadrilaterals are squares.) If two polygons (or any figures) have exactly the same size and shape, they are *congruent*. If they are the same shape but different sizes, they are *similar*.

Applying Geometric Concepts

Symmetry can be thought of as an imaginary fold line producing two congruent, mirror-image figures. Some geometric figures do not have symmetry. Polygons may have lines of symmetry, which can be thought of as imaginary fold lines that produce two congruent, mirror-image figures. Squares have four lines of symmetry, and nonsquare rectangles have two, as shown later. Circles have an infinite number of lines of symmetry; a few are shown on the circle below.

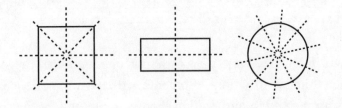

Geometric figures are **similar** if they have exactly the same shape, even if they are not the same size. In the following figure, triangles *A* and *B* are similar:

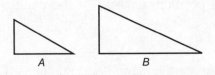

Corresponding angles of similar figures have the same measure, and the lengths of corresponding sides are proportional. In the following figure, which shows similar triangles, $\angle A \cong \angle D$ (meaning "angle *A* is congruent to angle *D*"), $\angle B \cong \angle E$, and $\angle C \cong \angle F$. The corresponding sides of the triangles are proportional, meaning that

$$\frac{AB}{DE} = \frac{BC}{EF} = \frac{CA}{FD}$$

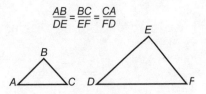

A **tessellation** is a collection of plane figures that fill the plane with no overlaps and no gaps. The following chart provides some examples:

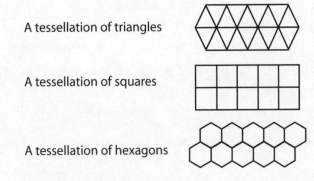

A tessellation of triangles

A tessellation of squares

A tessellation of hexagons

Scaling that is uniform is a linear transformation that enlarges or reduces an object; the scale factor is the same in all directions. The result of uniform scaling is an object that is similar (in the geometric sense) to the original. Scaling may be directional or may have a separate scale factor for each axis direction. This type of scaling may result in a change in shape.

Transformations include a variety of different operations from geometry, including rotations, reflections, and translations. Students will have experience with transformations such as flips, turns, slides, and scaling. For example, the teacher might ask students to select a shape that is a parallelogram. Then the teacher might ask the students to do the following:

- Describe the original position and size of the parallelogram. Students can use labeled sketches if necessary.

- Translate (or slide) the parallelogram several times. (A **translation** of a figure occurs if it is possible to give an object a straight shove for a certain distance and in a certain direction.) Rotate the parallelogram two times. Students should list the steps they followed.

- Challenge a friend to return the parallelogram to its original position.

- Determine if the friend used a reversal of the original steps or a different set of steps.

Determining and Locating Ordered Pairs

The **coordinate plane** is useful for graphing individual ordered pairs and relationships. The coordinate plane is divided into four quadrants by an x-axis (horizontal) and a y-axis (vertical). The upper-right quadrant is quadrant I, and the others (moving counterclockwise from quadrant I) are quadrants II, III, and IV.

Ordered pairs indicate the locations of points on the plane. For instance, the ordered pair $(-3, 4)$ describes a point that is three units *left* from the center of the plane (the **origin**) and four units *up*, as shown in the following diagram:

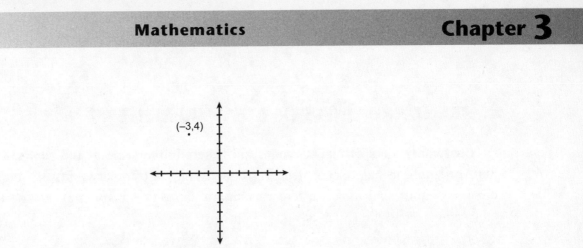

Ordered pairs are sets of data that one can display in a chart and graph on the coordinate plane. For example, the following set of data demonstrates four ordered pairs:

X	Y
3	5
4	6
5	7
6	8

Using Networks to Construct Three-Dimensional Geometric Shapes

A **network** (or net) is a union of points (its vertices or nodes) and the segments (its arcs) connecting them. The nets are, in effect, patterns for building three-dimensional triangles, cubes, and other geometric figures. The teacher may distribute the nets and the students may construct the figures by cutting, folding, and taping. Using the concrete level is an excellent way to develop geometric understanding in students; following the levels of learning mentioned earlier (concrete, semiconcrete, semiabstract, and abstract), the concrete level should come before using drawings alone to solve problems. Nets can help make this understanding possible. Below is a net for a tetrahedron—a tetranet.

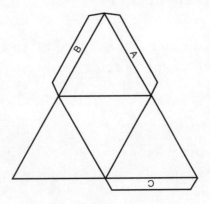

STANDARD UNITS OF MEASUREMENT

Customary units of measurement are generally the same as **U.S. units**. Customary units of length include inches, feet, yards, and miles. Customary units of weight include ounces, pounds, and tons. Customary units of capacity (or volume) include teaspoons, tablespoons, cups, pints, quarts, and gallons.

The **metric system of measurement** relates to the base-10 place-value scheme. The following chart lists the common metric prefixes:

Prefix	Meaning
Kilo-	Thousand (1,000)
Deci-	Tenth (0.1)
Centi-	Hundredth (0.01)
Milli-	Thousandth (0.001)

The basic unit of linear measure in the metric system is the **meter**, abbreviated as **m**. The relationships among the commonly used linear units of measurement in the metric system are

1 kilometer (km) = 1,000 m

1 meter (m) = 1.0 m

1 decimeter (dm) = 0.1 m

1 centimeter (cm) = 0.01 m

1 millimeter (mm) = 0.001 m

The centimeter is the metric unit of length used for short distances; about 2.5 centimeters equals 1 inch. The kilometer is a metric unit of length used for longer distances; slightly more than 1.5 kilometers equals a mile. A very fast adult runner could run a kilometer in about three minutes.

The basic unit of measurement for mass (or weight) in the metric system is the **gram**, abbreviated as **g**. The relationships among the commonly used units of measurement for mass in the metric system include:

1 kilogram (kg) = 1,000 g

1 gram (g) = 1.0 g

1 milligram (mg) = 0.001 g

A large paper clip weighs about 1 gram; it takes about 28 grams to make 1 ounce.

The basic unit of measurement for capacity (or volume) in the metric system is the **liter**, represented by **L** or **l**. The relationships among the most common metric units of capacity include

1 liter (l) = 1,000 milliliters (ml)

1 deciliter (dl) = 100 ml; 10 cl

1 centiliter (cl) = 10 ml

A liter is slightly smaller than a quart; it takes more than four liters to make a gallon.

Here are some frequently used customary-to-metric ratios. (Values are approximate.)

1 inch = 2.54 centimeters

1 yard = 0.91 meter

1 mile = 1.61 kilometers

1 ounce = 28.35 grams

1 pound = 2.2 kilograms

1 quart = 0.94 liter

One can determine the metric-to-customary conversions by taking the reciprocals of each of the factors just listed. For instance, 1 kilometer = 0.62 mile (computed by dividing 1 by 1.61).

An important step in solving problems involving measurement is to decide what is being measured. Generally, such problems fall under one of these categories: length, area, angles, volume, mass, time, money, and temperature. Solving measurement problems will likely require knowledge in several other areas of mathematics, especially algebra. The following is one example of a measurement problem that requires knowledge of several math topics (geometry, multiplication, conversions, estimation, measurement, etc.):

Sophie's Carpet Store charges $19.40 per square yard for the type of carpeting Tony would like in his bedroom (padding and labor included). How much would Tony pay to carpet his 9 × 12-foot room?

One way to find the solution is to convert the room dimensions to yards (3 × 4 yards) and multiply to get 12 square yards. The final step is to multiply 12 by the price of $19.40 per square yard, for a total price of $232.80.

PROBABILITY AND STATISTICS

Central Tendency and Range

Measures of central tendency of a set of values include the mean, median, and mode. The **mean** is found by adding all the values and then dividing the sum by the number of values. The **median** of a set is the middle number when the values are in numerical order. (If the set comprises an even number of values, and therefore no middle value, the mean of the middle two values gives the median.) The **mode** of a set is the value occurring most often. (Not all sets of values have a single mode; some sets have more than one.) Consider the following set:

$$6, 8, 14, 5, 6, 5, 5$$

The mean, median, and mode of the set are 7, 6, and 5, respectively. (Note that the mean is often referred to as the average, but all three measures are averages of sorts.)

The **range** of a set of numbers is a measure of the spread of, or variation in, the numbers.

Mean, Median, Mode, and Range

To determine the mean of a set of numbers, add the set of numbers and divide by the total number of elements in the set. For example, to find the mean of 15, 10, 25, 5, and 40, you would use the equation $(15 + 10 + 25 + 5 + 40) \div 5 = 19$.

To find the median, order a given set of numbers from smallest to largest; the median is the "middle" number. That is, half the numbers in the set of numbers are below the median and half the numbers in the set are above the median. For example, to find the median of the set of whole numbers 15, 10, 25, 5, and 40, the first step is to order the set of numbers: 5, 10, 15, 25, 40. Because 15 is the middle number (half of the numbers are below 15; half are above 15), 15 is the median of this set of whole numbers. If a set has an even number of numbers, the median is the mean of the middle two numbers. For instance, in the set of numbers 2, 4, 6, and 8, the median is the mean of 4 and 6, or 5.

The mode of the set of numbers 15, 10, 25, 10, 5, 40, 10, and 15 is the number 10 because it appears most frequently (three times).

The **range** of a set of numbers is obtained by subtracting the smallest number in the set from the largest number in the set. For example, to determine the range of the set 15, 10, 25, 5, and 40, you would use the equation $40 - 5 = 35$.

Probabilities of Dependent or Independent Events

Probability theory provides models for chance variations. The likelihood or chance that an event will take place is called the **probability** of the event. The probability of any event occurring is equal to the number of desired outcomes divided by the number of all possible events. Thus, the probability of blindly pulling a green ball out of a hat (in this case, the desired outcome) if the hat contains two green and five yellow balls is $^2/_7$ (about 29 percent).

The probability of 2/7 can also be expressed as the ratio of 2:7. We can also write the mathematical sentence with words:

$$\text{Probability of a particular event occurring} = \frac{\text{Number of ways the event can occur}}{\text{Total number of possible events}}$$

Determining Odds For and Against a Given Situation

Odds are related to but different from probability. The odds that any given event *will* occur can be expressed as the ratio of the probability that the event *will* occur to the probability that the event will *not* occur. In the example from the previous section, the odds that a green ball will be drawn are two to five (2:5) because two balls are green and five balls are not green.

If there are four marbles—three red and one blue—in a jar, the probability of drawing the blue is 1/4. There is one chance of a blue marble, and there are four total chances (marbles). Odds describe the number of chances for (or against) versus the number of chances against (or for). Because there is one chance of picking blue and three chances of picking red, the odds are three to one *against* picking the blue. For odds in favor, just reverse the numbers: the odds are one to three *in favor* of picking the blue. To repeat, if you express odds as *against*, you put the number of chances against first, versus the number of chances for. If you express odds as *in favor of*, you put the number of chances for first.

Note that the odds in the marbles example do not mean that the probability is 1/3 for or against. To convert odds to probability, one must add the chances. For example, if the odds against a horse winning are four to one, this means that, out of five (4 + 1) chances, the horse has one chance in favor of winning; the probability of the horse winning is 1/5 or 20 percent (*www.mathforum.org/library/drmath/view/56495.html*).

Applying Fundamental Counting Principles Such as Combinations to Solve Probability Problems

As noted earlier, probability is calculated as follows:

$$\text{Probability of a particular event occurring} = \frac{\text{Number of ways the event can occur}}{\text{Total number of possible events}}$$

Human sex type is determined by the genetic material in the sperm and egg. The genetic sex code for human females is XX. The genetic sex code for human males is XY. Eggs carry only X genes. Sperm carry both X and Y genes; the Y gene is the absence of the X gene. The following chart illustrates the probability of a fertilized human egg being male or female:

	Female	
	X	**X**
Male		
X	*XX*	*XX*
Y	*XY*	*XY*

The chart shows that the probability of a female (XX) is 2 out of 4, and the probability of a male (XY) is 2 out of 4. Therefore, there is a 50 percent chance of a boy and a 50 percent chance of a girl.

PROBLEM SOLVING

Selecting the Appropriate Operation(s) to Solve Problems Involving Ratios, Proportions, and Percents, and the Addition, Subtraction, Multiplication, and Division of Rational Numbers

The key to converting word problems into mathematical problems is attention to **reasonableness**, with the choice of operations being crucial to success. Often, individual words and phrases translate into numbers and operation symbols; making sure that the translations are reasonable is important.

Each word problem requires an individual approach, but keeping in mind the reasonableness of the computational setup should be helpful. Most modern math programs introduce the concept of ratio and use ratio to solve various problems. Consider this example:

> Pencils are priced at two for 25 cents. How many pencils can Teresa buy for 50 cents?

"Two pencils for 25 cents" suggests the fixed constant of 2/25:

$$\frac{2 \text{ (pencils)}}{25 \text{ (cents)}}$$

With a fixed ratio, it should be possible to figure out how many pencils Teresa can buy for 50 cents by setting up an equivalent ratio:

$$\frac{x \text{ (number of pencils)}}{50 \text{ (cents)}}$$

The relationship between the two ratios is one of equality; that is, they are equivalent ratios. As noted earlier in the chapter, an equation of two equivalent ratios is one of proportion. There are several ways to solve the equivalent ratios problem with the pencils, but one way to do it is to use **cross multiplication**:

$$\frac{x}{50} \times \frac{2}{25}$$

Cross multiplication gives $25x = 100$. Solving for x requires dividing 100 by 25 to get 4. Thus, Teresa can buy four pencils for 50 cents.

Another way to solve the problem is to set up a chart. You might even try extending the chart for several rows to be sure the values increase appropriately.

Pencils	Cost
2	25 cents
4	50 cents
6	75 cents

In solving problems involving percents, students must always consider reasonableness in their thinking and estimating. Mathematical reasoning includes analyzing problem situations, making conjectures, organizing information, and selecting strategies to solve problems. Students must rely on both formal and informal **reasoning processes**. A key informal process relies on reasonableness. Consider this problem:

> Center Town Middle School has an enrollment of 640 students. One day, 28 students were absent. What percent of the total number of students was absent?
>
> A. 28% C. 18%
>
> B. 1% D. 4%

Even a student who has forgotten how to compute percents would be able to reject some of the answer choices instantly: 28% is more than one-fourth, a "small-but-not-tiny" chunk of 640; answers like 1% and 18% are *unreasonable*. Look for **key words** in solving problems. The words may provide a clue as to which operation to use. The following chart gives some examples:

Operation	Key Words
Addition	*Added to, combined, increased by, more than, sum, together, total of*
Subtraction	*Decreased by, difference between, difference of, fewer than, less, less than, minus*
Multiplication	*Decreased by a factor of, increased by a factor of, multiplied by, product of, times*
Division	*Divide, equal groups, how many groups, how many to each, quotient, separate, share*

Using Estimation and Other Problem-Solving Strategies

Estimation is a useful tool in predicting and in checking the answer to a problem. Estimation is at the second level in Bloom's Taxonomy—the comprehension level. Thinking at the comprehension level requires students not only to recall or remember information but also to understand the meaning of information and to restate it in their own words.

The ability to render some real-life quandaries into mathematical or logical problems—workable using established procedures—is an important part of finding solutions. Because each quandary will be unique, so too will be students' problem-solving plans of attack. Still, many real-world problems that lend themselves to mathematical solutions are likely to require one of the following strategies:

Guess and Check

This is not the same as "wild guessing." With this problem-solving strategy, students make their best guess and then check the answer to see whether it is right. Even if the guess does not immediately provide the solution, it may help students get closer to it so that they can continue to work on it. Here's an example:

> The ages of three people add up to 72, and each person is one year older than the last person. What are their ages?

Because the three ages must add up to 72, it is reasonable to take one-third of 72 (24) as the starting point. Of course, even though 24 + 24 + 24 gives a sum of 72, those numbers do not match the information ("each person is one year older"). So, students might guess that the ages are 24, 25, and 26. Checking that guess by addition, students would see that the sum of 75 is too high. Lowering their guesses by one each, they then would try 23, 24, and 25, which indeed add up to 72, giving the students the solution. There are many variations of the guess-and-check method.

Make a Sketch or a Picture

Being able to visualize a problem can help to clarify it. Consider this problem:

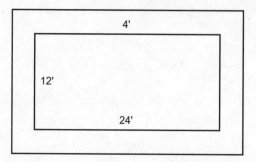

Mr. Rosenberg plans to put a 4-foot-wide concrete sidewalk around his backyard pool. The pool is rectangular, measuring 12 feet by 24 feet. The cost of the concrete is $1.28 per square foot. How much concrete is required for the job?

Students with exceptional visualization abilities will not need a sketch. For most, however, a drawing like the one shown here may be helpful in solving this and many other real-life problems.

Make a Table or a Chart

Sometimes organizing the information from a problem into a table or chart makes it easier to find the solution.

Make a List

Like a table or chart, a list can help organize information and perhaps provide or at least hint at a solution. The list-making strategy would work well for solving this problem:

How many different outcomes are there if you roll two regular six-sided dice?

Act it Out

Sometimes literally "doing" a problem—with physical objects or even their bodies—can help students produce a solution. A class problem that could be solved in this manner is the following:

If five strangers meet and everyone shakes everyone else's hand once, how many total handshakes will there be?

Look for Patterns

This technique encourages students to ask, "What's happening here?" Spotting a pattern would be helpful in solving a problem such as this:

Nevin's weekly savings account balances for 15 weeks are as follows: $125, $135, $148, $72, $85, $96, $105, $50, $64, $74, $87, $42, $51, $60, $70. If the pattern holds, what might Nevin's balance be the next week?

It appears that Nevin saves for two to three weeks; the following week he spends about half the accumulation. Because the total is $70, the observer would probably find about $35 in the savings account after Nevin's typical withdrawal.

Work a Simpler Problem

By finding the solution to a different but simpler problem, students might spot a way to solve the harder one. Estimating can be thought of as working a simpler problem. To find the product of 23×184 when no calculator or pencil and paper are handy, students could estimate the product by getting the exact answer to the simpler problem, 20×200.

Writing an Open Math Sentence (an equation with one or more variables, or unknowns) and Then Solving It

This is sometimes called "translating" a problem into mathematics. Here is a sample problem:

Tiana earned grades of 77%, 86%, 90%, and 83% on her first four weekly science quizzes. Assuming all grades are equally weighted, what score will she need on the fifth week's quiz to have an average (or mean) score of 88%?

Using the given information, students could set up and solve the following equation to answer the question:

$$\frac{(77 + 86 + 90 + 83 + x)}{5} = 88$$

Work Backward

Consider this problem:

If you add 12 to some number and then multiply the sum by 4, you will get 60. What is the number?

Students could find a solution by *starting at the end* with 60. The problem states that the 60 came from multiplying a sum by 4. When 15 is multiplied by 4, the result is 60. The sum must be 15; if 15 is the sum of 12 and something else, the "something else" can only be 3.

Selecting Appropriate Measurement Units to Solve Problems

Solving measurement problems requires first determining whether to use customary units or metric units. The next decision is whether the problem involves measurements of length, volume, mass, or temperature. Using the metric system requires choosing the appropriate prefix for *meter*.

There are, of course, hybrid approaches to problem solving. Students can mix and match strategies whenever they think they are appropriate. In general, attention to reasonableness may be most crucial to problem-solving success, especially in real-life situations.

Social Studies

GEOGRAPHY IN THE SOCIAL STUDIES CURRICULUM

Five Themes of Geography

The five themes of geography are place; location; human-environmental interaction; movement and connections; and regions, patterns, and processes. An understanding of these themes includes the ability to use them to analyze regions, states, countries, and the world to gain a perspective about interrelationships among those areas. When a teacher uses the five themes, students should gain the ability to compare regions:

1. In this world of fast-breaking news from throughout the globe, students must be able to recognize the **place** names of continents, countries, and even cities. In addition to geography, the theme of place encompasses the fields of political science.

2. An understanding of the theme of **location** requires knowledge of both absolute and relative location. **Absolute location** is determined by longitude and latitude. **Relative location** deals with the interactions that occur between and among places. Relative location involves the interconnectedness among people because of land, water, and technology. For example, the Silver River brought commerce and steamboats to

the Silver Springs area of Florida; the 99.8 percent pure artesian spring waters in one of the largest artesian spring formations in the world offered respite and beauty to settlers and tourists alike. Hullam Jones invented the glass-bottom boat there in 1878 and enabled visitors to view the underwater world of fish, turtles, crustaceans, and fossils more than 10,000 years old. The location of Silver Springs has contributed to the area's economic development and vitality. In addition to geography, the theme of location encompasses the fields of technology, history, and economics.

3. An understanding of the theme of **human-environmental interaction** involves consideration of how people rely on the environment, how people alter it, and how the environment may limit what people are able to do. For example, Silver Springs is at the headwaters of the Silver River. In the 1850s, barges carried cotton, lumber, and non-perishables up the Silver River to the area's growing population. The development of a stagecoach line and the arrival of conventional steamboats in Silver Springs in 1860 aided in the development of Silver Springs and the nearby areas. In addition to geography, the theme of human-environmental interaction encompasses the field of ecology.

4. An understanding of the theme of **movement and connections** requires identifying how people are connected through different forms of transportation and communication networks and how those networks have changed over time. This would include identifying channels for the movement of people, goods, and information. For example, the automobile industry had a profound impact on the number of visitors to Silver Springs, Florida, and on the movement patterns of ideas, fashion, and people. In addition to geography, the theme of movement and connections encompasses the fields of communications, history, anthropology, economics, and sociology.

5. An understanding of the theme of **regions, patterns, and processes** involves identifying climatic, economic, political, and cultural patterns within regions. To comprehend why these patterns were created, students need to understand how climatic systems, communication

networks, international trade, political systems, and population changes contributed to a region's development. With an understanding of a particular region, students can study its uniqueness and relationship to other regions. In addition to geography, the theme of regions, patterns, and processes encompasses the fields of economics, sociology, and politics.

The study of global issues and events includes comprehending the interconnectedness of peoples throughout the world (sociology and political science). For example, knowing the relationship between world oil consumption and oil production helps students understand the impact that increased demand for oil in China would have on the price of a barrel of oil, which in turn could affect the decisions of consumers of new vehicles in the United States.

Using Geologic Maps

Any study of maps should begin with a study of the globe—a model of the earth with a map on its surface. The globe is more accurate than a flat map. Constantly using the globe helps bring understanding of the earth's shape and structure.

Some of the points on the globe that students should be able to locate include the equator, Antarctic Circle, Arctic Circle, prime meridian, international date line, North Pole, South Pole, meridians, parallels, the Great Circle Route, and time zones. The use of maps requires students to identify four main types of map projections: conic, cylindrical, interrupted, and plane. Additional graphics that students use in geography include charts, graphs, and picture maps.

Interpreting Geologic Maps

Geologic maps provide much information about the earth and present a perfect opportunity to integrate social studies and science. By reading a **topographical map**, a student can find out about **altitudes** (heights above and below sea level) and landforms. **Symbols** on the map may represent rivers, lakes, rapids, and forests. **Map scales** allow the student to determine distances. The **legends** of a map furnish additional information, including the locations of mineral deposits and quarries, dams and boat ramps, fire and ranger stations, and more. Often a map displays a **compass rose**, which gives the cardinal directions: north, south, east, and west.

Parallels and meridians grid the earth. **Meridians** run from pole to pole, and 360 of them surround the earth in one-degree increments. Every hour a given location on the earth's surface rotates through 15 degrees of longitude. Meridians help measure longitude, the distance east and west of the prime meridian, which has a measurement of 0° east-west. **Parallels** are the lines that run in an east-west direction; parallels help measure **latitude**, the distance north and south of the equator. Geologic maps often contain all this information. A geologic map usually differs from a political map, which shows political boundaries, counties, cities, towns, churches, schools, and other representations of government and people.

Factors That Influence the Selection of a Location for a Specific Activity

Factors that influence the selection of a location for a specific activity include the area's population density, government, latitude (distance from the equator), altitude (height above sea level), distance from bodies of water, culture, economics, landforms, sociology, vegetation, and climate (temperature, rainfall, etc.).

The human development of the area also affects selection. For instance, methods of transportation, highways, airports, communication, waterways, water travel, buildings, industries, and facilities are only a few of the factors that influence location for a specific activity. For some industries, nearness to sources of raw materials for production and ways of transporting the goods after production may be important in selecting an area in which to locate.

Two types of location—absolute and relative—describe the positions of people and places on the earth's surface. Determining **absolute location** requires the use of longitude and latitude on a grid system. The longitude and latitude coordinates identify exact (absolute) location. **Relative location**, on the other hand, recognizes the interdependence of people and places. Places do not exist in isolation. Geographers attempt to identify relationships between or among places and to determine the factors that might encourage those relationships.

The Relationship Between Natural Physical Processes and the Environment

One can approach geography—the study of places on the earth's surface—from various perspectives. One study approach is **physical geography**—locating and describing places according to physical features (climate, soil, landforms, vegetation, etc.). Physical geography must take into account how the earth's movements around the sun, the tilt of the earth, the sea, weather patterns, the distance from the equator, the altitude, and the air affect the earth's surface. The physical approach alone, however, is a narrow methodology from the social science point of view because it ignores the human factor.

How Places Differ in Their Human and Physical Characteristics

For geography (the study of the earth) to be a true social science, it must take into account the human factor. Some notice of the interaction of the humans and animals that live on the earth—whether the interaction is deliberate or incidental—is an important part of the social sciences. The relationship between a place and the humans and animals that inhabit it is called **cultural geography**.

Location affects both plant and animal life. The physical environment—climate, resources, terrain, and so on—impinges on the life of people by affecting diet, shelter, clothing, accessibility, inventions, religion, resources, and prosperity. In fact, in prehistoric times—even before history, government, or economics—the earth (geography) was the most important element in human life. Geography is still important in society today. Studying a map of the rivers and the fall line (a physical feature that indicates the navigability of rivers) in North Carolina, for example, reveals why many people decided to settle there. In the late 1800s, textile mills were often built near the fall line so they could use water as a power source. Many people who needed employment and were not highly skilled sought work in the textile mills. This example shows how the physical characteristics of a place can affect the people who move there.

How Conditions of the Past, Such as Wealth and Poverty, Land Tenure, Exploitation, Colonialism, and Independence, Affect Present Human Characteristics of Places

Three generalizations of geography relate the past to human characteristics of places:

1. Physical factors and cultural factors are related. For instance, the types of houses that families build reflect the available materials and climates. Therefore, physical differences can arise among houses in various places. The richness of the physical environment can affect the wealth of the people.

2. Change is a constant. The effects of change on people are both physical and cultural. For example, the people themselves bring about some changes; they may modify the environment by cutting trees and affecting the landscape now and in years to come.

3. People modify the environment to suit their changing needs and wants. For example, when tenant farmers lived on another person's land, they had little say over the use of the land; planting gardens for their own families' uses may have been out of the question. Once they were able to purchase land, their use of the land changed; many began planting gardens and fruit trees for their families. Today, people living in an area damaged by a storm may be able to repair the damages caused by the storm and even change the place to suit their current needs and wants.

How People Adapt to an Environment

Although the environment can affect the way people live, people can change the environment to meet their wants and needs. For example, the jobs that people hold enable them to get money for food, clothing, and shelter. Some jobs—farming, logging, and mining, for example—have a profound effect on the environment. In parts of the world without adequate rainfall, farmers have to use irrigation to grow their crops. Through their adaptation of the environment, the farmers acquire the things they need to survive but, in the process, may damage their environment and ultimately threaten the survival of future generations.

Ideally, people will explore a damaged environment to determine the causes of water and air pollution, for example. They will also determine whether there is any harm to local plants and animals, and they will ascertain the cause if there is damage. People will ideally work to change damages to the environment and prevent further harm.

How Tools and Technology Affect the Environment

The period from the emergence of the first-known hominids, or humans, around 2.5 million years ago until approximately 10,000 B.C.E. has been designated as the Paleolithic period, or the Old Stone Age. During that period, human beings lived in very small groups of perhaps 10 to 20 nomadic people who were constantly moving from place to place. Human beings had the ability to make tools and weapons from stone and the bones of the animals they killed. Hunting large game such as mammoths, which the hunters sometimes drove off cliffs in large numbers, was crucial to the survival of early humans. The meat, fur, and bones of the hunted animals were essential to the survival of prehistoric people, who supplemented their diets by foraging for food.

Early human beings found shelter in caves and other natural formations and took the time to paint and draw on the walls of their shelters. Created during the prehistoric period, cave paintings in France and northern Spain depict scenes of animals, such as lions, owls, and oxen. Around 500,000 years ago, humans developed the means of creating fire and used it to provide light and warmth in shelters and to cook meat and other foods. They also developed improved techniques of producing tools and weapons. Tools and technology can improve the lives of people; needless to say, tools and technology can also harm the lives of people. Likewise, people can use tools and technology both to improve their environment and to harm or even destroy their immediate areas or even the world. For example, as Alfred Nobel learned after he developed dynamite, escalating the power of weapons has never successfully prevented war. As weapons become more powerful, the danger from the technology increases.

Reasons for the Movement of People in the World, Nation, or State

The people living in a particular area determine the characteristics of that area. The physical, cultural, economic, and political characteristics are important to most area residents and may affect their original decision to settle there.

If the characteristics of an area become unacceptable to residents, the residents may consider moving to a different location. With the ease of transportation today, most people can move more easily than they could a generation ago. The move may be to another region of their state, the nation, or the world.

Economic reasons for moving include the finances of the individual considering relocation and the economic level required to live comfortably in the area. Some residents may move to a more expensive area, but others may decide to go to a less expensive area. Many change their places of residence, therefore, to get ahead economically or to raise their standard of living.

Some people decide to relocate for **cultural reasons**. These people might consider their neighbors too similar to them and decide to move to an area with more diversity. On the other hand, some people would rather live with others who are similar to them.

Physical reasons can also affect a person's decision to relocate. An understanding of the theme of human-environmental interaction involves considering how people rely on the environment, how they alter it, and how the environment can limit what people are able to do. Sometimes people move to a place where they can satisfy their physical wants or needs. In some cases, people can modify their environment or bring the needed goods to their area without having to relocate. For example, an adaptation of the environment that aided the Illinois shipping industry was the development of the lock and dam system on the Mississippi River.

An understanding of the theme of location, movement, and connections involves identifying how people are connected through different forms of transportation and communication networks and how those networks have changed over time. This would include identifying the channels of movement for people, goods, and information. For example, the textile industry in North Carolina in the 1930s had a profound impact on the movement patterns of ideas and people; many of those without work came to the textile regions seeking jobs. When the textile mills began closing in the 1990s, many people began to leave the area in search of other employment.

Political reasons also compel the movement of people. Many people equate the political system with government. There is a distinction, however. Government carries out the decisions of the political system. The organizations and processes that contribute to the decision-making process make up the political system. Individuals may move to another region or area if they are unhappy with the government and/or political systems in their area and are unable to bring about change. On the other hand, an attractive system of government may bring people to an area.

Comparing and Contrasting Major Regions of the World

There are many ways of dividing the world into regions. Perhaps the simplest is to consider the equator as a dividing line between the Northern Hemisphere and the Southern Hemisphere. Another way of dividing the world into regions is to draw a line from pole to pole. Such a line may separate the globe into the Eastern Hemisphere and Western Hemisphere. Another way geographers might divide the world into regions is by landmasses, or continents, specifically Africa, Asia, Australia, Europe, North America, and South America; some geographers also include Antarctica as a separate continent. Other geographers prefer to group the regions according to political characteristics. Still others prefer to designate regions by latitudes: low, middle, and high.

Two important higher-order thinking skills that teachers should encourage among their students are comparing and contrasting. The use of regions is an ideal place to work with these skills of comparing and contrasting two (or more) things (or concepts). The process of finding similarities between or among the things or concepts that appear dissimilar on the surface requires deeper thought. W. J. J. Gordon describes a process of synectics, which forces students to make an analogy between two concepts, one familiar and the other new. At first, the concepts might seem completely different, but through a series of steps, the students discover underlying similarities. By comparing something new with something familiar, students have a "hook" that will help them remember and understand the new information (Huitt 1998; Gordon 1961).

For example, a biology teacher might ask students to draw an analogy between a cell (new concept) and a city government (familiar concept). Although they seem impossibly different, both concepts involve systems for transportation, systems for disposing of unwanted materials, and parts that govern those systems. After discussion of this analogy, students trying to remember the functions of a cell would find help by relating the functions of the cell to the systems of city government.

WORLD HISTORY

Prehistory and Early Civilization

Major Leaders and Events

The earth is estimated to be approximately 6 billion years old. The earliest known humans, called **hominids**, lived in Africa 3 to 4 million years ago. Of the several species of hominids that developed, all modern humans descended from just one group, the *Homo sapiens sapiens*. *Homo sapiens sapiens* is a subspecies of *Homo sapiens* (along with Neanderthals, who became extinct) and appeared in Africa between 200,000 and 150,000 years ago.

Historians divide prehistory into three periods. The period when people first appeared (around 2.5 million years ago until approximately 10,000 B.C.E.) is the **Paleolithic period**, or **Old Stone Age**. These nomads lived in groups of 10 to 20 and **made tools and weapons** from stone and from the bones of the animals they killed. Large animals were crucial to their survival; they sometimes drove the animals off cliffs. The early people foraged for food and took shelter in caves and other natural formations. About 500,000 years ago humans began to use fire for light, cooking, and warmth. They improved their methods of making tools and weapons, and learned how to create fire.

The **Mesolithic period**, or **Middle Stone Age**, from 10,000 to 7000 B.C.E., marks the beginning of a major transformation known as the Neolithic Revolution. Previously, historians and archeologists thought this change occurred later. Thus, they called it the Neolithic Revolution because they thought it took place entirely within the Neolithic period, or New Stone Age. Beginning in the Mesolithic period, humans domesticated plants and began to shift away from a reliance on hunting large game and foraging. Human beings had previously relied on gathering food where they found it and had moved almost constantly in search of game and wild berries and other vegetation. During the Mesolithic period, humans were able to **plant and harvest** some crops and began to stay in one place for longer periods. Early humans also improved their tool-making techniques and developed various kinds of tools and weapons.

During the **Neolithic period**, or **New Stone Age**, this revolution was complete, and humans engaged in systematic agriculture and began domesticating animals. Although humans continued to hunt animals to supplement their diet with **meat** and to use the skins and bones to make clothing and weapons, major changes in society occurred. Human beings became settled and lived in farming villages or towns, the population increased, and people began to live in much larger communities. A more settled way of life led to a **more structured social system**; a higher level of organization within societies; the development of **crafts**, such as the production of **pottery**; and a rise in **trade** or exchange of goods among groups.

Between 4000 and 3000 B.C.E., **writing** developed, and the towns and villages settled during the Neolithic period developed a more complex pattern of existence. The establishment of written records marks the **end of the prehistoric period**. The beginning of history coincides with the emergence of the earliest societies that exhibit characteristics enabling them to be considered civilizations. The first civilizations emerged in Mesopotamia and Egypt.

Ancient and Medieval Times

Appearance of Civilization and Related Cultural and Technological Developments

Between 6000 and 3000 B.C.E., humans invented the **plow**, developed the **wheel**, harnessed the **wind**, discovered how to smelt **copper ores**, and began to develop accurate **solar calendars**. Small villages gradually grew into populous cities. The **invention of writ-**

ing in 3500 B.C.E. in Mesopotamia marks the beginning of civilization and divides prehistoric from historic times.

Mesopotamia

Sumer (4000–2000 B.C.E.) included the city of Ur. The Sumerians constructed **dikes and reservoirs** and established a loose confederation of **city-states**. They probably invented writing (called **cuneiform** because of its wedge-shaped letters). After 538 B.C.E., the peoples of Mesopotamia, whose natural boundaries were insufficient to thwart invaders, were absorbed into other empires and dynasties.

Egypt. During the end of the Middle Archaic Period (6000–3000 B.C.E.), in about 3200 B.C.E., Menes, or Narmer, probably unified Upper and Lower Egypt. The capital moved to Memphis during the Third Dynasty (ca. 2650 B.C.E.). The **pyramids** were built during the Fourth Dynasty (ca. 2613–2494 B.C.E.). After 1085 B.C.E., in the Post-Empire period, Egypt came under the successive control of the Assyrians; the Persians; Alexander the Great; and finally, in 30 B.C.E., the Roman Empire. The Egyptians developed papyrus and made many medical advances.

Palestine and the Hebrews. Phoenicians settled along the present-day Lebanon coast (Sidon, Tyre, Beirut, Byblos) and established colonies at Carthage and in Spain. They spread **Mesopotamian culture** through their trade networks. The Hebrews probably moved to Egypt in about 1700 B.C.E. and suffered enslavement in about 1500 B.C.E. The Hebrews fled Egypt under Moses and, around 1200 B.C.E., returned to Palestine. King David (reigned ca. 1012–972 B.C.E.) defeated the Philistines and established Jerusalem as a capital. The poor and less attractive state of Judah continued until 586 B.C.E., when the Chaldeans transported the Jews ("the people of Judah" or, in some translations, "the people of God") to Chaldea as advisors and slaves (Babylonian captivity). The Persians conquered Babylon in 539 B.C.E. and allowed the Jews to return to Palestine.

Greece. In the period from about 800–500 B.C.E., the Greeks organized around the **polis**, or city-state. Oligarchs controlled most of the polis until near the end of the sixth century, when individuals holding absolute power (tyrants) replaced them. By the end of the sixth century, **democratic governments** in turn replaced many tyrants.

The Classical Age. The fifth century B.C.E. was the high point of Greek civilization. It opened with the Persian Wars (560–479 B.C.E.), after which Athens organized the Delian League. **Pericles** (ca. 495–429 B.C.E.) used money from the league to rebuild Athens, includ-

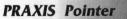

PRAXIS Pointer

Don't make questions more difficult than they are—there are no "trick" questions or hidden meanings.

ing construction of the Parthenon and other buildings on the Acropolis hill. Athens's dominance spurred war with Sparta. At the same time, a revolution in philosophy occurred in classical Athens. The **Sophists** emphasized the individual and the attainment of excellence through rhetoric, grammar, music, and mathematics. **Socrates** (ca. 470–399 B.C.E.) criticized the Sophists' emphasis on rhetoric and emphasized a process of questioning, or dialogue, with his students. Like Socrates, **Plato** (ca. 428–348 B.C.E.) emphasized ethics. Aristotle (ca. 384–322 B.C.E.) was Plato's pupil. He criticized Plato and argued that ideas or forms did not exist outside things. He contended that, in treating any object, it was necessary to examine four factors: its matter, its form, its cause of origin, and its end or purpose.

Rome. The traditional founding date for Rome is 753 B.C.E. Between 800 and 500 B.C.E., Greek tribes colonized southern Italy, bringing their alphabet and religious practices to Roman tribes. In the sixth and seventh centuries B.C.E., the Etruscans expanded southward and conquered Rome. In the early Republic, power was in the hands of the patricians (wealthy landowners). During the 70s and 60s, **Pompey** (106–48 B.C.E.) and **Julius Caesar** (100–44 B.C.E.) emerged as the most powerful men.

In 60 B.C.E., Caesar convinced Pompey and Crassus (ca. 115–53 B.C.E.) to form the First Triumvirate. When Crassus died, Caesar and Pompey fought for leadership. In 47 B.C.E., the Senate proclaimed Caesar dictator and later named him consul for life. **Brutus** and **Cassius** believed that Caesar had destroyed the Republic. They formed a conspiracy, and on March 15, 44 B.C.E. (the Ides of March), Brutus and Cassius assassinated Caesar in the Roman forum. Caesar's 18-year-old nephew and adopted son, Octavian, succeeded him.

The Roman Empire. After a period of struggle, Octavian (reigned 27 B.C.E.–14 C.E.), named as Caesar's heir, gained absolute control while maintaining the appearance of a republic. When he offered to relinquish his power in 27 B.C.E., the Senate gave him a vote of confidence and a new title, Augustus. He introduced many reforms, including new coinage, new tax collection, fire and police protection, and land for settlers in the provinces. By the first century C.E., Christianity had spread throughout the Empire. Around 312 C.E., Emperor Constantine converted to Christianity and ordered toleration in the Edict of Milan (ca. 313 C.E.). In 391 C.E., Emperor Theodosius I (reigned 371–395 C.E.) proclaimed Christianity the empire's official religion.

The Byzantine Empire. Emperor Theodosius II (reigned 408–450 C.E.) divided his empire between his two sons, one ruling the East and the other ruling the West. After the Vandals sacked Rome in 455 C.E., Constantinople was the undisputed leading city of the Byzantine Empire. In 1453 C.E., Constantinople fell to the Ottoman Turks.

Islamic Civilization in the Middle Ages. Mohammed was born about 570 C.E. In 630 C.E., he marched into Mecca. The Shari'ah (code of law and theology) outlines five pillars of faith for Muslims to observe. The beliefs that there is one God and that Mohammed is his prophet form the first pillar. Second, the faithful must pray five times a day. Third, they must perform charitable acts. Fourth, they must fast from sunrise to sunset during the holy month of Ramadan. Finally, they must make a *haj*, or pilgrimage, to Mecca. The Koran, which consists of 114 *suras* (verses), contains Mohammed's teachings.

The Umayyad caliphs, with their base in Damascus, governed from 661–750 C.E. They called themselves **Shiites** and believed they were Mohammed's true successors. (Most Muslims were **Sunnis**, from the word *sunna*, meaning "oral traditions about the prophet.")

The Abbāsid caliphs ruled from 750–1258 C.E. They moved the capital to Baghdad and treated Arab and non-Arab Muslims as equals. Genghis (or Chingis) Khan (reigned 1206–1227 C.E.) and his army invaded the Abbāsids. In 1258 C.E., they seized Baghdad and murdered the last caliph.

Feudalism in Japan. Feudalism in Japan began with the arrival of mounted nomadic warriors from throughout Asia during the Kofun Era (300–710 C.E.). Some members of the nomadic groups formed an elite class and became part of the court aristocracy in the capital city of Kyoto, in western Japan. During the Heian Era (794–1185 C.E.), a hereditary military aristocracy arose in the Japanese provinces; by the late Heian Era, many of these formerly nomadic warriors had established themselves as independent landowners, or as managers of landed estates, or *shoen* owned by Kyoto aristocrats. These aristocrats depended on the warriors to defend their *shoen,* and in response to this need, the warriors organized into small groups called *bushidan.*

After victory in the Taira-Minamoto War (1180–1185 C.E.), Minamoto no Yorimoto forced the emperor to award him the title of **shogun**, which is short for "barbarian-subduing generalissimo." Yorimoto used this power to found the Kamakura shogunate, a feudal military dictatorship that survived for 148 years.

By the fourteenth century C.E., the great military governors (*shugo*) had augmented their power enough to become a threat to the Kamakura, and in 1333 C.E., they led a rebellion that overthrew the shogunate. The Tokugawa shogunate was the final and most unified of the three shogunates. Under the Tokugawa, the *daimyo* were direct vassals of the shoguns and were under strict control. The warriors gradually became scholars and bureaucrats under the *bushido*, or code of chivalry, and the principles of neo-Confucianism. Under the Meji Restoration of 1868, the emperor again received power and the samurai class lost its special privileges.

Chinese and Indian Empires. In the third century B.C.E., the Indian kingdoms fell under the Mauryan Empire. The grandson of the founder of this empire, named Ashoka, opened a new era in the cultural history of India by believing in the Buddhist religion.

Buddha had disregarded the Vedic gods and the institutions of caste and had preached a relatively simple ethical religion that advocated two levels of aspiration—a monastic life that renounced the world and a high, but not too difficult, morality for the layperson. Although the two religions of Hinduism and Buddhism flourished together for centuries in a tolerant rivalry, Buddhism almost disappeared from India by the thirteenth century C.E.

Chinese civilization originated in the Yellow River Valley, only gradually extending to the southern regions. Three dynasties ruled early China: the Xia or Hsia, the Shang (ca. 1500 to 1122 B.C.E.), and the Zhou (ca. 1122 to 211 B.C.E.). After the Zhou Dynasty fell, China welcomed the teachings of **Confucius**; warfare between states and philosophical speculation created circumstances ripe for such teachings. Confucius made the good order of society depend on an ethical ruler, who would receive advice from scholar-moralists like Confucius himself. In contrast to the Confucians, the Chinese Taoists professed a kind of anarchism; the best kind of government was none at all. Wise people did not concern themselves with political affairs but with mystical contemplation that identified them with the forces of nature.

African Kingdoms and Cultures. The **Bantu** peoples lived across large sections of Africa. Bantu societies lived in tiny chiefdoms, starting in the third millennium B.C.E., and each group developed its own version of the original Bantu language.

The **Nok** people lived in the area now known as Nigeria. Artifacts indicate that they were peaceful farmers who built small communities consisting of houses of wattle and daub (poles and sticks). The **Ghanaians** lived about 500 miles from what is now Ghana. Their kingdom fell to a Berber group in the late eleventh century C.E., and Mali emerged as the next great kingdom in the thirteenth century. The Malians lived in a huge kingdom that lay mostly on the savanna bordering the Sahara Desert. Timbuktu, built in the thirteenth century C.E., was a thriving city of culture where traders visited **stone houses, shops, libraries, and mosques**. The Songhai lived near the Niger River and gained their independence from the Mali in the early 1400s. The major growth of the empire came after 1464 C.E., under the leadership of Sunni 'Alī, who devoted his reign to warfare and expansion of the empire.

Civilizations of the Americas. The great civilizations of early America were agricultural, and the foremost civilization was the Mayan in Yucatan, Guatemala, and eastern Honduras. Farther north, in present-day Mexico, a series of advanced cultures derived much of their substance from the Maya. Peoples, such as the Zapotecs, Totonacs, Olmecs, and Toltecs, evolved into a high level of civilization. By 500 B.C.E., agricultural peoples had begun to use a **ceremonial calendar** and had built **stone pyramids** on which they held religious observances.

The Aztecs then took over Mexican culture, and a major feature of their culture was human sacrifice in repeated propitiation of their chief god. Aztec government was centralized, with an elective king and a large army. Andean civilization was characterized by the evolution of **beautifully made pottery, intricate fabrics, and flat-topped mounds**, or *huacas*.

In the interior of South America, the Inca, who called themselves "Children of the Sun," controlled an area stretching from Ecuador to central Chile. As sun worshippers, they believed that they were the sun god's vice regents on earth and were more powerful than any other humans. They believed that every person's place in society was fixed and immutable and that the state and the army were supreme. They were at the apex of their power just before the Spanish conquest.

In the present-day southwestern United States and northern Mexico, two varieties of ancient culture are still identifiable. The Anasazi developed **adobe architecture**, worked the land extensively, had a highly developed system of **irrigation**, and made cloth and baskets. The Hohokam built separate stone and timber houses around a central plaza.

Europe in Antiquity. The Frankish Kingdom was the most important medieval Germanic state. Under Clovis I (reigned 481–511 C.E.), the Franks finished conquering France and the Gauls in 486 C.E. Clovis converted to Christianity and founded the Merovingian dynasty.

Charles the Great, or **Charlemagne** (reigned 768–814 C.E.), founded the Carolingian dynasty. In 800 C.E., Pope Leo III named Charlemagne emperor of the Holy Roman Empire. In the Treaty of Aix-la-Chapelle (812 C.E.), the Byzantine emperor recognized Charles's authority in the West. The purpose of the Holy Roman Empire was to reestablish the Roman Empire in the West. Charles's son, Louis the Pious (reigned 814–840 C.E.), succeeded him. On Louis's death, his three sons vied for control of the Empire. The three eventually signed the Treaty of Verdun in 843 C.E. This gave Charles the Western Kingdom (France), Louis the Eastern Kingdom (Germany), and Lothair the Middle Kingdom, a narrow strip of land running from the North Sea to the Mediterranean.

In this period, **manorialism** developed as an economic system in which large estates, granted by the king to nobles, strove for self-sufficiency. The lord and his serfs (also called villeins) divided the ownership. The church was the only institution to survive the Germanic invasions intact. The power of the popes grew in this period. **Gregory I** (reigned 590–604 C.E.) was the first member of a monastic order to rise to the papacy. He advanced the ideas of penance and purgatory. He centralized church administration and was the first pope to rule as the secular head of Rome. Monasteries preserved the few remnants that survived the decline of antiquity.

The year 1050 marked the beginning of the High Middle Ages. Europe was poised to emerge from five centuries of decline. Between 1000 and 1350, the population of Europe grew from 38 million to 75 million. New technologies, such as **heavy plows**, and a slight temperature rise produced a longer growing season and contributed to agricultural productivity.

The Holy Roman Empire. Charlemagne's grandson, Louis the German, became Holy Roman Emperor under the Treaty of Verdun. Otto became Holy Roman Emperor in 962. His descendants governed the empire until 1024, when the Franconian dynasty assumed power, reigning until 1125. Under the leadership of **William the Conqueror** (reigned 1066–1087), the Normans conquered England in 1066. William stripped the Anglo-Saxon nobility of its privileges and instituted feudalism. He ordered a survey of all property of the realm; the Domesday Book (1086) records the findings.

William introduced feudalism to England. **Feudalism** was the decentralized political system of personal ties and obligations that bound vassals to their lords. Serfs were peasants who were bound to the land. They worked on the *demesne*, or lord's property, three or four days a week in return for the right to work their own land. In 1215, the English barons forced King John I to sign the **Magna Carta Libertatum**, acknowledging their "ancient" privileges. The Magna Carta established the principle of a limited English monarchy.

From 710 to 711, the Moors conquered Spain, which had been ruled by the Visigoths. Under the Moors, Spain enjoyed a stable, prosperous government. The caliphate of Córdoba became a center of scientific and intellectual activity. The Reconquista (1085–1340) wrested control from the Moors. The fall of Córdoba in 1234 completed the Reconquista, except for the small state of Granada.

Most of eastern Europe and Russia was never under Rome's control; Germanic invasions separated the areas from Western influence. In Russia, Vladimir I converted to Orthodox Christianity in 988. He established the basis of Kievian Russia. After 1054, Russia broke into competing principalities. The **Mongols (Tartars)** invaded in 1221. They completed their conquest in 1245 and cut Russia's contact with the West for almost a century.

The **Crusades** attempted to liberate the Holy Land from infidels. Seven major crusades occurred between 1096 and 1300. Urban II called Christians to the First Crusade (1096–1099) with the promise of a plenary indulgence (exemption from punishment in purgatory). Younger sons who would not inherit their fathers' lands were also attracted. The Crusades helped to renew interest in the ancient world. The Crusaders massacred thousands of Jews and Muslims, however, and relations between Europe and the Byzantine Empire collapsed.

Scholasticism. Scholasticism was an effort to reconcile reason and faith and to instruct Christians on how to make sense of the pagan tradition. The most influential proponent of this effort was Thomas Aquinas (ca. 1225–1274), who believed that there were two orders of truth. The lower level, reason, could demonstrate propositions such as the existence of God, but the higher level necessitated that some of God's mysteries, such as the nature of the Trinity, be accepted on faith. Aquinas viewed the universe as a great chain of being, with humans midway on the chain, between the material and the spiritual.

Late Middle Ages and the Renaissance

The Black Death

Conditions in Europe encouraged the quick spread of disease. Refuse, excrement, and dead animals filled the streets of the cities, which lacked any form of urban sanitation.

Living conditions were overcrowded, with families often sleeping in one room or one bed; poor nutrition was rampant; and there was often little personal cleanliness. Merchants helped bring the plague to Asia; carried by fleas on rats, the disease arrived in Europe in 1347. By 1350, the disease had killed 25 percent to 40 percent of the European population.

Literature, Art, and Scholarship. Humanists, as both orators and poets, often imitated the classical works that inspired them. The literature of the period was more secular and wide ranging than that of the Middle Ages. **Dante Alighieri** (1265–1321) was a Florentine writer whose *Divine Comedy*, describing a journey through hell, purgatory, and heaven, shows that reason can take people only so far and that attaining heaven requires God's grace and revelation. Francesco Petrarch (1304–1374) encouraged the study of ancient Rome, collected and preserved works of ancient writers, and produced a large body of work in the classical literary style.

Giovanni Boccaccio (1313–1375) wrote *The Decameron*, a collection of short stories that the Italian author meant to amuse, not edify, the reader. Artists also broke with the medieval past in both technique and content. Renaissance art sometimes used religious topics but often dealt with secular themes or portraits of individuals. Oil paints, chiaroscuro, and linear perspectives produced works of energy in three dimensions. **Leonardo da Vinci** (1452–1519) produced numerous works, including *The Last Supper* and *Mona Lisa*. Raphael Santi (1483–1520), a master of Renaissance grace and style, theory, and technique, brought all his skills to his painting *The School of Athens*. **Michelangelo** Buonarroti (1475–1564) produced masterpieces in architecture, sculpture (*David*), and painting (the Sistine Chapel ceiling). His work was a bridge to a new, non-Renaissance style: mannerism.

Renaissance scholars were more practical and secular than medieval ones. **Manuscript collections** enabled scholars to study the primary sources and to reject traditions established since classical times. Also, scholars participated in the lives of their cities as active politicians. Leonardo Bruni (1370–1444), a civic humanist, served as chancellor of Florence, where he used his rhetorical skills to rouse the citizens against external enemies. Niccolo **Machiavelli** (1469–1527) wrote *The Prince*, which analyzed politics from the standpoint of expedience rising above morality in the name of maintaining political power.

The Reformation. The Reformation destroyed western Europe's religious unity and introduced new ideas about the relationships among God, the individual, and society. Politics greatly influenced the course of the Reformation and led, in most areas, to the subjection of the church to the political rulers.

Martin Luther (1483–1546), to his personal distress, could not reconcile the sinfulness of humans with the justice of God. During his studies of the Bible, Luther came to believe that personal efforts—good works such as a Christian life and attention to the sacraments of the church—could not "earn" the sinner salvation but that belief and faith were the only way to obtain grace. By 1515, Luther believed that "justification by faith alone" was the road to salvation.

On October 31, 1517, Luther nailed 95 theses, or statements, about **indulgences** (the cancellation of a sin in return for money) to the door of the Wittenberg church and challenged the practice of selling them. At this time he was seeking to reform the church, not divide it. In 1519, Luther presented various criticisms of the church and declared that only the Bible, not religious traditions or papal statements, could determine correct religious practices and beliefs. In 1521, Pope Leo X excommunicated Luther for his beliefs.

In 1536, **John Calvin** (1509–1564), a Frenchman, arrived in Geneva, a Swiss city-state that had adopted an anti-Catholic position. In 1540, Geneva became the center of the Reformation. Calvin's *Institutes of the Christian Religion* (1536), a strictly logical analysis of Christianity, had a universal appeal. Calvin emphasized the doctrine of **predestination**, which indicated that God knew who would obtain salvation before those people were born. Calvin believed that church and state should unite. Calvinism triumphed as the majority religion in Scotland under the leadership of John Knox (ca. 1514–1572), and in the United Provinces of the Netherlands. Puritans in England and New England also accepted Calvinism.

The Thirty Years' War. Between 1618 and 1648, the European powers fought a series of wars. The reasons for the wars varied; religious, dynastic, commercial, and territorial rivalries all played a part. The battles were fought over most of Europe and ended with the Treaty of Westphalia in 1648. The Thirty Years' War changed the boundaries of most European countries.

Explorations and Conquests. Between 1394 and 1460 (Prince Henry the Navigator's lifespan) and afterward, a period of exploration and conquests characterized European history. The discussion on *Causes and Consequences of Exploration, Settlement, and Growth* includes more information on the people and the explorations of the period.

Revolution and the New World Order

The Scientific Revolution

For the first time in human history, the eighteenth century saw the appearance of a secular worldview: the Age of Enlightenment. The philosophical starting point for the Enlightenment was the belief in the autonomy of man's intellect apart from God's. The most basic assumption was faith in reason rather than faith in revelation. René Descartes (1596–1650) sought a basis for logic and believed he found it in man's ability to think. "I think; therefore, I am" was his most famous statement.

Benedict de Spinoza (1632–1677) developed a rational pantheism in which he equated God and nature. He denied all freewill and ended up with an impersonal, mechanical universe. Gottfried Wilhelm Leibniz (1646–1716) worked on symbolic logic and calculus and invented a calculating machine. He, too, had a mechanistic view of the world and life and thought of God as a hypothetical abstraction rather than a persona. **John Locke** (1632–1704) pioneered the empiricist approach to knowledge; he stressed the importance of the environment in human development. Locke classified knowledge as either (1) according to reason, (2) contrary to reason, or (3) above reason. Locke thought reason and revelation were complementary and from God.

The Enlightenment's Effect on Society

The Enlightenment affected more than science and religion. New political and economic theories originated as well. John Locke and **Jean-Jacques Rousseau** (1712–1778) believed that people were capable of governing themselves, either through a political (Locke) or social (Rousseau) contract forming the basis of society.

Most philosophers opposed democracy, preferring a limited monarchy that shared power with the nobility. The assault on mercantilist economic theory was begun by the physiocrats in France; the physiocrats proposed a laissez-faire (minimal governmental interference) attitude toward land use. The culmination of their beliefs was the theory of economic capitalism, which was associated with Adam Smith (1723–1790) and his notions of free trade, free enterprise, and the law of supply and demand.

The French Revolution

The increased criticism directed toward governmental inefficiency and corruption and toward the privileged classes demonstrated the rising expectations of "enlightened" society in France. The remainder of the population (called the Third Estate) consisted of the middle class, urban workers, and the mass of peasants, who bore the entire burden of taxation and the imposition of feudal obligations.

The most notorious event of the French Revolution was the so-called Reign of Terror (1793–1794), the government's campaign against its internal enemies and counterrevolutionaries. **Louis XVI** faced charges of treason, was declared guilty, and suffered execution on January 21, 1793. Later the same year, the queen, **Marie Antoinette**, met the same fate. The middle class controlled the Directory (1795–1799). Members of the Directory believed that, through peace, they would gain more wealth and establish a society in which money and property would become the only requirements for prestige and power. Rising inflation and mass public dissatisfaction led to the downfall of the Directory.

The Era of Napoleon

On December 25, 1799, a new government and constitution concentrated supreme power in the hands of **Napoleon**. Napoleon's domestic reforms and policies affected every aspect of society.

French-ruled peoples viewed Napoleon as a tyrant who repressed and exploited them for France's glory and advantage. Enlightened reformers believed Napoleon had betrayed the ideals of the Revolution. The downfall of Napoleon resulted from his inability to conquer England, economic distress caused by the Continental System (boycott of British goods), the Peninsular War with Spain, the German War of Liberation, and the invasion of Russia. The actual defeat of Napoleon occurred at the **Battle of Waterloo** in 1815.

The Industrial Revolution

The term *Industrial Revolution* describes a period of transition, when machines began to significantly displace human and animal power in methods of producing and distributing goods and when an agricultural and commercial society became an industrial one.

Roots of the Industrial Revolution are evident in

- the Commercial Revolution (1500–1700) that spurred the great economic growth of Europe and brought about the Age of Discovery and Exploration, which in turn helped to solidify the economic doctrines of mercantilism;

- the effect of the Scientific Revolution, which produced the first wave of mechanical inventions and technological advances;

- the increase in population in Europe from 140 million people in 1750 to 266 million people by the mid-nineteenth century (more producers, more consumers); and

- the nineteenth-century political and social revolutions that began the rise to power of the middle class and that provided leadership for the economic revolution.

A transportation revolution ensued to distribute the productivity of machinery and to deliver raw materials to the eager factories. This led to the growth of canal systems; the construction of hard-surfaced **"macadam" roads**; the commercial use of the **steamboat**, which **Robert Fulton** (1765–1815) demonstrated; and the **railway locomotive**, which **George Stephenson** (1781–1848) made commercially successful. The Industrial Revolution created a unique new category of people who depended on their jobs for income and who needed job security. Until 1850, workers as a whole did not share in the general wealth produced by the Industrial Revolution. Conditions improved as the century neared an end. Union action, general prosperity, and a developing social conscience all combined to improve the working conditions, wages, and hours of skilled labor first and unskilled labor later.

Socialism

The Utopian Socialists were the earliest writers to propose an equitable solution to improve the distribution of society's wealth. The name of this group comes from *Utopia*, **Saint Thomas More's** (1478–1535) book on a fictional ideal society. While they endorsed the productive capacity of industrialism, the Utopian Socialists denounced its mismanagement. Human society was ideally a community rather than a mixture of competing, selfish individuals. All the goods a person needed could be produced in one community.

Scientific socialism, or **Marxism**, was the creation of **Karl Marx** (1818–1883), a German scholar who, with the help of **Friedrich Engels** (1820–1895), intended to replace utopian hopes and dreams with a militant blueprint for socialist working-class success. The principal works of this revolutionary school of socialism were *The Communist Manifesto* and *Das Kapital*. Marxism has four key propositions:

1. An economic interpretation of history that asserts that economic factors (mainly centered on who controls the means of production and distribution) determines all human history

2. The belief that there has always been a class struggle between the rich and the poor (or the exploiters and the exploited)

3. The theory of surplus value, which holds that the true value of a product is labor; because workers receive a small portion of their just labor price, the difference is surplus value "stolen" from workers by capitalists

4. The belief that socialism is inevitable because capitalism contains the seeds of its own destruction (overproduction, unemployment, etc.): The rich grow richer and the poor grow poorer until the gap between each class (proletariat and bourgeoisie) becomes so great that the working classes rise up in revolution and overthrow the elite bourgeoisie to install a "dictatorship of the proletariat." The creation of a classless society guided by the principle "from each according to his abilities, to each according to his needs" is the result of dismantling capitalism.

Causes and Consequences of Exploration, Settlement, and Growth

Beginnings of European Exploration

Europeans were largely unaware of the existence of the American continent, even though a Norse seaman, **Leif Eriksson**, had sailed within sight of the continent in the eleventh century. Few other explorers ventured nearly as far as America. Before the fifteenth century, Europeans had little desire to explore and were not ready to face the many challenges of a long sea voyage. Just as developments led to changes and conflict in North America and produced an increasing number of distinct cultures and systems, developments in Europe were about to make possible the great voyages that led to contact between Europe and the Americas. In the fifteenth and sixteenth centuries, technological devices such as the **compass** and **astrolabe** freed explorers from some of the constraints that had limited early voyages. Three primary factors—God, gold, and glory—led to increased interest in exploration and eventually to a desire to settle in the newly discovered lands.

Although Europeans, such as Italians, participated in overland trade with the East and sailed through the Mediterranean and beyond, it was the Arabs who played the largest part in such trade and who benefited the most economically. **Prince Henry the Navigator**, ruler of Portugal, sponsored voyages aimed at adding territory and gaining control of trading routes to increase the power and wealth of Portugal. Prince Henry also wanted to spread Christianity and prevent the further expansion of Islam in Africa. Prince Henry the Navigator brought a number of Italian merchant traders to his court at Cape St. Vincent, and subsequently they sailed in Portuguese ships down the western coast of Africa. These initial voyages were extremely difficult because the voyagers lacked navigational instruments and any kind of maps or charts. Europeans had charted the entire Mediterranean Sea, including harbors and the coastline, but they had no knowledge or maps of the African coast.

The first task of the explorers was to create accurate charts of the African shoreline. The crews on these initial voyages did not encounter horrible monsters or boiling water, which rumors had said existed in the ocean beyond Cape Bojador, the farthest point Europeans had previously reached. They did discover, however, that strong southward winds made it easy to sail out of the Mediterranean but difficult to return. Most people believed that Africa and China were joined by a southern continent, eliminating any possibility of an eastern maritime route to the Indian Ocean. Prince Henry, however, sent ships along the coast of Africa because he believed it was possible to sail east through the Atlantic and reach the Indian Ocean.

Technical Innovations Aiding Exploration

One of the reasons that the explorers sailing from Portugal traveled along the coast was to avoid losing sight of land. By the thirteenth century, explorers were using the compass, borrowed from China, to determine direction; it was more difficult to determine the relative position from the North and South Poles and from landmasses or anything else. In the Northern Hemisphere, a navigator could determine the relative north-south position, or latitude, by calculating the height of the **Pole Star** from the horizon. South of the equator, one cannot see the Pole Star; until around 1460, captains had no way to determine their position if they sailed too far south. Although longitude (relative east-west position) remained unknown until the eighteenth century, the introduction of the astrolabe allowed sailors to calculate their latitude south of the equator.

Along with navigational aids, improvements in shipbuilding and in weaponry also facilitated exploration. Unlike the Mediterranean, it was not possible to use ships propelled only by oarsmen in the Atlantic because the waves were high and the currents and winds were strong. Europeans had initially used very broad sails on ships that went out into the Atlantic; the ships were heavy and often became stranded by the absence of the favorable tailwinds upon which the ships and sailors depended. The Portuguese borrowed techniques from Arab and European shipbuilding and developed the Caravela Redondo. This ship proved to be more worthy of long voyages because it combined square rigging for speed with lateen sails that were more responsive and easier to handle. Other European states adopted the ship and also the practice of mounting artillery and other weapons on exploration vessels.

Main Elements of European Exploration

As the Portuguese began to trade and explore along the coast of Africa, they brought back slaves, ivory, gold, and knowledge of the African coast. It looked as though the Portuguese might find a route to the Indian Ocean, and it was clear that the voyages sponsored by Prince Henry were benefiting Portugal in many ways.

Other European states wanted to increase their territory and wealth and to establish trade routes to the East. Although the desire for control of trade routes and wealth was a primary motive in launching voyages of exploration, it was not the only incentive. Europe in the fifteenth and sixteenth centuries, despite the increase in dissenting views, was still extremely religious. The Catholic Church continued to exert a tremendous influence, and some Christians were motivated to go on voyages of discovery to conduct missionary activities and spread the word of God. In addition, after the beginning of the Reformation, many Lutherans, Calvinists, and other groups who had left the Catholic Church emigrated from Europe in the hope of settling where they would be free from religious persecution or violent conflicts.

Other individuals sponsored or participated in voyages in the hope of gaining wealth or increased opportunities. For example, younger sons of families in Europe were able to secure prominent positions in the church, but they were often not able to find lucrative opportunities at home because the eldest son usually inherited lands and wealth. The voyages of exploration were a means of securing fame and fortune and of obtaining opportunities that would not be available otherwise.

Although the motivation of fame and fortune was often secondary to God and glory, many individuals were attracted to exploration by the possibility of adventure and by their desire to explore uncharted territory. These three factors—gold, God, and glory—operated on both individual and state levels; kings and heads of states were as interested as the seamen were in spreading their faith and increasing the wealth and prestige of their states.

Portugal was the first European state to establish sugar plantations on an island off the west coast of Africa and to import slaves from Africa to labor there. This marked the beginning of the slave trade. The level of trading was initially far less extensive and intense than during the later period of the slave trade, when Spain and England became involved. In an attempt to maintain control of the slave trade and of the eastern routes to India, the Portuguese appealed to the pope; he ruled in their favor and forbade the Spanish and others to sail south and east in an attempt to reach India or Asia.

When **Ferdinand and Isabella** married and united Spain's two largest provinces (Castile and Aragon), they not only began the process of uniting all of Spain but also agreed to sponsor **Christopher Columbus** in his voyage of exploration. Only the heads of states had the necessary resources and could afford the risk involved in sponsoring a major voyage across the oceans of the world, but most monarchs were unwilling to take such a risk. Columbus was an Italian explorer looking for a sponsor and had approached Ferdinand and Isabella after being turned down by the English government. He convinced the Spanish monarchs that a western route to the Indian Ocean existed and that it would be possible to make the voyage.

However, Columbus had miscalculated the distance of the voyage from Europe to Asia. His estimate of the circumference of the earth was much less than it should have been for an accurate calculation, and no Europeans were aware of the existence of the American continents. One of the reasons that Ferdinand and Isabella were willing to support Columbus was that the previous agreements prevented all states but Portugal from sailing east to reach India. Therefore, the only chance for Spain to launch an expedition to India and to participate in trade and exploration was in the discovery of a western route to India.

European Contact with the Americas

In 1492, Columbus sailed from Spain with 90 men on three ships, the *Niña*, the *Pinta*, and the *Santa María*. After a 10-week voyage, they landed in the Bahamas. On his second trip, Columbus reached Cuba; and then in 1498, during his third trip, he reached the mainland and sailed along the northern coast of South America. Columbus originally thought he had reached India; he referred to the people he encountered in the Bahamas and on his second landing in Cuba as Indians.

There is considerable debate over whether Columbus realized, either during his third voyage or just before his death, that he had landed not in India but on an entirely unknown continent between Europe and Asia. Another question is whether Columbus, who died in obscurity despite his fame for having discovered America, should receive credit for this discovery; earlier explorers had reached the American continent.

However, because Columbus's voyages prompted extensive exploration and settlement of the Americas, it is accurate to state that he was responsible for the discovery of the New World by Europeans. Another result of Columbus's voyages was the increased focus of Spain on exploration and conquest. Nevertheless, the New World took its name from the Florentine merchant **Amerigo Vespucci**—not Columbus. Vespucci took part in several voyages to the New World and wrote a series of descriptions that not only gave Europeans an image of this "New World" but also spread the idea that the discovered lands were not part of Asia or India. Vespucci, then, popularized the image of the Americas and the idea that the Americas were continents separate from those previously known.

A Portuguese navigator, **Vasco da Gama**, crossed the Isthmus of Panama and came to another ocean, which separates the American continents from China. The Spanish sponsored another Portuguese sailor, **Ferdinand Magellan**, who discovered at the southern end of South America a strait that provided access to the ocean west of the Americas. Magellan named this ocean the Pacific because it was much calmer than the strait through which he had sailed to reach it. Later, he reached the Philippines and met his death in a conflict with the natives. Magellan's voyage, nevertheless, was the final stage of the process whereby Europeans completed the first known circumnavigation of the globe. Although initially the Spanish were eager to find a route around the Americas that would enable them to sail on toward their original goal, the treasures of the Far East, they began to consider the Americas as a possible source of untapped wealth.

The Spanish claimed all the New World except Brazil, which papal decree gave to the Portuguese. The first Spanish settlements were on the islands of the Caribbean Sea. It was not until 1518 that Spain appointed **Hernando Cortez** as a government official in Cuba; Cortez led a small military expedition against the Aztecs in Mexico. Cortez and his men failed in their first attack on the Aztec capital city, Tenochtitlán, but were ultimately successful.

A combination of factors allowed the small force of approximately 600 Spanish soldiers to overcome the extensive Aztec Empire. The Spanish were armed with rifles and bows, which provided an advantage over Aztec fighters armed only with spears. However, weapons and armor were not the main reason that the Spanish were able to overcome the military forces of the natives.

The Aztec ruler, Montezuma, allowed a delegation, which included Cortez, into the capital city because the description of the Spanish soldiers in their armor and with feathers in their helmets was similar to the description in Aztec legend of messengers who would be sent by the chief Aztec god, Quetzalco'atl. The members of Cortez's expedition exposed the natives to smallpox and other diseases that devastated the native population. Finally, the Spanish expedition was able to form alliances with other native tribes that the Aztecs had conquered; these tribes were willing to cooperate to defeat the Aztecs and thus break up their empire.

Twenty years after Cortez defeated the Aztecs, another conquistador, **Francisco Pizarro**, defeated the Incas in Peru. Pizarro's expedition enabled the Spanish to begin to explore and settle South America. Spain funded the conquistadors, or conquerors, who were the first Europeans to explore some areas of the Americas. However, the sole purpose of the conquistadors' explorations was defeating the natives to gain access to gold, silver, and other wealth. Spain established mines in the territory it claimed and produced a tremendous amount of gold and silver. In the 300 years after the Spanish conquest of the Americas in the sixteenth century, those mines produced 10 times more gold and silver than the total produced by all the mines in the rest of the world.

Spain had come to view the New World as more than an obstacle to voyages toward India; over time, Spain began to think that it might be possible to exploit this territory for more than just mining. The conquistadors made it possible for the Spanish to settle the New World, but they were not responsible for forming settlements or for overseeing Spanish colonies there. Instead, Spain sent officials and administrators from Spain to oversee settlements after their initial formation.

Spanish settlers came to the New World for various reasons: Some went in search of land to settle or buy, others went looking for opportunities that were not available to them in Europe, and priests and missionaries went to spread Christianity to the natives. By the end of the sixteenth century, Spain had established firm control over not only the several islands in the Caribbean, Mexico, and southern North America but also in the territory currently within the modern states of Chile, Argentina, and Peru.

Spanish Settlements in the New World

The first permanent settlement established by the Spanish was the predominantly military fort of St. Augustine, located in present-day Florida. In 1598, Don Juan de Oñate led a group of 500 settlers north from Mexico and established a colony in what is now New Mexico.

Oñate granted *encomiendas* to the most prominent Spaniards who had accompanied him. Under the *encomienda* system, which the Spanish in Mexico and parts of North America established, these distinguished individuals had the right to exact tribute and/or labor from the native population, which continued to live on the land in exchange for the services the native peoples provided. Spanish colonists founded Santa Fe in 1609, and by 1680 about 2,000 Spaniards were living in New Mexico. Most of the colonists raised sheep and cattle on large ranches and lived among approximately 30,000 Pueblo Indians. The Spanish crushed a major revolt that threatened to destroy Santa Fe in 1680. Attempts to prevent the natives—both those who had converted to Catholicism and those who had not—from performing religious rituals that predated the Spaniards' arrival provoked the revolt. The natives drove the Spanish from Santa Fe, but they returned in 1696, crushed the Pueblos, and seized the land.

Although the Spanish ultimately quelled the revolt, they began to change their policies toward the natives, who still greatly outnumbered the Spanish settlers. The Spanish continued to try to Christianize and "civilize" the native population, but they also began to allow the Pueblos to own land. In addition, the Spanish unofficially tolerated native religious rituals, although Catholicism officially condemned all such practices. By 1700, the Spanish population in New Mexico had increased and reached about 4,000 and the native population had decreased to about 13,000; intermarriage between natives and Spaniards increased. Nevertheless, disease, war, and migration resulted in the steady decline in the Pueblo population. New Mexico had become a prosperous and stable region, but it was still relatively weak and, as the only major Spanish settlement in northern Mexico, was isolated.

Effects of Contact between Europe and the Americas

One cannot underestimate the impact of the Europeans on the New World, both before and after the arrival of the English and French. The most immediate effect was the spread of disease, which decimated the native population. In some areas of Mexico, for example, 95 percent of the native population died as a result of contact with Europeans and the subsequent outbreaks of diseases like smallpox. In South America, the native population was devastated not only by disease but also by deliberate policies instituted to control and in some cases eliminate native peoples.

Although Europeans passed most diseases to the natives, the natives passed syphilis to the Europeans, who carried it back to Europe. The European and American continents exchanged plants and animals. Europeans brought animals to the New World, and they took plants, such as potatoes, corn, and squash, back to Europe, where introduction of these crops led to an explosion of the European population. The decimation of the native population and the establishment of large plantations led to a shortage of workers, and Europeans began to transport slaves from Africa to the New World to fill the shortage.

UNITED STATES HISTORY

European Exploration and Colonization

Identifying Individuals and Events That Have Influenced Economic, Social, and Political Institutions in the United States

In 1497, King Henry VIII of England sponsored a voyage by **John Cabot** to try to discover a northwest passage through the New World to the Orient. However, the English made no real attempt to settle in the New World until nearly a century later. By the 1600s, the English became interested in colonizing the New World for several reasons.

Many people in England emigrated overseas because the country's population was increasing and because much of the land was being used for raising sheep for wool rather than for growing foodstuffs for survival. Scarce opportunities, like those for buying land, were primary motivators for emigration from England. Some people in England left their homeland because of the religious turmoil that engulfed England after the beginning of the Protestant Reformation. In addition to converts to Lutheranism and Calvinism, a major emigrating group was the Puritans, who called for reforms to "purify" the church.

Mercantilism also provided a motive for exploration and for the establishment of colonies. According to mercantile theories, an industrialized nation needed an inexpensive source of raw materials and markets for finished products. Colonies provided a way to obtain raw materials and to guarantee a market for industrial goods. Economic reasons, among others, motivated the French and the Dutch to explore and establish colonies in the New World.

In 1609, the year after the first English settlement, the French established a colony in Quebec. Overall, far fewer French settlers traveled to the New World than did English settlers, but the French were able to exercise a tremendous influence through the establishment of strong ties with the natives. The French created trading partnerships and a vast trading network; they often intermarried with the local native population. The Dutch financed an English explorer, **Henry Hudson**, who claimed for Holland the territory that is now New York. The Dutch settlements along the Hudson, Delaware, and Connecticut rivers developed into the colony of New Netherlands and established a vast trading network that effectively separated the English colonies of Jamestown and Plymouth.

One reason that English settlements became more prominent after 1600 was the defeat of the Spanish fleet, the supposedly invincible Armada, by the English in 1588. The changing power balance on the seas encouraged the English to increase their exploration and to attempt colonization of the Americas. The first few colonies founded by the English in America did not flourish. Sir Humphrey Gilbert, who had obtained a six-year grant giving him the exclusive rights to settle any unclaimed land in America, was planning to establish a colony in Newfoundland, but a storm sank his ship. Instead, **Sir Walter Raleigh** received the six-year grant. Raleigh explored the North American coast and named the territory through which he traveled Virginia, in honor of the "Virgin Queen" Elizabeth I of England. In addition, Raleigh convinced his cousin Sir Grenville to establish a colony on the island of Roanoke. **Roanoke** was off the coast of what later became North Carolina. The first settlers lived there for a year while Sir Grenville returned to England for supplies and additional settlers. However, when Sir Francis Drake arrived in Roanoke nearly a year later and found that Sir Grenville had not yet returned, the colonists left on his ship and abandoned the settlement. In 1587, Raleigh sent another group of colonists to Roanoke, but a war with Spain broke out in 1588 and kept him from returning until 1590. When Raleigh returned to Roanoke, the colonists had vanished and had left only one clue: a single word, *Croatan*, carved into a tree. This word could have referred to a nearby settlement of natives whom they might have joined or who might have attacked them. This suggested a number of possibilities in regard to the missing settlers; conclusive proof of their fate was never found.

Colonization: The Jamestown Settlement

In 1606, King James I of England granted to the Virginia Company a charter for exploration and colonization. This charter marked the beginning of ventures sponsored by merchants rather than directly by the Crown. The charter of the Virginia Company had two branches. James I gave one branch to the English city of Plymouth, which had the right to the northern portion of territory on the eastern coast of North America, and he granted the London branch of the company the right to the southern portion.

Considerable difficulties prevented the English from founding and maintaining a permanent settlement in North America. The Plymouth Company failed to establish a lasting settlement. The company itself ran out of money, and the settlers who had gone to the New World gave up and abandoned their established Sagadahoc Colony in Maine. Having decided to colonize the Chesapeake Bay area, the London Company sent three ships with about 104 sailors to that area in 1607. The company's ships sailed up a river, which they named the James in honor of the English king, and they established the fort and permanent settlement of Jamestown. The London Company and the men who settled Jamestown were hoping to find a northwest passage to Asia, gold, and silver or to be able to find lands capable of producing valuable goods, such as grapes, oranges, or silk. The colony at Jamestown did not allow the settlers to accomplish any of those things. Its location on the river, which became contaminated every spring, led to the outbreak of diseases such as typhoid, dysentery, and malaria. Over half the colonists died the first year, and by the spring of 1609, only one-third of the total number of colonists who had joined the colony were still alive.

The survival of the colony initially was largely accomplished through the efforts of **Captain John Smith**. Smith was a soldier who turned the colony's focus from exploration to obtaining food. Initially, Smith was able to obtain corn from the local Indians led by **Powhatan** and his 12-year-old daughter, **Pocahontas**. Smith also forced all able men in the colony to work four hours a day in the wheat fields. Attempts by the London Company to send additional settlers and supplies encountered troubles and delays. **Thomas Gates** and some 600 settlers, who left for Jamestown in 1609, ran aground on Bermuda and had to build a new ship. Although some new settlers did arrive in Jamestown, disease continued to shrink the population. When a seriously injured Smith had to return to England, his departure deprived the colony of its most effective and resourceful leader. It was not long after Smith left that the colonists provoked a war with Powhatan, who was beginning to tire of the colonists' demands for corn. Powhatan realized that the settlers intended to stay indefinitely and might challenge the Indians for control of the surrounding territory. Gates finally arrived in June 1610 with only 175 of the original 600 settlers. He found only 60 colonists who had survived the war with the Indians and the harsh winter of 1610, during which they had minimal food and other resources. Gates decided to abandon Jamestown and was sailing down the river with the surviving colonists on board when he encountered the new governor from England, **Thomas West**, Baron de la Warr. Gates and West returned to Jamestown, imposed martial law, responded to Indian attacks, and survived a five-year war with the Indians. Although the war did not end until 1614, when the colonists were able to negotiate a settlement by holding Pocahontas hostage, the situation in Jamestown began to improve in 1610. Some of the settlers went to healthier locations, and in 1613 one of them, **John Rolfe**, married Pocahontas. In 1614, the settlers planted a mild strain of tobacco, which gave them a crop they could sell for cash. The Crown issued two new charters that allowed Virginia to extend its borders all the way to the Pacific and made the London Company a joint-stock company. Changes in the company led to a new treasurer, **Sir Edwin Sandy**, who tried to reform Virginia.

Sandy encouraged settlers in Virginia to try to produce grapes and silkworms and to diversify the colony's economy in other ways. Sandy also replaced martial law with English common law. The colonists established a council to make laws, and settlers now had the right to own land. By 1623, about 4,000 additional settlers had arrived in Virginia. Attempts to produce and sell crops other than tobacco failed, however, and the arrival of large numbers of new colonists provoked renewed conflict with the Indians. A major Indian attack launched in March 1622 killed 347 colonists. Investors in the London Company withdrew their capital and appealed to the king, and a royal commission visited the colony. As a result of this investigation, the king declared the London Company bankrupt and assumed direct control of Virginia in 1624. Virginia became the first royal colony, and the Crown appointed a governor and a council to oversee its administration.

Three trends continued after the Crown assumed control. The first was unrelenting conflict with the Indians. By 1632, through war and raids, the colonists had killed or driven out most of the Indians in the area immediately around Jamestown. The other two trends were the yearly influx of thousands of new settlers and the high death rate in the colony. Despite the high mortality rate, the population of the colony began to increase gradually. The expansion of tobacco production led to a demand for labor, and thousands of the young men who came were indentured servants. In exchange for their passage to America and food and shelter during their terms of service, these men were bound to work for their masters for four or five years. After that time, they gained their freedom and often a small payment to help them become established. Most of these men were not able to participate in the running of the colony even after they became free, but some were able to acquire land.

In 1634, the Crown divided Virginia into counties, each with appointed justices and the right to fill all other positions. Under this type of system, individuals from a few wealthy families tended to dominate the government. Most of the counties became Anglican, and the colony continued to elect representatives to its House of Burgesses, an assembly that met with the governor to discuss issues of common law. The king, however, refused to recognize the colony's House of Burgesses. After 1660, the colony became even more dominated by the wealthiest 15 percent of the population, and these individuals and their sons continued to be the only colonists to serve as justices and burgesses. Settlement of the colonies continued, primarily for religious and economic reasons. Conflict between the colonists and the natives was constant.

Growth of the Slave Trade

The shortage of labor in the southern colonies and a drop in the number of people coming to the colonies as indentured servants forced the colonists to search for other sources of labor. Although the colonists began using African servants and slaves almost immediately after settling in the New World, the slave trade and the slave population in British North America remained small in the first half of the seventeenth century. Toward the end of the seventeenth century, increasing numbers of slaves from Africa became available, and the demand for them in North America further stimulated the growth of the transatlantic slave trade.

By the nineteenth century, millions of Africans had been forcibly taken from their native lands and sold into perpetual slavery. The Europeans sold slaves at forts that the slave traders had established on the African coast; the Europeans packed the slaves as closely as possible into the lower regions of ships for the long journey to the Americas. Chained slaves traveled in deplorable unsanitary conditions and received only enough food and water to keep them alive. Many slaves died during this Middle Passage voyage. Plantation owners in the Caribbean, Brazil, or North America bought the slaves to do the work. It was only after 1697 that English colonists began

to buy large numbers of slaves. By 1760, the slave population had reached approximately a quarter of a million, with most of the slaves concentrated in the southern colonies. Slave labor replaced indentured servitude, and a race-based system of perpetual slavery developed. Colonial assemblies began to pass "slave codes" in the eighteenth century. These codes identified all nonwhites or dark-skinned people as slaves, made their condition permanent, and legalized slavery in British North America.

Salem Witch Trials

During this period of increasing tensions brought about by fears of the occult, intolerance, and conflicts between the religious community and some less-understood individuals, several areas held witchcraft trials. In Salem, Massachusetts, a group of young girls accused servants from West India and older white members of the community, mostly women, of exercising powers that Satan had given to them. Other towns also experienced turmoil and charged residents with witchcraft. In Salem alone, the juries pronounced 19 people guilty; in 1692, after the execution of all 19 victims, the girls admitted their stories were not true.

The witchcraft trials illustrate the highly religious nature of New England society, but they also suggest that individuals who did not conform to societal expectations were at risk. Most of the accused were outspoken women who were often critical of their communities, were older, and were either widowed or unmarried. Some of these women had acquired property despite the accepted views and limitations regarding women's role in society.

Religion in the Colonies and the Great Awakening

The religious nature of colonial settlers did not lead to the kind of intolerance or persecution that had plagued Europe since the Reformation. Conflict among various religious groups did break out occasionally, but British North America enjoyed a far greater degree of religious toleration than anywhere else. Among the reasons this toleration existed were that several religious groups had immigrated to North America and that every colony, except Virginia and Maryland, ignored the laws establishing the Church of England as the official faith of the colony. Even among the Puritans, differences in religious opinion led to the establishment of different denominations.

Although there was some religious toleration, Protestants still tended to view Roman Catholics as threatening rivals. In Maryland, Catholics numbered about 3,000, the largest population of all the colonies, and were the victims of persecution. Jews were often victims of persecution; they could not vote or hold office in any of the colonies, and only in Rhode Island could they practice the Jewish religion openly. The other main trends in addition to toleration were the westward spread of communities, the rise of cities, and a decline in religious piousness. This sense of the weakening of religious authority and faithfulness led to the Great Awakening. The Great Awakening refers to a period beginning in the 1730s in which several well-known preachers traveled through British North America giving speeches and arguing for the need to revive religious piety and closer relationships with God. The main message of the preachers was that everyone has the potential, regardless of past behavior, to reestablish their relationship with God. This message appealed to many women and younger sons of landowners who stood to inherit very little. The best-known preacher during this period was **Jonathan Edwards**. Edwards denounced some current beliefs as doctrines of easy salvation. At his church in Northampton, Massachusetts, Edwards sermonized about the absolute sovereignty of God, predestination, and salvation by grace alone.

The Great Awakening further divided religion in America by creating distinctions among New Light groups (revivalists), Old Light groups (traditionalists), and new groups that incorporated elements of both. The various revivalists, or New Light groups, did not agree on every issue. Some revivalists denounced education and learning from books, while others founded schools in the belief that education was a means of furthering religion. While some individuals were stressing a need for renewed spiritual focus, others were beginning to embrace the ideas of the Enlightenment. As discussed earlier, the Scientific Revolution had demonstrated the existence of natural laws that operated in nature, and enlightened thinkers began to argue that humans had the ability to improve their own situation through the use of rational thought and acquired knowledge. Intellectuals of the **Enlightenment** shifted the focus from God to humans, introduced the idea of progress, and argued that people could improve their own situations and make decisions on how to live rather than just having faith in God and waiting for salvation and a better life after death.

Enlightenment thought had a tremendous impact on the North American colonists, who began to establish more schools, encourage the acquisition of knowledge, and become more interested in gaining scientific knowledge. The colleges founded in North America taught the scientific theories held by **Copernicus**, who argued that the planets rotated around the sun not the earth, and **Sir Isaac Newton**, who introduced the key principles of physics, including gravity. The colonists did not just learn European theories. **Benjamin Franklin** was among the colonists who began to carry out their own experiments and form their own theories. Franklin experimented with electricity and was able to demonstrate in 1752, by using a kite, that electricity and lightning were the same. Scientific theories also led to inoculations against smallpox. The Puritan theologian **Cotton Mather** convinced the population of Boston that injections with a small amount of the smallpox virus would build up their resistance to the disease and reduce the likelihood of reinfection. Leading theologians and scientists spread European scientific ideas and developed their own theories and applications using their acquired knowledge.

The American Revolution

The Coming of the American Revolution

In 1764, George Grenville pushed through Parliament the **Sugar Act** (the Revenue Act), which aimed to raise revenue by taxing goods imported by Americans. The **Stamp Act** (1765) imposed a direct tax on the colonists for the first time. By requiring Americans to purchase revenue stamps on everything from newspapers to legal documents, the Stamp Act would have created an impossible drain on hard currency in the colonies.

Americans reacted first with restrained and respectful petitions and pamphlets in which they pointed out that "taxation without representation is tyranny." The colonists began to limit their purchase of imported goods. From there, resistance progressed to stronger protests that eventually became violent. In October 1765, delegates from nine colonies met as the Stamp Act Congress, passed moderate resolutions against the act, and asserted that Americans could not be taxed without the consent of their representatives. The colonists now ceased all importation. In March 1766, Parliament repealed the Stamp Act. At the same time, however, it passed the **Declaratory Act**, which claimed for Parliament the power to tax or make laws for the Americans "in all cases whatsoever." In 1766, Parliament passed a program of taxes on items imported into the colonies. The taxes came to be known as the Townsend duties, a name that came from Britain's chancellor of the exchequer, Charles Townsend. American reaction was at first slow, but the sending of troops aroused them to resistance.

Again the colonies halted importation, and soon British merchants were calling on Parliament to repeal the Townsend duties. In March 1770, Parliament repealed all the taxes except that on tea; Parliament wanted to prove that it had the right to tax the colonies if it so desired. When Parliament ended the **Tea Act** in 1773, a relative peace ensued. In desperate financial condition—partially because the Americans were buying smuggled Dutch tea rather than the taxed British product—the British East India Company sought and obtained from Parliament concessions that allowed it to ship tea directly to the colonies rather than only by way of Britain. The result would be that the East India Company tea, even with the tax, would be cheaper than smuggled Dutch tea. The company hoped that the colonists would thus buy the tea—tax and all—save the East India Company, and tacitly accept Parliament's right to tax them. The Americans, however, proved resistant to this approach. Rather than acknowledge Parliament's right to tax, they refused to buy the cheaper tea and resorted to various methods, including tar and feathers, to prevent the collection of the tax on tea. In most ports, Americans did not allow ships carrying the tea to land. In Boston, however, the pro-British governor **Thomas Hutchinson** forced a confrontation by ordering Royal Navy vessels to prevent the tea ships from leaving the harbor. After 20 days, this would, by law, result in selling the cargoes at auction and paying the tax. The night before the time was to expire, December 16, 1773, Bostonians thinly disguised as Native Americans boarded the ships and threw the tea into the harbor. This was the **Boston Tea Party**. The British responded with four acts collectively titled the **Coercive Acts** (1774), in which they strengthened their control over the colonists. The **First Continental Congress** (1774) met in response to the acts. The First Continental Congress called for strict nonimportation and rigorous preparation of local militia companies.

The War for Independence

British troops went to Massachusetts, which the Crown had officially declared to be in a state of rebellion. General Thomas Gage received orders to arrest the leaders of the resistance or, failing that, to provoke any sort of confrontation that would allow him to turn British military might loose on the Americans. Americans detected the movement of Gage's troops toward Concord, however, and dispatch riders, like **Paul Revere** and **William Dawes**, spread the news throughout the countryside.

In Lexington, about 70 **minutemen** (trained militiamen who would respond at a moment's notice) awaited the British on the village green. A shot was fired; it is unknown which side fired first. This became **"the shot heard 'round the world."** The British opened fire and charged. Casualties occurred on both sides. The following month, the Americans tightened the noose around Boston by fortifying Breed's Hill (a spur of Bunker Hill). The British were determined to remove them by a frontal attack. Twice thrown back, the British finally succeeded when the Americans ran out of ammunition. There were more than 1,000 British casualties in what turned out to be the bloodiest battle of the war (June 17, 1775), yet the British had gained very little and remained "bottled up" in Boston.

Congress put **George Washington** (1732–1799) in charge of the army; called for more troops; and adopted the Olive Branch Petition, which pleaded with **King George III** to intercede with Parliament to restore peace. However, the king gave his approval to the Prohibitory Act, declaring the colonies in rebellion and no longer under his protection. Preparations began for full-scale war against America. In 1776, the colonists formed two committees to establish independence and a national government. One was to work out a framework for a national government. The other was to draft a statement of the reasons for declaring independence. The statement, called the **Declaration of Independence**, was primarily the work of Thomas Jefferson (1743–1826) of Virginia. It was a restatement of political ideas by then commonplace in America and showed why the former colonists felt justified in separating from Great Britain. Congress formally adopted the Declaration of Independence on **July 4, 1776**. The British landed that summer at New York City. Washington, who had anticipated the move, was waiting for them. However, the undertrained, underequipped, and badly outnumbered American army was no match for the British and had to retreat. By December, what was left of Washington's army had made its way into Pennsylvania.

With his small army melting away as demoralized soldiers deserted, Washington decided on a bold move. On Christmas night 1776, his army crossed the **Delaware River** and struck the Hessians (German mercenaries who often served with the British) at **Trenton, New Jersey**. Washington's troops easily defeated the Hessians, still groggy from their hard-drinking Christmas party. A few days later, Washington defeated a British force at **Princeton, New Jersey**. The Americans regained much of New Jersey from the British and saved the American army from disintegration. Hoping to weaken Britain, France began making covert shipments of arms to the Americans early in the war. These French shipments were vital for the Americans. The American victory at Saratoga, New York, convinced the French to join openly in the war against England. Eventually, the Spanish (1779) and the Dutch (1780) joined as well. The final peace agreement between the new United States and Great Britain became known as the Treaty of Paris of 1783. Its terms stipulated the following:

1. The recognition by the major European powers, including Britain, of the United States as an independent nation

2. The establishment of America's western boundary at the Mississippi River

3. The establishment of America's southern boundary at latitude 31° north (the northern boundary of Florida)

4. The surrender of Florida to Spain and the retainment of Canada by Britain

5. The enablement of private British creditors to collect any debts owed by United States citizens

6. The recommendation of Congress that the states restore confiscated loyalist property

New Politicians, New Governments, and Social Change

After the adoption and failure of the Articles of Confederation, Congress adopted a new constitution and the Americans elected George Washington as president under its guidelines.

The Federalist Era. George Washington received almost all the votes of the presidential electors. **John Adams** (1735–1826) received the next highest number and became the vice president. After a triumphant journey from his home at Mount Vernon in Virginia, Washington attended his inauguration in New York City, the temporary seat of government.

To oppose the antifederalists, the states ratified 10 amendments—the Bill of Rights—by the end of 1791. The first nine spelled out specific guarantees of personal freedoms, and the Tenth Amendment reserved to the states all powers not specifically withheld or granted to the federal government. **Alexander Hamilton** (1757–1804) interpreted the Constitution as having vested extensive powers in the federal government. This "implied powers" stance claimed that the federal government had all powers that the Constitution had not expressly denied it. Hamilton's was the "broad" interpretation of the Constitution. By contrast, Thomas Jefferson and **James Madison** (1751–1836) held the view that the Constitution prohibited any action not specifically permitted in the Constitution. Based on this view of government, adherents of this "strict" interpretation opposed the establishment of Hamilton's national bank. The Jeffersonian supporters, primarily under the guidance of Madison, began to organize political groups in opposition to Hamilton's program. The groups opposing Hamilton's view called themselves Democratic-Republicans or Jeffersonians.

The Federalists, Hamilton's supporters, received their strongest confirmation from the business and financial groups in the commercial centers of the Northeast and from the port cities of the South. The strength of the Democratic-Republicans lay primarily in the rural and frontier areas of the South and West. Federalist candidate John Adams won the election of 1796. The elections in 1798 increased the Federalists' majorities in both houses of Congress that used their "mandate" to enact legislation to stifle foreign influences.

The **Alien Act** raised new hurdles in the path of immigrants trying to obtain citizenship, and the **Sedition Act** widened the powers of the Adams administration to muzzle its newspaper critics. Democratic-Republicans were convinced that the Alien and Sedition Acts were unconstitutional, but the process of deciding on the constitutionality of federal laws was as yet undefined.

The Jeffersonian Era. Thomas Jefferson and **Aaron Burr** ran for the presidency on the Democratic-Republican ticket, though not together, against John Adams and Charles Pinckney for the Federalists. Both Jefferson and Burr received the same number of votes in the electoral college, so the election went to the House of Representatives. After a lengthy deadlock, Alexander Hamilton threw his support to Jefferson. Burr had to accept the vice presidency, the result obviously intended by the electorate.

The adoption and ratification of the Twelfth Amendment in 1804 ensured that a tie vote between candidates of the same party could not again cause the confusion of the Jefferson-Burr affair. Following the constitutional mandate, an 1808 law prevented the importation of slaves. An American delegation purchased the trans-Mississippi territory from Napoleon for $15 million in April 1803 (the Louisiana Purchase), even though they had no authority to buy more than the city of New Orleans.

The War of 1812. Democratic-Republican **James Madison** won the election of 1808 over Federalist Charles Pinckney, but the Federalists gained seats in both houses of Congress.

PRAXIS Pointer

When you feel anxious, close your eyes and take a couple of long, deep breaths. Then hold it and exhale slowly. Imagine a peaceful place to visit.

The Native American tribes of the Northwest and the **Mississippi Valley** were resentful of the government's policy of pressured removal to the West, and the British authorities in Canada exploited their discontent by encouraging border raids against the American settlements. At the same time, the British interfered with American transatlantic shipping, including impressing sailors and capturing ships. On June 1, 1812, President Madison asked for a declaration of war, and Congress complied. After three years of inconclusive war, the British and Americans signed the Treaty of Ghent (1815). It provided for the acceptance of the status quo that had existed at the beginning of hostilities, and both sides restored their wartime conquests against the other.

The Monroe Doctrine. As Latin American nations began declaring independence, British and American leaders feared that European governments would try to restore the former New World colonies to their erstwhile royal owners. In December 1823, **President James Monroe** (1758–1831) included in his annual message to Congress a statement that the peoples of the American hemisphere were "henceforth not to be considered as subjects for future colonization by any European powers."

The Marshall Court. Chief Justice **John Marshall** (1755–1835) delivered the majority opinions in several critical decisions in the formative years of the U.S. Supreme Court. These decisions served to strengthen the power of the federal government (and of the Court itself) and restrict the powers of state governments. Here are two key examples:

- *Marbury v. Madison* (1803) established the Supreme Court's power of judicial review over federal legislation.

- In *Gibbons v. Ogden* (1824), a case involving competing steamboat companies, Marshall ruled that commerce includes navigation and that only Congress has the right to regulate commerce among states. Marshall's ruling voided the state-granted monopoly.

The Missouri Compromise. The Missouri Territory, the first territory organized from the Louisiana Purchase, applied for statehood in 1819. Because the Senate membership was evenly divided between slaveholding and free states at that time, the admission of a new state would give the voting advantage to either the North or the South. As the debate dragged on, the northern territory of Massachusetts applied for admission as the state of Maine. By combining the two admission bills, the Senate hoped to reach a compromise by admitting Maine as a free state and Missouri as a slave state. To make the Missouri Compromise palatable for the House of Representatives, the Senate added a provision prohibiting slavery in the remainder of the Louisiana Territory north of the southern boundary of Missouri (latitude 36°30′).

Jacksonian Democracy. Andrew Jackson (1767–1845), the candidate of a faction of the emerging Democratic Party, won the election of 1828. Jackson was popular with the common man. He seemed to be the prototype of the self-made westerner: rough-hewn, violent, vindictive, with few ideas but strong convictions. He ignored his appointed cabinet officers and relied instead on the counsel of his "Kitchen Cabinet," a group of partisan supporters. He exercised his veto power more than any other president before him.

Jackson supported the removal of all Native American tribes to an area west of the Mississippi River. The **Indian Removal Act** of 1830 provided for the federal enforcement of that process. One of the results of this policy was the **Trail of Tears**, the forced march under U.S. Army escort of thousands of Cherokee Indians to the West. One-quarter or more of them, mostly women and children, perished on the journey.

The National Bank. The Bank of the United States had operated under the direction of Nicholas Biddle since 1823. He was a cautious man, and his conservative economic policy enforced conservatism among state and private banks—which many bankers resented. In 1832, Jackson vetoed the national bank's renewal, and it ceased being a federal institution in 1836.

The Antislavery Movement. In 1831, **William Lloyd Garrison** started his newspaper, *The Liberator*, and began to advocate total and immediate emancipation. He founded the New England Antislavery Society in 1832 and the American Antislavery Society in 1833. Theodore Weld pursued the same goals but advocated more gradual means.

The movement split into two wings: Garrison's radical followers and the moderates who favored "moral suasion" and petitions to Congress. In 1840, the Liberty Party, the first national antislavery party, fielded a presidential candidate on the platform of "free soil" (preventing the expansion of slavery into the new western territories).

The Role of Minorities. The women's rights movement focused on social and legal discrimination, and women like Lucretia Mott and Sojourner Truth became well-known figures on the speakers' circuit. By 1850, roughly 200,000 free blacks lived in the North and West. Prejudice restricted their lives, and "Jim Crow" laws separated the races.

Manifest Destiny and Westward Expansion. The coining of the term *Manifest Destiny* did not occur until 1844, but the belief that the destiny of the American nation was expansion all the way to the Pacific Ocean—and possibly even to Canada and Mexico—was older than that. A common conviction was that Americans should share American liberty and ideals with everyone possible, by force if necessary. In the 1830s, American missionaries followed the traders and trappers to the Oregon country and began to publicize the richness and beauty of the land. The result was the Oregon Fever of the 1840s, as thousands of settlers trekked across the Great Plains and the Rocky Mountains to settle the new Shangri-la.

Texas had been a state in the Republic of Mexico since 1822, following the Mexican revolution against Spanish control. The new Mexican government invited immigration from the North by offering land grants to Stephen Austin and other Americans. By 1835, approximately 35,000 "gringos" were homesteading on Texas land. Mexican officials saw their power base eroding as the foreigners flooded in, so they moved to tighten control through restrictions on immigration and through tax increases. The Texans responded in 1836 by proclaiming independence and establishing a new republic. Texas requested that the United States annex it. Many American citizens protested this annexation; they feared retaliation from Mexico and expressed concern about the annexation of such a large area with slavery. Congress learned that Great Britain might serve as protector for Texas, and this was a major reason for changing its vote. In 1845, after a series of failed attempts at annexation, the U.S. Congress admitted Texas to the Union.

The Mexican War

Though Mexico broke diplomatic relations with the United States immediately after Texas's admission to the Union, there was still hope of a peaceful settlement. In the fall of 1845, President **James K. Polk** (1795–1849) sent **John Slidell** to Mexico City with a proposal for a peaceful settlement, but like other attempts at negotiation, nothing came of it. Racked by coups and countercoups, the Mexican government refused even to receive Slidell. Polk responded by sending U.S. troops into the disputed territory. On April 5, 1846, Mexican troops attacked an American patrol. When news of the clash reached

Washington, Polk sought and received from Congress a declaration of war against Mexico.

Negotiated peace came with the signing of the Treaty of Guadalupe Hidalgo on February 2, 1848. Under the terms of the treaty, Mexico ceded to the United States the southwestern territory from Texas to the California coast.

Sectional Conflict and the Causes of the Civil War

The Crisis of 1850. The Mexican War had barely started when, on August 8, 1846, a freshman Democratic congressman, **David Wilmot** of Pennsylvania, introduced his **Wilmot Proviso** as a proposed amendment to a war appropriations bill. It stipulated that "neither slavery nor involuntary servitude shall ever exist" in any territory to be acquired from Mexico. The House passed the proviso, but the Senate did not; Wilmot introduced his provision again amidst increasingly acrimonious debate.

One compromise proposal called for the extension of the 36°30′ line of the Missouri Compromise westward through the Mexican cession to the Pacific, with territory north of the line closed to slavery. Another compromise solution was *popular sovereignty*, which held that the residents of each territory should decide for themselves whether to allow slavery. Having more than the requisite population and being in need of better government, California petitioned in September 1849 for admission to the Union as a free state. Southerners were furious. Long outnumbered in the House of Representatives, the South would find itself, should Congress admit California as a free state, similarly outnumbered in the Senate. At this point, the aged **Henry Clay** proposed a compromise. For the North, Congress would admit California as a free state; the land in dispute between Texas and New Mexico would go to New Mexico; popular sovereignty would decide the issue of slavery in the New Mexico and Utah territories (all of the Mexican cession outside California); and there would be no slave trade in the District of Columbia. For the South, Congress would enact a tougher fugitive slave law, promise not to abolish slavery in the District of Columbia, and declare that it did not have jurisdiction over the interstate slave trade; the federal government would pay Texas's $10 million preannexation debt.

The Kansas-Nebraska Act. All illusion of sectional peace ended abruptly in 1854 when Senator **Stephen A. Douglas** of Illinois introduced a bill in Congress to organize the area west of Missouri and Iowa as the territories of Kansas and Nebraska on the basis of popular sovereignty. The **Kansas-Nebraska Act** aroused a storm of outrage in the North, which viewed the repeal of the Missouri Compromise as the breaking of a solemn agreement; hastened the disintegration of the Whig Party; and divided the Democratic Party along North-South lines.

Springing to life almost overnight as a result of northern fury at the Kansas-Nebraska Act was the Republican Party. This party included diverse elements whose sole unifying principle was banning slavery from all the nation's territories, confining slavery to the states where it already existed, and preventing the further spread of slavery.

The Dred Scott Decision. In *Dred Scott v. Sanford* (1857), the Supreme Court attempted to settle the slavery question. The case involved a Missouri slave, **Dred Scott**, whom the abolitionists had encouraged to sue for his freedom on the basis that his owner had taken him to a free state, Illinois, for several years and then to a free territory, Wisconsin.

The Court attempted to read the extreme southern position on slavery into the Constitution, ruling not only that Scott had no standing to sue in federal court but also that temporary residence in a free state, even for several years, did not make a slave free. In addition, the Court ruling signified that the Missouri Compromise (already a dead letter by that time) had been unconstitutional all along because Congress did not have the authority to exclude slavery from a territory, nor did territorial governments have the right to prohibit slavery.

The Election of 1860. As the 1860 presidential election approached, the Republicans met in Chicago, confident of victory and determined to do nothing to jeopardize their favorable position. Accordingly, they rejected as too radical the front-running candidate, New York Senator **William H. Seward**, in favor of Illinois's favorite son **Abraham Lincoln** (1809–1865). The platform called for federal support of a transcontinental railroad and for the containment of slavery. On Election Day, the voting went along strictly sectional lines. Lincoln led in popular votes; though he was short of a majority of popular votes, he did have the needed majority in electoral college votes and won the election.

The Secession Crisis. On December 20, 1860, South Carolina, by vote of a special convention, seceded from the Union. By February 1, 1861, six more states (Alabama, Georgia, Florida, Mississippi, Louisiana, and Texas) had followed suit.

Representatives of the seceded states met in Montgomery, Alabama, in February 1861 and declared themselves to be the Confederate States of America. They elected former secretary of war and United States senator **Jefferson Davis** (1808–1889) of Mississippi as president and Alexander Stephens (1812–1883) of Georgia as vice president.

Civil War and Reconstruction

Hostilities Begin. In his inaugural address, Lincoln urged Southerners to reconsider their actions but warned that the Union was perpetual; that states could not secede; and that he would, therefore, hold the federal forts and installations in the South. Only two remained in federal hands: Fort Pickens, off Pensacola, Florida; and Fort Sumter, in the harbor of Charleston, South Carolina.

From **Major Robert Anderson**, commander of the small garrison at Sumter, Lincoln soon received word that supplies were running low. Desiring to send in the needed supplies, Lincoln informed the governor of South Carolina of his intention but promised that no attempt would be made to send arms, ammunition, or reinforcements unless Southerners initiated hostilities. Confederate **General P. G. T. Beauregard**, acting on orders from President Davis, demanded Anderson's surrender. Anderson said he would surrender if the fort were not resupplied. Knowing supplies were on the way, the Confederates opened fire at 4:30 AM on April 12, 1861. The next day, the fort surrendered. The day following Sumter's surrender, Lincoln declared an insurrection and called for the states to provide 75,000 volunteers to put it down. In response, Virginia, Tennessee, North Carolina, and Arkansas declared their secession. The remaining slave states—Delaware, Kentucky, Maryland, and Missouri—wavered but stayed with the Union.

The North enjoyed many advantages over the South. It had the majority of wealth and was vastly superior in industry. The North also had an advantage of almost three to one in labor; over one-third of the South's residents were slaves, whom Southerners would not use as soldiers. Unlike the South, the North received large numbers of **immigrants** during the war. The North retained control of the U.S. Navy; it could command the sea and blockade the South. Finally, the North enjoyed a much superior system of railroads.

The South did, however, have some advantages. It was vast in size and difficult to conquer. In addition, its troops would be fighting on their own ground, a fact that would give them the advantage of familiarity with the terrain and the added motivation of defending their homes and families.

The Homestead Act and the Morrill Land Grant Act. In 1862, Congress passed two highly important acts dealing with domestic affairs in the North. The Homestead Act granted 160 acres of government land free of charge to any person who would farm it for at least five years. Many of the settlers of the West used the provisions of this act. The Morrill Land Grant Act offered large amounts of the federal government's land to states that would establish "agricultural and mechanical" colleges. The founding of many of the nation's large state universities occurred under the provisions of this act.

The Emancipation Proclamation. By mid-1862, Lincoln, acting under pressure from radical elements of his own party and hoping to make a favorable impression on foreign public opinion, determined to issue the **Emancipation Proclamation**, which declared free all slaves in areas still in rebellion as of January 1, 1863. At the recommendation of William Seward, former New York senator and now his secretary of state, Lincoln waited to announce the proclamation until the North won some sort of victory. The Battle of Antietam (September 17, 1862) provided this victory.

Northern Victory

Lincoln ran on the ticket of the National Union Party—essentially, the Republican Party with the addition of loyal or "war" Democrats. His vice presidential candidate was **Andrew Johnson** (1808–1875), a loyal Democrat from Tennessee.

In September 1864, word came that **General William Sherman** (1820–1891) had taken Atlanta. The capture of this vital southern rail and manufacturing center brought an enormous boost to northern morale. Along with other northern victories that summer and fall, it ensured a resounding election victory for Lincoln and the continuation of the war to complete victory for the North. **General Robert E. Lee** (1807–1870) abandoned Richmond, Virginia, on April 3, 1865, and attempted to escape with what was left of his army. Under the command of **Ulysses S. Grant** (1822–1885), Northern forces cornered Lee's troops and forced his surrender at Appomattox, Virginia, on April 9, 1865. Other Confederate troops still holding out in various parts of the South surrendered over the next few weeks. Lincoln did not live to receive news of the final surrenders. On April 14, 1865, **John Wilkes Booth** shot Lincoln in the back of the head while the president was watching a play in Ford's Theater in Washington, D.C.

Reconstruction. In 1865, Congress created the **Freedman's Bureau** to provide food, clothing, and education and generally to look after the interests of former slaves. To restore legal governments in the seceded states, Lincoln had developed a policy that made it relatively easy for Southern states to enter the collateral process.

Congress passed a **Civil Rights Act** in 1866, declaring that all citizens born in the United States are, regardless of race, equal citizens under the law. This act became the model of the Fourteenth Amendment to the Constitution. **President Andrew Johnson** obeyed the letter but not the spirit of the Reconstruction acts. Congress, angry at his refusal to cooperate, sought in vain for grounds to impeach him. In August 1867, Johnson violated the Tenure of Office Act, which forbade the president from removing from office those officials who had been approved by the Senate. This test of the act's constitutionality took place not in the courts but in Congress. The House of Representatives impeached Johnson, who came within one vote of being removed from office by the Senate.

The Fifteenth Amendment. In 1868, the Republicans nominated Ulysses S. Grant for president. His narrow victory prompted Republican leaders to decide that it would be politically expedient to give the vote to all blacks, Northern as well as Southern. For this purpose, leaders of the North drew up and submitted to the states the Fifteenth Amendment. Ironically, the idea was so unpopular in the North that it won the necessary three-fourths approval only because Congress required the Southern states to ratify it.

Industrialism, War, and the Progressive Era

The Economy. Captains of industry—such as **John D. Rockefeller** in oil, **J. P. Morgan** in banking, **Gustavus Swift** in meat processing, **Andrew Carnegie** in steel, and **E. H. Harriman** in railroads—created major industrial empires. In 1886, **Samuel Gompers** and **Adolph Strasser** put together a combination of national craft unions, the **American Federation of Labor (AFL)**, to represent labor's concerns about wages, hours, and safety conditions. Although aggressive in its use of the strike and in its demand for collective bargaining in labor contracts with large corporations, the AFL did not promote violence or radicalism.

The Spanish-American War. The Cuban revolt against Spain in 1895 threatened American business interests in Cuba. Sensational "yellow" journalism and nationalistic statements from officials such as Assistant Secretary of the Navy **Theodore Roosevelt** (1858–1919) encouraged popular support for direct American military intervention on behalf of Cuban independence.

On March 27, 1897, President **William McKinley** (1843–1901) asked Spain to call an armistice, accept American mediation to end the war, and stop using concentration camps in Cuba. Spain refused to comply. On April 21, Congress declared war on Spain, with the objective of establishing Cuban independence (the Teller Amendment). The first U.S. forces landed in Cuba on June 22, 1898, and by July 17, they had defeated the Spanish forces. Spain ceded the Philippines, Puerto Rico, and Guam to the United States in return for a payment of $20 million to Spain for the Philippines.

Theodore Roosevelt and Progressive Reforms. On September 6, 1901, while attending the Pan American Exposition in Buffalo, New York, President McKinley was shot by Leon Czolgosz, an anarchist. The president died on September 14. Theodore Roosevelt, at age 42, became the nation's twenty-fifth president and its youngest president to date.

In accordance with the Antitrust Policy (1902), Roosevelt ordered the Justice Department to prosecute corporations pursuing monopolistic practices. Attorney General P. C. Knox first brought suit against the Northern Securities Company, a railroad holding corporation put together by J. P. Morgan, and then moved against John D. Rockefeller's Standard Oil Company. By the time he left office in 1909, Roosevelt had indictments against 25 monopolies. Roosevelt engineered the separation of Panama from Colombia and the recognition of Panama as an independent country.

The **Hay-Bunau-Varilla Treaty** of 1903 granted the United States control of the Canal Zone in Panama for $10 million and an annual fee of $250,000; the control would begin nine years after ratification of the treaty by both parties. Construction of the **Panama Canal** began in 1904 and was completed in 1914.

In 1905, the African American intellectual and militant **W. E. B. DuBois** founded the **Niagara Movement**, which called for federal legislation to protect racial equality and to grant full citizenship rights. Formed in 1909, the **National Association for the Advancement of Colored People** pressed actively for the rights of African Americans. A third organization of the time, the radical labor organization called the **Industrial Workers of the World** (IWW, or Wobblies; 1905–1924) promoted violence and revolution. The IWW organized effective strikes in the textile industry (1912) and among a few western miners' groups, but it had little appeal to the average American worker. After the Red Scare of 1919, the government worked to smash the IWW and deported many of its immigrant leaders and members.

The Wilson Presidency. The nation elected Democratic candidate **Woodrow Wilson** (1856–1924) as president in 1912. Before the outbreak of World War I in 1914, Wilson, working with cooperative majorities in both houses of Congress, achieved much of the remaining progressive agenda, including tariff reform (Underwood-Simmons Act, 1913); the Sixteenth Amendment (graduated income tax, 1913); the Seventeenth Amendment (direct election of senators, 1913); the Federal Reserve banking system (regulation of and flexibility to monetary policy, 1913); the Federal Trade Commission (to investigate unfair business practices, 1914); and the Clayton Antitrust Act (improving the old Sherman Act and protecting labor unions and farm cooperatives from prosecution, 1914).

Wilson's Fourteen Points. When America entered World War I in 1917, President Wilson maintained that the war would make the world safe for democracy. In an address to Congress on January 8, 1918, he presented his specific peace plan in the form of the Fourteen Points. The first five points called for open rather than secret peace treaties, freedom of the seas, free trade, arms reduction, and a fair adjustment of colonial claims. The next eight points addressed national aspirations of various European peoples and the adjustment of boundaries. The fourteenth point, which he considered the most important and which he had espoused as early as 1916, called for a "general association of nations" to preserve the peace.

Social Conflicts. Although many Americans had called for immigration restriction since the late nineteenth century, the only major restriction imposed on immigration by 1920 had been the Chinese Exclusion Act of 1882. Labor leaders believed that immigrants depressed wages and impeded unionization. Some progressives believed that they created social problems. In June 1917, Congress, over Wilson's veto, imposed a **literacy test for immigrants** and **excluded many Asian nationalities**.

In 1921, Congress passed the **Emergency Quota Act.** In practice, the law admitted almost as many immigrants as the nation wanted from nations such as Britain, Ireland, and Germany but severely restricted Italians, Greeks, Poles, and eastern European Jews hoping to enter the country. The law became effective in 1922 and reduced the number of immigrants annually to about 40 percent of the 1921 total. Congress then passed the National Origins Act of 1924, which further reduced the number of southern and eastern European immigrants and cut the annual immigration total to 20 percent of the 1921 figure. In 1927, the nation set the annual maximum number of immigrants allowed into the United States to 150,000.

On Thanksgiving Day in 1915, **William J. Simmons** founded the **Knights of the Ku Klux Klan**. Its purpose was to intimidate African Americans, who were experiencing an apparent rise in status during World War I. The Klan's methods of repression included cross burnings, tar and featherings, kidnappings, lynchings, and burnings. The Klan was not a political party, but it endorsed and opposed candidates and exerted considerable control over elections and politicians in at least nine states.

Fundamentalist Protestants, under the leadership of **William Jennings Bryan**, began a campaign in 1921 to prohibit the teaching of evolution in the schools and protect the belief in the literal biblical account of creation. The South especially received the idea enthusiastically.

The Great Depression and the New Deal

The Crash. Signs of recession were apparent before the stock market crash in 1929. The farm economy, which involved almost 25 percent of the population; coal; railroads; and New England textiles had not been prosperous during the 1920s.

After 1927, new construction declined and auto sales began to sag. Many workers lost their jobs before the crash of 1929. Stock prices increased throughout the decade. The boom in prices and volume of sales was especially active after 1925 and was intensive from 1928 to 1929. Careful investors recognized the overpricing of stocks and began to sell to take their profits. During October 1929, prices declined as more people began to sell their stock. **Black Thursday**, October 24, 1929, saw the trading of almost 13 million shares; this was a large number for that time, and prices fell precipitously. Investment banks tried to boost the market by buying, but on October 29, **Black Tuesday**, the market fell about 40 points, with 16.5 million shares traded.

Hoover's Depression Policies. The nation had elected **Herbert Hoover** (1874–1964) to the presidency in 1928. In June 1929, Congress passed the Agricultural Marketing Act, which created the Federal Farm Board. The board had a revolving fund of $500 million to lend agricultural cooperatives to buy commodities, such as wheat and cotton, and hold them for higher prices.

The Hawley-Smoot Tariff of June 1930 raised duties on both agricultural and manufactured imports. Chartered by Congress in 1932, the Reconstruction Finance Corporation loaned money to railroads, banks, and other financial institutions. It prevented the failure of basic firms, on which many other elements of the economy depended, but many people criticized it as relief for the rich.

The Federal Home Loan Bank Act, passed in July 1932, created home loan banks, which made loans to building and loan associations, savings banks, and insurance companies. Its purpose was to help avoid foreclosures on homes.

The First New Deal. Franklin D. Roosevelt (1882–1945), governor of New York, easily defeated Hoover in the election of 1932. By the time of Roosevelt's inauguration on March 4, 1933, the American economic system seemed to be on the verge of collapse. In his inaugural address, Roosevelt assured the nation that "the only thing we have to fear is fear itself," called for a special session of Congress to convene on March 9, and asked for "broad executive powers to wage war against the emergency." Two days later, he closed all banks for a brief time and forbade the export of gold or the redemption of currency in gold. A special session of Congress from March 9 to June 16, 1933 ("The Hundred Days") passed a great body of legislation that has left a lasting mark on the nation. Historians have called Roosevelt's 1933–1935 legislation the First New Deal and a new wave of programs beginning in 1935 the Second New Deal.

Passed on March 9, the first day of the special session, the Emergency Banking Relief Act provided additional funds for banks from the Reconstruction Finance Corporation and the Federal Reserve, allowed the Treasury to open sound banks after 10 days and to merge or liquidate unsound ones, and forbade the hoarding or exporting of gold. On March 12, Roosevelt assured the public of the soundness of the banks in the first of many "fireside chats," or radio addresses. People believed him. Most banks were soon open, and their deposits were outnumbering withdrawals.

The **Banking Act of 1933,** or the Glass-Steagall Act, established the Federal Deposit Insurance Corporation to insure individual deposits in commercial banks and to separate commercial banking from the more speculative activity of investment banking. The Federal Emergency Relief Act appropriated $500 million for state and local governments to distribute to the poor. The act also established the Federal Emergency Relief Administration under **Harry Hopkins** (1890–1946). The **Civilian Conservation Corps** enrolled 250,000 young men aged 18 to 24 from families on relief to go to camps where they worked on flood control, soil conservation, and forest projects under the direction of the War Department. The **Public Works Administration** had $3.3 billion to distribute to state and local governments for building projects such as schools, highways, and hospitals. The Agricultural Adjustment Act of 1933 created the **Agricultural Adjustment Administration**. Farmers agreed to reduce production of principal farm commodities and received subsidies in return. Farm prices increased; when owners took land out of cultivation, however, tenants and sharecroppers suffered. The repeal of the law came in January 1936 on the grounds that the processing tax was not constitutional.

The **National Industrial Recovery Act** was the cornerstone of the recovery program; Congress passed it in June 1933. In executing the provisions of the code, President Roosevelt established the National Recovery Administration (NRA); the goal was the self-regulation of business and the development of fair prices, wages, hours, and working conditions. Section 7-a of the NRA permitted collective bargaining for workers; laborers would test the federal support for their bargaining in the days to come. The slogan of the NRA was, "We do our part." The economy improved but did not recover.

The Second New Deal. The **Works Progress Administration (WPA)** began in May 1935, following the passage of the Emergency Relief Appropriations Act of April 1935. The WPA employed people from the relief rolls for 30 hours of work a week at pay double that of the relief payment but less than private employment.

Created in May 1935, the **Rural Electrification Administration** provided loans and WPA labor to electric cooperatives so they could build lines into rural areas that the private companies did not serve. Passed in August 1935, the **Social Security Act** established for persons over age 65 a retirement plan to be funded by a tax on wages paid equally by employees and employers. The government paid the first benefits, ranging from $10 to $85 per month in 1942. Another provision of the act forced states to initiate unemployment insurance programs.

Labor Unions. The 1935 passage of the National Labor Relations Act, or the **Wagner Act**, resulted in massive growth in union membership—but at the expense of bitter conflict within the labor movement. Primarily craft unions made up the **American Federation of Labor (AFL),** formed in 1886. Some leaders wanted to unionize mass-production industries, such as automobile and rubber manufacturing, with industrial unions.

In November 1935, **John L. Lewis** formed the **Committee for Industrial Organization (CIO)** to unionize basic industries, presumably within the AFL. **President William Green** of the AFL ordered the CIO to disband in January 1936. When the rebels refused, the AFL expelled them. The insurgents then reorganized the CIO as the independent Congress of Industrial Organizations. Labor strikes, particularly in the textile mills, marked the end of the 1930s. Soon the nation would receive another test.

World War II

The American Response to the War in Europe. In August 1939, Roosevelt created the War Resources Board to develop a plan for industrial mobilization in the event of war. The next month, he established the Office of Emergency Management in the White House to centralize mobilization activities.

Roosevelt officially proclaimed the neutrality of the United States on September 5, 1939. The Democratic Congress, in a vote that followed party lines, passed a new Neutrality Act in November. It allowed the cash-and-carry sale of arms and short-term loans to belligerents but forbade American ships from trading with belligerents or Americans from traveling on belligerent ships.

Roosevelt determined that to aid Britain in every way possible was the best way to avoid war with Germany. In September 1940, he signed an agreement to give Britain 50 American destroyers in return for a 99-year lease on air and naval bases in British territories in Newfoundland, Bermuda, and the Caribbean.

The Road to Pearl Harbor. In late July 1941, the United States placed an embargo on the export of aviation gasoline, lubricants, and scrap iron and steel to Japan and granted an additional loan to China. In December, additional articles—iron ore and pig iron, some chemicals, machine tools, and other products—fell under the embargo.

In October 1941, a new military cabinet headed by **General Hideki Tojo** took control of Japan. The Japanese secretly decided to make a final effort to negotiate with the United States and to go to war if there was no solution by November 25. A new round of talks followed in Washington, but neither side would make a substantive change in its position. The Japanese secretly gave final approval on December 1 for a surprise attack on the United States.

The Japanese planned a major offensive to take the Dutch East Indies, Malaya, and the Philippines and to obtain the oil, metals, and other raw materials they needed. At the same time, they would attack Pearl Harbor in Hawaii to destroy the American Pacific fleet and keep it from interfering with their plans. At 7:55 AM on Sunday, December 7, 1941, the first wave of Japanese carrier-based planes unexpectedly attacked the American fleet in **Pearl Harbor**. A second wave followed at 8:50 AM. The United States suffered the loss of two battleships sunk, six damaged and out of action, three cruisers and three destroyers sunk or damaged, several lesser vessels destroyed or damaged, and the destruction of all 150 aircraft on the ground at Pearl Harbor. Worst of all, 2,323 American servicemen were killed and about 1,100 were wounded. The Japanese lost 29 planes, five midget submarines, and one fleet submarine.

Declared War Begins. On December 8, 1941, Congress declared war on Japan, with one dissenting vote—Representative Jeanette Rankin of Montana. On December 11, Germany and Italy declared war on the United States. Great Britain and the United States established the Combined Chiefs of Staff, headquartered in Washington, to direct Anglo-American military operations. On January 1, 1942, representatives of 26 nations met in Washington, DC, and signed the Declaration of the United Nations, pledged themselves to the principles of the Atlantic Charter, and promised not to make a separate peace with their common enemies.

The Home Front. In *Korematsu v. United States* (1944), the Supreme Court upheld sending the Issei (Japanese Americans from Japan) and Nisei (native-born Japanese Americans) to concentration camps. The camps did not close until March 1946—after the end of World War II.

President Roosevelt died on April 12, 1945, at Warm Springs, Georgia. **Harry S Truman** (1884–1972), formerly a senator from Missouri and vice president of the United States, became president on April 12, 1945. (Harry Truman did not have a middle name; he used only the letter *S*, which he did not follow with a period.)

The Atomic Bomb. The Army Corps of Engineers established the Manhattan Engineering District in August 1942 for the purpose of developing an atomic bomb; the program eventually took the name the **Manhattan Project**. **J. Robert Oppenheimer** directed the design and construction of a transportable atomic bomb at Los Alamos, New Mexico. On July 16, 1945, the Manhattan Project exploded the first atomic bomb at Alamogordo, New Mexico.

The *Enola Gay* dropped an atomic bomb on Hiroshima, Japan, on August 6, 1945, killing about 78,000 people and injuring 100,000 more. On August 9, the United States dropped a second bomb on Nagasaki, Japan. Japan surrendered on August 14, 1945, and signed the formal surrender on September 2.

The Postwar Era

The Cold War and Containment. In February 1947, Great Britain notified the United States that it could no longer aid the Greek government in its war against Communist insurgents. The next month, President Truman asked Congress for $400 million in military and economic aid for Greece and Turkey. In his **Truman Doctrine**, Truman argued that the United States must support free peoples who were resisting Communist domination.

Secretary of State George C. Marshall proposed in June 1947 that the United States provide economic aid to help rebuild Europe. The following March, Congress passed the European Recovery Program; popularly known as the **Marshall Plan**, the program provided more than $12 billion in aid.

Anticommunism. On February 9, 1950, Senator **Joseph R. McCarthy** of Wisconsin stated that he had a list of known Communists who were working in the State Department. He later expanded his attacks. After McCarthy made charges against the army, the Senate censured and discredited him in 1954.

Korean War. On June 25, 1950, North Korea invaded South Korea. President Truman committed U.S. forces to the United Nations (UN) military effort; **General Douglas MacArthur** would command the troops. By October, UN forces (mostly American) had driven north of the thirty-eighth parallel, which divided North and South Korea.

Chinese troops attacked MacArthur's forces on November 26, pushing them south of the thirty-eighth parallel, but by spring 1951, UN forces had recovered their offensive. The armistice of June 1953 left Korea divided along nearly the same boundary that had existed before the war.

Eisenhower-Dulles Foreign Policy. Dwight D. Eisenhower (1890–1969), elected president in 1952, chose **John Foster Dulles** as secretary of state. Dulles talked of a more aggressive foreign policy, calling for "massive retaliation" and "liberation" rather than containment. He wished to emphasize nuclear deterrents rather than conventional armed forces.

In July 1954, after several years of nationalist (Vietnamese) war against French occupation in Vietnam, France, Great Britain, the Soviet Union, and China signed the Geneva Accords, which divided Vietnam along the seventeenth parallel. The North would be under the leadership of **Ho Chi Minh** and the South under **Emperor Bao Dai**. The purpose of the scheduled elections was to unify the country, but **Ngo Dinh Diem** overthrew Bao Dai and prevented the elections from taking place. The United States supplied economic aid to **South Vietnam**.

In January 1959, **Fidel Castro** overthrew the dictator of Cuba. Castro criticized the United States, aligned Cuba more closely with the Soviet Union, and signed a trade agreement with the Soviets in February 1960. The United States prohibited the importation of Cuban sugar in October 1960 and broke off diplomatic relations in January 1961.

Space Exploration. The launching of the Soviet space satellite *Sputnik* on October 4, 1957, created fear that the United States was falling behind technologically. Although the United States launched *Explorer I* on January 31, 1958, the concern continued. In 1958, Congress established the **National Aeronautics and Space Administration** (NASA) to coordinate research and development, and passed the National Defense Education Act to provide grants and loans for education.

Civil Rights. Eisenhower completed the formal integration of the armed forces; desegregated public services in Washington, D.C., naval yards, and veterans' hospitals; and appointed a civil rights commission. In *Brown v. Board of Education of Topeka* (1954), **Thurgood Marshall**, lawyer for the National Association for the Advancement of Colored People, challenged the doctrine of "separate but equal" (***Plessy v. Ferguson*, 1896**). The Court declared that separate educational facilities were inherently unequal. In 1955, the Court ordered states to integrate "with all deliberate speed."

On December 11, 1955, in Montgomery, Alabama, **Rosa Parks** refused to give up her seat on a city bus to a white man and faced arrest. Under the leadership of **Martin Luther King Jr.** (1929–1968), an African American pastor, African Americans in Montgomery organized a bus boycott that lasted for a year until, in December 1956, the Supreme Court refused to review a lower-court ruling that stated that "separate but equal" was no longer legal.

In February 1960, a segregated lunch counter in Greensboro, North Carolina, denied four African American students service; the students staged a sit-in. This action inspired sit-ins elsewhere in the South and led to the formation of the Student Nonviolent Coordinating Committee, whose chief aim was to end segregation in public accommodations.

The New Frontier, Vietnam, and Social Upheaval

Kennedy's New Frontier. Democratic Senator **John F. Kennedy** (1917–1963) won the presidential election of 1960. The Justice Department, under Attorney General **Robert F. Kennedy**, began to push for civil rights, including desegregation of interstate transportation in the South, integration of schools, and supervision of elections. President Kennedy presented a comprehensive civil rights bill to Congress in 1963. With the bill held up in Congress, 200,000 people marched and demonstrated on its behalf, and Martin Luther King Jr. gave his "I Have a Dream" speech.

Cuban Missile Crisis. Under Eisenhower, the **Central Intelligence Agency** had begun training some 2,000 men to invade Cuba and to overthrow Fidel Castro. On April 19, 1961, this force invaded at the **Bay of Pigs**; opposing forces pinned them down, demanded their surrender, and captured some 1,200 men.

On October 14, 1962, a U-2 reconnaissance plane brought photographic evidence of the construction of missile sites in Cuba. On October 22, Kennedy announced a blockade of Cuba and called on the Soviet premier, **Nikita Khrushchev** (1894–1971), to dismantle the missile bases and remove all weapons capable of attacking the United States from Cuba. Six days later, Khrushchev backed down and withdrew the missiles. Kennedy lifted the blockade.

Johnson and the Great Society. On November 22, 1963, **Lee Harvey Oswald** assassinated President Kennedy in Dallas, Texas; **Jack Ruby** killed Oswald two days later. Debate still continues as to whether the assassination was a conspiracy. **Lyndon B. Johnson** (1908–1973) succeeded John Kennedy as president of the United States.

The **1964 Civil Rights Act** outlawed racial discrimination by employers and unions, created the Equal Employment Opportunity Commission to enforce the law, and eliminated the remaining restrictions on black voting. Michael Harrington's *The Other America: Poverty in the United States* (1962) showed that 20 to 25 percent of American families were living below the governmentally defined poverty line. The Economic Opportunity Act of 1964 sought to address the problem by establishing a job corps, community action programs, education programs, work-study programs, job training, loans for small businesses and farmers, and a "domestic peace corps" called Volunteers in Service to America. The Office of Economic Opportunity administered many of these programs.

Emergence of Black Power. In 1965, Dr. Martin Luther King Jr. announced a voter registration drive. With help from the federal courts, he dramatized his effort by leading a march from Selma, Alabama, to Montgomery, Alabama, between March 21 and 25. The Voting Rights Act of 1965 authorized the attorney general to appoint officials to register voters.

Seventy percent of African Americans lived in city ghettos. In 1966, New York and Chicago experienced riots, and the following year there were riots in Newark and Detroit. The Kerner Commission, appointed to investigate the riots, concluded that the focus of the riots was a social system that prevented African Americans from getting good jobs and crowded them into ghettos. On April 4, 1968, **James Earl Ray** assassinated Martin Luther King Jr. in Memphis, Tennessee. Ray was an escaped convict; he pled guilty to the murder and received a sentence of 99 years in prison. Riots in more than 100 cities followed.

Vietnam. After the defeat of the French in Vietnam in 1954, the United States sent military advisors to South Vietnam to aid the government of **Ngo Dinh Diem**. The pro-Communist Vietcong forces gradually grew in strength because Diem failed to follow through on promised reforms and because of the support from North Vietnam, the Soviet Union, and China.

"Hawks" in Congress defended President Johnson's policy and, drawing on the containment theory, said that the nation had the responsibility to resist aggression. The claim was that, if Vietnam should fall, all Southeast Asia would eventually go. Antiwar demonstrations were attracting large crowds by 1967. "Doves" argued that the war was a civil war in which the United States should not meddle. On January 31, 1968, the first day of the Vietnamese New Year (Tet), the Vietcong attacked numerous cities and towns, American bases, and even Saigon. Although they suffered large losses, the Vietcong won a psychological victory as American opinion began turning against the war.

The Nixon Conservative Reaction. Republican **Richard M. Nixon** (1913–1994), emphasizing stability and order, defeated Democratic nominee Hubert Humphrey by a margin of one percentage point. The Nixon administration sought to block renewal of the Voting Rights

Act and delay implementation of court-ordered school desegregation in Mississippi. In 1969, Nixon appointed **Warren E. Burger**, a conservative, as chief justice. Although more conservative than the Warren court, the Burger court did declare in 1972 that the death penalty in use at the time was unconstitutional; it struck down state antiabortion legislation in 1973.

The president turned to Vietnamization, the effort to build up South Vietnamese forces while withdrawing American troops. In 1969, Nixon reduced American troop strength by 60,000 but at the same time ordered the bombing of Cambodia, a neutral country. In the summer of 1972, negotiations between the United States and North Vietnam began in Paris. A few days before the 1972 presidential election, **Henry Kissinger**, the president's national security advisor, announced that "peace was at hand." Nixon resumed the bombing of North Vietnam in December 1972; he claimed that the North Vietnamese were not bargaining in good faith. In January 1973, the two sides reached a settlement in which the North Vietnamese retained control over large areas of the South and agreed to release American prisoners of war within 60 days. Nearly 60,000 Americans had been killed and 300,000 more wounded, and the war had cost American taxpayers $109 billion. On March 29, 1973, the last American combat troops left South Vietnam. The North Vietnamese forces continued to push back the South Vietnamese, and in April 1975, Saigon fell to the North.

Watergate, Carter, and the New Conservatism

Watergate. The Republicans renominated Nixon, who won a landslide victory over the Democratic nominee, Senator **George McGovern**. What became known as the Watergate crisis began during the 1972 presidential campaign. Early on the morning of June 17, a security officer for the Committee for the Reelection of the President, along with four other men, broke into Democratic headquarters at the Watergate apartment complex in Washington, DC. The authorities caught the men going through files and installing electronic eavesdropping devices.

In March 1974, a grand jury indicted some of Nixon's top aides and named Nixon an unindicted co-conspirator. Meanwhile, the House Judiciary Committee televised its debate over impeachment. The committee charged the president with obstructing justice, misusing presidential power, and failing to obey the committee's subpoenas. Before the House began to debate impeachment, Nixon announced his resignation on August 8, 1974, to take effect at noon the following day.

Gerald Ford (1913–2006) then became president. Ford was in many respects the opposite of Nixon. Although a partisan Republican, he was well liked and free of any hint of scandal. Ford almost immediately encountered controversy when, in September 1974, he offered to pardon Nixon. Nixon accepted the offer, although he admitted no wrongdoing and had not yet received any criminal charges.

Carter's Moderate Liberalism. In 1976, the Democrats nominated **James Earl Carter** (1924–), formerly governor of Georgia, who ran on the basis of his integrity and lack of Washington connections. Carter narrowly defeated Ford in the election.

Carter offered amnesty to Americans who had fled the draft and gone to other countries during the Vietnam War. He established the departments of energy and education and placed the civil service on a merit basis. He created a superfund for cleanup of chemical waste dumps, established controls over strip mining, and protected 100 million acres of Alaskan wilderness from development.

Carter's Foreign Policy. Carter negotiated a controversial treaty with Panama, affirmed by the Senate in 1978, that provided for the transfer of ownership of the canal to Panama in 1999 and guaranteed its neutrality. In 1978, Carter negotiated the Camp David Accords between Israel and Egypt. Israel promised to return occupied land in the Sinai to Egypt in exchange for Egyptian recognition, a process completed in 1982. An agreement to negotiate the Palestinian refugee problem proved ineffective.

The Iranian Crisis. In 1978, a revolution forced the **shah of Iran** to flee the country and replaced him with a religious leader, **Ayatollah Ruhollah Khomeini** (ca. 1900–1989). Because the United States had supported the shah with arms and money, the revolutionaries were strongly anti-American, calling the United States the "Great Satan."

After Carter allowed the exiled shah to come to the United States for medical treatment in October 1979, some 400 Iranians broke into the American embassy in Teheran on November 4 and took the occupants captive. They demanded the return of the shah to Iran for trial, the confiscation of his wealth, and the presentation of his wealth to Iran. Carter rejected these demands; instead, he froze Iranian assets in the United States and established a trade embargo against Iran. After extensive negotiations with Iran, in which Algeria acted as an intermediary, the Iranians freed the American hostages on January 20, 1981.

Attacking Big Government. Republican **Ronald Reagan** (1911–2004) defeated Carter by a large electoral majority in 1980. Reagan placed priority on cutting taxes. He based his approach on supply-side economics, the idea that if government left more money in the hands of the people, they would invest rather then spend the excess on consumer goods. The results would be greater production, more jobs, and greater prosperity, resulting in more income for the government despite lower tax rates. However, the federal budget deficit ballooned from $59 billion in 1980 to $195 billion by 1983. Reagan ended ongoing antitrust suits against IBM and AT&T and fulfilled his promise to reduce government interference with business.

Iran-Contra. In 1985 and 1986, several Reagan officials sold arms to the Iranians in hopes of encouraging them to use their influence in obtaining the release of American hostages being held in Lebanon. Profits from these sales went to the Nicaraguan *contras*—a militant group opposed to the left-leaning elected government—thus circumventing congressional restrictions on funding the *contras*. The attorney general appointed a special prosecutor, and Congress held hearings on the affair in May 1987.

The Election of 1988. Vice President George H. W. Bush (1924–) won the Republican nomination. Bush defeated Democrat **Michael Dukakis**, but the Republicans were unable to make any inroads in Congress.

Operation Just Cause. Since coming to office, the Bush administration had been concerned that Panamanian dictator **Manuel Noriega** was providing an important link in the drug traffic between South America and the United States. After economic sanctions, diplomatic efforts, and an October 1989 coup failed to oust Noriega, Bush ordered 12,000 troops into Panama on December 20 for what became known as Operation Just Cause.

On January 3, 1990, Noriega surrendered to the Americans and faced drug-trafficking charges in the United States. Found guilty in 1992, his sentence was 40 years.

Persian Gulf Crisis. On August 2, 1990, Iraq invaded Kuwait, an act that Bush denounced as "naked aggression." The United States quickly banned most trade with Iraq, froze Iraq's and Kuwait's assets in the United States, and sent aircraft carriers to the Persian Gulf. On August 6, after the UN Security Council condemned the invasion, Bush ordered the deployment of air, sea, and land forces to Saudi Arabia and dubbed the operation Desert Shield.

On February 23, the allied air assault began. Four days later, Bush announced the liberation of Kuwait and ordered offensive operations to cease. The UN established the terms for the ceasefire, which Iraq accepted on April 6.

The Road to the Twenty-First Century

The Election of 1992. William Jefferson Clinton (1946–) won 43 percent of the popular vote and 370 electoral votes, while President Bush won 37 percent of the popular vote and 168 electoral votes. Although he won no electoral votes, the Independent Party candidate Ross Perot (1930–) gained 19 percent of the popular vote.

Domestic Affairs. The **North American Free Trade Agreement (NAFTA),** negotiated by the Bush administration, eliminated most tariffs and other trade barriers among the United States, Canada, and Mexico. Passed by Congress and signed by Clinton in 1993, NAFTA became law in January 1994.

In October 1993, the Clinton administration proposed legislation to reform the health care system, which included universal coverage with a guaranteed benefits package, managed competition through health care alliances that would bargain with insurance companies, and employer mandates to provide health insurance for employees. With most Republicans and small business, insurance, and medical business interests opposed to the legislation, the Democrats dropped their attempt at a compromised package in September 1994.

Impeachment and Acquittal. Clinton received criticism for alleged wrongdoing in connection with a real estate development called Whitewater. While governor of Arkansas, Clinton had invested in Whitewater, along with **James B. and Susan McDougal**, owners of a failed savings and loan institution. After Congress renewed the independent counsel law, a three-judge panel appointed **Kenneth W. Starr** to the new role of independent prosecutor.

The Starr investigation yielded massive findings in late 1998, roughly midway into Clinton's second term, including information on an adulterous affair that Clinton had had with Monica Lewinsky while she was an intern at the White House. It was on charges stemming from this report that the House of Representatives impeached Clinton in December 1998 for perjury and obstruction of justice. The Senate acquitted him of all charges in February 1999.

Continuing Crisis in the Balkans. During Clinton's second term, continued political unrest abroad and civil war in the Balkans remained major foreign policy challenges. In 1999, the Serbian government attacked ethnic Albanians in Kosovo, a province of Serbia. In response, North Atlantic Treaty Organization (NATO) forces, led by the United States, bombed Serbia. Several weeks of bombing forced Serbian forces to withdraw from Kosovo.

The Election of 2000. Preelection polls indicated that the election would be close, and few ventured to predict the outcome. Indeed, the election outcome was much in doubt for several weeks after the election. Though Clinton's vice president, **Al Gore** (1948–), won the popular vote, the electoral college was very close, and Florida (the state governed by George W. Bush's brother) was pivotal in deciding the election.

George W. Bush (1946–), son of the former president **George H. W. Bush**, appeared to win Florida, but by a very small margin; a recount began. Then controversy over how to conduct the recount led to a series of court challenges, with the matter ultimately decided by the U.S. Supreme Court, which ruled in favor of Bush. George W. Bush thus became the forty-third president of the United States.

Terrorism Hits Home. The new president would soon face the grim task of dealing with a massive terrorist attack on major symbols of U.S. economic and military might. On the morning of September 11, 2001, hijackers deliberately crashed two U.S. commercial jetliners into the World Trade Center in New York City—toppling its 110-story twin towers. They crashed another plane into the Pentagon, just outside Washington, D.C. Passengers on yet another hijacked airplane took over the plane; by crashing it in Pennsylvania, they likely saved the lives of many others. Some 2,750 people died in the destruction of the World Trade Center, the deadliest act of terrorism in American history. One hundred eighty-four people died at the Pentagon and 40 in Pennsylvania.

Though the person behind the attacks was not immediately known, Bush cast prime suspicion on the Saudi exile Osama bin Laden, the alleged mastermind of the bombings of two U.S. embassies in 1998 and of a U.S. naval destroyer in 2000. The United States had earlier seen terrorism on its home soil carried out by Islamic militants in the 1993 bombing of the World Trade Center and by a member of the American militia movement in the bombing of the Oklahoma City federal building in 1995.

In retaliation for the terrorism brought against the United States, U.S. forces attacked Afghanistan. Many of these forces remain in Afghanistan to this day. The final outcome of the troop invasion is still uncertain. Disputes with Iraq continued when the United States reported that the country held weapons of mass destruction. Bush declared war (a disputed option) with Iraq. The outcome of sending troops to Iraq is undetermined.

Immigration and Settlement Patterns

"The United States is a nation of immigrants" is a frequently quoted remark. The quotation, however, may cause some to forget that the Europeans came to a country already occupied by Native Americans.

The New World that Columbus and other explorers discovered in the late fifteenth and early sixteenth centuries was neither recently formed nor recently settled. It had actually been settled between 15,000 and 35,000 years before. As in other areas of the world, the native peoples of the so-called New World formed communities but did not immediately develop written languages. The lack of any kind of written record makes interpreting the prehistorical past more difficult. Archeologists and anthropologists working in North and South America have unearthed the remains of these early communities, and based on this evidence, anthropologists have formed the earliest theories about the origins, movements, and lifestyles of native people.

It is important to remember that there is not one universally accepted theory regarding the earliest history of the people who settled North and South America. By the time Europeans came into contact with the indigenous peoples of the Americas, more than 2,000 distinct cultures and hundreds of distinct languages existed. It is therefore necessary to trace not just the origins but also the developments, affected by various factors, e.g. the environment, that took place before the Europeans arrived. This provides an understanding of the various Indian cultures and societies and the resulting impact of contact with Europeans.

Previous sections and topics relate to the topic, "Identifying Immigration and Settlement Patterns That Have Shaped the History of the United States." The reader may wish to review the earlier sections/topics, such as "Prehistory and Early Civilization," "Causes and Consequences of Exploration, Settlement, and Growth," and "The Continued Exploration, Settlement, and Revolution in the 'New World' " to review some of the groups that came to America, their reasons for being here, and where they settled. The previous passages also give some attention to the legislation surrounding these immigrants, the Native Americans, human rights, and calls for immigration restriction.

Calls for immigration restriction had begun in the late nineteenth century, but the only major restriction imposed on immigration at the time had been the Chinese Exclusion Act of 1882. Labor leaders believed that immigrants depressed wages and impeded unionization. Some progressives believed that they created social problems. In June 1917, Congress, over President Wilson's veto, had imposed a literacy test for immigrants and excluded many Asian nationalities. In 1921, Congress passed the Emergency Quota Act. In practice, the law admitted almost as many immigrants as wanted to come from nations such as Britain, Ireland, and Germany but severely restricted Italians, Greeks, Poles, and eastern European Jews wanting to enter the country. The law became effective in 1922 and reduced the number of immigrants annually to about 40 percent of the 1921 total. Congress then passed the National Origins Act of 1924, which further reduced the number of southern and eastern European immigrants and cut the annual immigration total to 20 percent of the 1921 figure. In 1927, the annual maximum number of immigrants allowed into the United States was reduced to 150,000.

On Thanksgiving Day in 1915, William J. Simmons founded the Knights of the Ku Klux Klan (KKK) to intimidate African Americans, who were experiencing an apparent rise in status during World War I. The Klan's methods of repression included cross burnings, tar and featherings, kidnappings, lynchings, and burnings. The Klan was not a political party, but it endorsed and opposed candidates and exerted considerable control over elections and politicians in at least nine states. As a result of KKK activity, many of the immigrants—especially those from African nations—moved to sections of the North.

In *Korematsu v. United States* (1944), the Supreme Court upheld sending the Issei (Japanese Americans from Japan) and Nisei (native-born Japanese Americans) to concentration camps. The camps closed in March 1946. Some of the concentration camp victims remained on the West Coast, although some did return to their previous area of residence in the United States; some elected to relocate in Japan.

Since the United States first began tracking the arrival of immigrants within its boundaries in 1820, the United States has accepted 66 million legal immigrants, with 11 percent arriving from Germany and 10 percent from Mexico. However, two centuries of immigration and integration have not yielded consensus on the three major immigration questions: How many? From where? and What status should newcomers have when they arrive?

The U.S. immigration system in the early twenty-first century recognizes 800,000 to 900,000 foreigners a year as legal immigrants, admits 35 million nonimmigrant tourists and business visitors a year, and knows of another 300,000 to 400,000 unauthorized foreigners who settle in the country annually. Recent decades have witnessed contentious debates over the place of immigrants and their children in the educational, welfare, and political systems of the United States, or more broadly, whether the immigration system serves U.S. national interests (Martin 2002). Restrictions have been more frequently proposed after the 9/11 attack, the war in Iraq, health care concerns for the population, and increased controversy surrounding illegal immigrants.

Table 4-1 on the next page ranks the ten leading countries of birth of the foreign-born resident population from 1850 to 2000. In 2003, the U.S. Census Bureau, in its Current Population Survey, indicated the regions of residence of foreign-born residents. Of the 33,500,000 foreign-born residents in the United States in 2000, 37 percent (12,395,000) resided in the West. The South had the second highest percentage, with 29 percent (9,715,000). The region with the third highest number of foreign-born residents (7,370,000) was the Northeast, which had almost 22 percent. Eleven percent (3,685,000) of the foreign-born residents lived in the Midwest (U.S. Census Bureau, *Current Population Survey*, March 2003, *www.census.gov/prod/2004pubs/p20-551.pdf*). Martin (2002) predicts that immigration is likely to continue at current levels of 900,000 legal and 300,000 unauthorized a year. In the words of Kenneth Prewitt, a former director of the U.S. Census Bureau, America is "the first country in world history which is literally made up of every part of the world" (Alvarez 2001). Setting limits on the numbers of immigrants, providing services for those who are illegal immigrants in the United States, locating the immigrants who come to the United States, and finding work for those who are newly arrived without taking jobs from those who are already settled are some of the debates that concern legislators and citizens of the country.

ECONOMICS

How Resources Affect Economic Choices

A basic understanding relating to economics is that wants are unlimited while resources are limited. When resources are limited, the limitation affects prices (the amount of money needed to buy goods, services, or resources). Therefore, individuals and institutions must make choices when purchasing. These seemingly local decisions may affect other people and even other nations.

Table 4-1. Countries of Birth of the Foreign-Born Population, 1850–2000 (Resident Population)

Ten leading countries	1850	1880	1900	1930	1960	1970	1980	1990	2000
1	Ireland 962,000	Germany 1,967,000	Germany 2,663,000	Italy 1,790,000	Italy 1,257,000	Italy 1,009,000	Mexico 2,199,000	Mexico 4,298,000	Mexico 7,841,000
2	Germany 584,000	Ireland 1,855,000	Ireland 1,615,000	Germany 1,609,000	Germany 990,000	Germany 833,000	Germany 849,000	China 921,000	China 1,391,000
3	Great Britain 379,000	Great Britain 918,000	Canada 1,180,000	United Kingdom 1,403,000	Canada 953,000	Canada 812,000	Canada 843,000	Philippines 913,000	Philippines 1,222,000
4	Canada 148,000	Canada 717,000	Great Britain 1,168,000	Canada 1,310,000	United Kingdom 833,000	Mexico 760,000	Italy 832,000	Canada 745,000	India 1,007,000
5	France 54,000	Sweden 194,000	Sweden 582,000	Poland 1,269,000	Poland 748,000	United Kingdom 686,000	United Kingdom 669,000	Cuba 737,000	Cuba 952,000
6	Switzerland 13,000	Norway 182,000	Italy 484,000	Soviet Union 1,154,000	Soviet Union 691,000	Poland 548,000	Cuba 608,000	Germany 712,000	Vietnam 863,000
7	Mexico 13,000	France 107,000	Russia 424,000	Ireland 745,000	Mexico 576,000	Soviet Union 463,000	Philippines 501,000	United Kingdom 640,000	El Salvador 765,000
8	Norway 13,000	China 104,000	Poland 383,000	Mexico 641,000	Ireland 339,000	Cuba 439,000	Poland 418,000	Italy 581,000	Korea 701,000
9	Holland 10,000	Switzerland 89,000	Norway 336,000	Sweden 595,000	Austria 305,000	Ireland 251,000	Soviet Union 406,000	Korea 568,000	Dominican Republic 692,000
10	Italy 4,000	Bohemia 85,000	Austria 276,000	Czechoslovakia 492,000	Hungary 245,000	Austria 214,000	Korea 290,000	Vietnam 543,000	Canada 678,000

Source: U.S. Census Bureau. "Countries of Birth of the Foreign-Born Population, 1850–2000." *Profile of the Foreign-Born Population in the United States: 2001*

A true sense of global interdependence results from an understanding of the relationship between local decisions and global issues. For example, individual or community actions regarding waste disposal or recycling can affect the availability of resources worldwide. A country's fuel standards can affect air pollution, oil supplies, and gas prices. The government can provide the legal structure and help needed to maintain competition, redistribute income, reallocate resources, and promote stability. There are two main types of resources: economic resources and human resources.

Economic resources. The land (natural), labor (human), capital, and entrepreneurial ability used in the production of goods and services; productive agents; factors of production.

Human resources. The physical and mental talents and efforts of people; these resources are necessary to help produce goods and services.

The result of combining resources may be entrepreneurship. As a human resource that also takes advantage of economic resources to create a product, **entrepreneurship** is characterized by nonroutine decisions, innovation, and the willingness to take risks.

Characteristics of Different Economic Institutions

Two important higher-order thinking skills that teachers should encourage in their students are comparing and contrasting. The study of various economic institutions is an ideal place to work with these two skills. The following are the main economic institutions of the United States: banks, credit unions, the Federal Reserve System, and the stock market.

Banks. Banks serve anyone in the general public. Small groups of investors who expect a certain return on their investments own the banks. Only the investors have voting privileges; customers do not have voting rights, cannot be elected board members, and do not participate in governing the institution. The Federal Deposit Insurance Corporation insures the banks. Typically, banks do not share information, ideas, or resources.

> **PRAXIS Pointer**
>
> Double-check the numbers on the question and on the answer sheet each time you mark your sheet. Marking one wrong answer can throw off your entire answer sheet and sink your score.

Credit unions. Credit unions are owned by members. Each person who deposits money is a member, not a customer. Surplus earnings go to the members in higher dividends, low-cost or free services, and lower loan rates. The National Credit Union Share Insurance Fund insures credit unions. All credit unions share ideas, information, and resources.

Federal Reserve System. The Federal Reserve System is the central banking system of the United States. It has a central board of governors in Washington, DC. There are 12 Federal Reserve Bank districts in major cities throughout the nation. The district banks issue bank notes, lend money to member banks, maintain reserves, supervise member banks, and help set the national monetary policy. Alan Greenspan served as the chairman of the board of governors for 18 years. After Greenspan's retirement on January 31, 2005, Ben Bernanke became chairman.

Stock market. The stock market is an abstract concept. It is the mechanism that enables the trading of company stocks. It is different from the **stock exchange**, which is a corporation in the business of bringing together stock buyers and sellers.

The Role of Markets

A **market** is the interaction between potential buyers and sellers of goods and services. Money is the usual medium of exchange. **Market economies** have no central authority; custom plays a very small role. Every consumer makes buying decisions based on his or her own needs, desires, and income; individual self-interest rules. Every producer decides personally what goods or services to produce, what price to charge, what resources to employ, and what production methods to use. Profits motivate the producers. There is vigorous competition in a market economy. **Supply and demand** may affect the availability of resources needed for production, distribution, and consumption.

After production, the producer ideally distributes the product to the places where consumers need or want the product—and have the money to pay for the goods or services. In the United States, there is a large and active government (command) sector, but there is a greater emphasis on the market economy.

The following are the major types of economies in the world today:

Command economies. Command economies rely on a central authority to make decisions. The central authority may be a dictator or a democratically constituted government.

Although a command economy relies mainly on the government to direct economic activity, there is a small market sector as well.

Traditional economies. Traditional economies largely rely on custom to determine production and distribution issues. While not static, traditional systems are slow to change and are not well-equipped to propel a society into sustained growth. Many of the poorer countries of the developing world have traditional systems.

Mixed economies. Mixed economies contain elements of each of the two previously defined systems. All real-world economies are mixed economies, but the proportions of the mixture can vary greatly.

Capitalist economies. Capitalist economies produce resources owned by individuals.

Socialist economies. Socialist economies produce resources owned collectively by society. In other words, resources are under the control of the government.

Efficiency occurs when a society produces the types and quantities of goods and services that most satisfy its people. Failure to do so wastes resources. **Technical efficiency** occurs when a society is able to use its resources to the best advantage and thus produce the most types and the largest quantity of goods and services. Again, failure to do so wastes resources. **Equity** occurs when the distribution of goods and services conforms to a society's notions of "fairness." These goals often determine the type of economic system that a country has.

Factors Affecting Consumer Decisions

Adam Smith (1723–1790) was a Scottish economist whose writings may have inaugurated the modern era of economic analysis. Published in 1776, *An Inquiry into the Nature and Causes of the Wealth of Nations* is an analysis of a market economy.

Smith believed that a market economy was a superior form of organization from the standpoint of both economic progress and human liberty. Smith acknowledged that **self-interest** was a dominant motivating force in a market economy; this self-interest, he said, was ultimately consistent with the **public interest**. An "invisible hand" guided market participants to act in ways that promoted the public interest. **Profits** may be the main concern of firms, but only firms that **satisfy** consumer demand and offer **suitable prices** earn profits. Goods and services refer to things that satisfy human **needs**, **wants**, or **desires**. **Goods** are tangible items, such as food, cars, and clothing; **services** are intangible items such as education and health care. A market is the interaction between potential buyers and sellers of goods and services. **Money** is usually the medium of exchange. The **supply** of a good is the quantity of that good that producers offer at a certain price. The collection of all such points for every price is the **supply curve**. **Demand** for a good is the quantity of a good that consumers are willing and able to purchase at a certain price. The **demand curve** is the combination of quantity and price, at all price levels.

Economic Interdependence Among Nations

Understanding global interdependence begins with recognizing that world regions include economic, political, historical, ecological, linguistic, and cultural regions. This understanding should include knowledge of military and economic alliances such as NATO, of cartels, and of the ways in which their existence affects political and economic policies within regions. Knowledge of world regions and alliances leads to identification of issues that affect people worldwide. Common issues that affect people everywhere include **finances**, **movement of labor**, **trade**, food production, human rights, use of natural resources, prejudice, and poverty.

A true sense of global interdependence results from an understanding of the relationship between local decisions and global issues; for example, how individual or community actions regarding waste disposal or recycling can affect the availability of resources worldwide. Fuel emission standards, for example, can affect air pollution, oil supplies, and gas prices. **Microeconomics** focuses on problems specific to a household, firm, or industry, rather than national or global issues. Microeconomics gives particular emphasis to how these units make decisions and the consequences of those decisions. **Macroeconomics** is the study of the economy as a whole. Some of the topics considered include inflation, unemployment, and economic growth. **Economic theory** is an explanation of why certain economic phenomena occur. For example, there are theories explaining the rate of inflation, how many hours people choose to work, and the amount of goods and services a specific country will import. Economic theory is essentially a set of statements about cause-and-effect relationships in the economy.

Human, Natural, and Capital Resources and How These Resources Are Used in the Production of Goods and Services

Necessary for the production of goods and services are human resources, natural resources, and capital resources. **Human resources** are the people employed in a business or organization; in other words, a firm's human resources are its personnel. Originally, the term for human resources was *labor*. **Natural resources** are the material sources of wealth. Examples of natural or material resources are timber, fresh water, and mineral deposits that occur in a natural state and have economic value.

The word *capital* comes from the Latin word *caput*, which means "head." In economics, capital originally meant the profit that one made; the measure of profit was probably heads (*caput*) of cattle. In finance and economics today, **capital** means how much real, usable money a person or a company has.

How Transportation and Communication Networks Contribute to the Level of Economic Development in Different Regions

Economics is the study of society's choices among a limited amount of resources to attain the highest practical satisfaction. It is the allocation of scarce resources among competing ends.

Because people across the globe can now interact with each other almost instantly, the choices available to them throughout the world are more readily apparent today than they have been in the past. For example, advances in communication—especially through the satellites—made it possible for someone in Los Angeles to witness the devastation Hurricane Katrina wrought on the Gulf Coast in August 2005 and to become aware of the wants and needs there. Similarly, a person in Tokyo can see the goods and products readily available to American consumers in the newscasts and movies shown in Japan. People in New York can pick up the phone and call a person in London without delay to discuss the latest automobile styles. It is evident that people can see and hear about the goods and services available in other parts of the world; such knowledge affects the needs and wants of the world's people. Convenient transportation and even world travel is now possible for a large number of people throughout the world. Around the globe, people are becoming more aware of the world's products, services, and even clothing styles (blue jeans) as they see people who live an ocean away using the products, services, and clothing. Even fast-food chains are familiar throughout the globe. As people become aware of lifestyles in other places, their wants and needs may change. People may aspire to what they perceive as a higher economic level. Transportation and communication networks, therefore, have helped initiate many changes in people's needs and wants and have ultimately contributed to the economic development of many regions.

POLITICAL SCIENCE

The Structure, Functions, and Purposes of Government

Many people equate the terms *political system* and *government*, but the two concepts are distinct.

Definitions

Government is the agency for regulating the activities of people. It is the system that carries out the decisions of the political system or, in some countries, the decisions of the ruler. The organizations and processes that contribute to the decision-making process comprise the **political system**.

Structure

The distribution of power within the various **structures** of government is a key variable. Separation of powers among branches of the federal government is another aspect of structure useful in comparing political systems. The following are among the most important structures of government:

Confederation. A weak central government delegates principal authority to smaller units, such as states. The United States had this structure under the Articles of Confederation, before the Constitution was ratified in 1789.

Federal. Sovereignty is divided between a central government and a group of states. Contemporary examples of federal republics are the United States, Brazil, and India.

Unitary. The centralized government holds the concentration of power and authority. Examples include France and Japan.

Authoritarian. A government's central power is in a single or collective executive, with the legislative and judicial bodies having little input. Some examples of this include the former Soviet Union, the People's Republic of China, and Nazi Germany.

Parliamentary. The legislative and executive branches are combined, with a prime minister and cabinet selected from within the legislative body. They maintain control as long as the legislative assembly supports their major policies. Great Britain is an example of this form of government.

Presidential. The executive branch is clearly separate from the legislative and judicial branches. However, all three (particularly the executive and legislative branches) must cooperate for policy to be consistent and for smooth government operation. An example of this is the United States.

As just noted, the government of the United States is both a federal system, which divides the sovereignty between the central government and the states, and a presidential system, which has the executive branch clearly separated from the legislative and judicial branches. All countries, of course, do not have a division of power.

Functions

The *Merit Students Encyclopedia* (Halsey and Johnston 1991) notes that the **functions** of a government include (1) political functions, to maintain order within its territories and to protect its borders; (2) legal functions (in fact the word *anarchy*—meaning "lack of government"—has come to mean lawlessness); (3) economic functions, or those concerned with the economic activity of citizens; and/or (4) social functions, which may include civil rights, religion, and education.

Purposes

The question of how to define the purpose of government has been puzzling scholars from Plato's time to the present day. Although some say that government's purpose is to protect all people's rights and preserve justice, others contend that its purpose is to preserve and protect the rights of the few. From these diverging definitions, myriad ideologies—such as communism, liberalism, conservatism, and many others—have evolved. Although most thinkers agree that government is morally justified, they disagree on the role and form of government. News commentator Bob Schieffer stated boldly in 2005, following Hurricane Katrina, "There is no purpose for government except to improve the lives of its citizens."

The Rights and Responsibilities of a Citizen in the World, Nation, State, and/or Community

Essential democratic principles include those fundamental to the American judicial system, such as the right to due process of law, the right to a fair and speedy trial, protection from unlawful search and seizure, and the right to avoid self-incrimination. The democratic values include life, liberty, the pursuit of happiness, the common good, justice, equality, truth, diversity, popular sovereignty, and patriotism. Furthermore, the ideals of American democracy include the following essential constitutional principles: the rule of law, separation of powers, representative government, checks and balances, individual rights, freedom of religion, federalism, limited government, and civilian control of the military.

It is essential—indeed, a responsibility—for citizens to be active in maintaining a democratic society. Active citizens participate in the political process by voting, providing services to their communities, and regulating themselves in accordance with the law. Citizens of the United States need also to assume responsibilities to their communities, their states, the nation, and the world.

Major Concepts of the U.S. Constitution and Other Historical Documents

Historical Documents

The **Articles of Confederation**, adopted in 1777 after the quarrel with Great Britain, provided for a **unicameral** Congress, in which each state would have one vote, as had been the case in the Continental Congress. Executive authority under the articles would be vested in a committee of 13, with one member from each state. Amending the articles required the unanimous consent of all the states. Under the Articles of Confederation, the government could declare war, make treaties, determine the number of troops and amount of money each state should contribute to a war effort, settle disputes between states, admit new states to the Union, and borrow money. It could not levy taxes, raise troops, or regulate commerce.

As time went on, the inadequacy of the Articles of Confederation became increasingly apparent. In 1787 there was a call for a convention of all the states in Philadelphia for the purpose of revising the Articles of Confederation. The assembly unanimously elected George Washington to preside, and the enormous respect that he commanded helped hold the convention together through difficult times. The 55 delegates who met in Philadelphia in 1787 to draft a constitution drew on a variety of sources to shape the government that would be outlined in the document. Three British documents were important to the delegates' work: the **Magna Carta (1215)**, the **Petition of Right (1628)**, and the **Bill of Rights (1689)**. These three documents promoted the concept of limited government and were influential in shaping the fundamental principles embodied in the Constitution. The British philosopher John Locke, who wrote about the social contract concept of government and the right of people to alter or abolish a government that did not protect their interests, was another guiding force in the drafting of the Constitution.

Crises in Establishing the U.S. Constitution

One major problem that the delegates faced involved the number of state representatives. With George Washington presiding over the discussions, the delegates finally adopted a proposal known as the **Great Compromise**, which provided for a president, two senators per state, and representatives elected to the House according to their states' populations.

Another major crisis involved disagreement between the North and the South over slavery. To reach a compromise this time, the delegates decided that each slave was to count as three-fifths of a person for purposes of apportioning representation and direct taxation on the states (the Three-Fifths Compromise). Before 1808, the federal government could not stop the importation of slaves. The delegates had to compromise on the nature of the presidency. The result was a strong presidency with control over foreign policy and the power to veto Congress's legislation. Should the president commit an actual crime, Congress would have the power of impeachment. Otherwise, the president would serve for a term of four years and was eligible for reelection without limit. As a check to the possible excesses of democracy, an electoral college elected the president; each state would have the same number of electors as it did senators and representatives combined.

The U.S. Constitution

The new Constitution was to take effect when nine states, through special state conventions, had ratified it. By June 21, 1788, the required nine states had ratified, but the crucial states of New York and Virginia still had not. Ultimately, the promise of the addition of a bill of rights helped win the final states. At his inauguration in March 1789, George Washington became the nation's first president.

One of the most significant principles embodied in the Constitution is the concept of a federal system that divides the powers of government between the states and the national government. The local level handles local matters; those issues that affect all citizens are the responsibility of the federal government. Such a system was a natural outgrowth of the colonial relationship between the Americans and the mother country of England. The Tenth Amendment declares: "Those powers not delegated to the United States by the Constitution, nor prohibited by it to the States, are reserved to the States respectively, or to the people." The federal government and those of the separate states have powers that may in practice overlap, but in cases where they conflict, the federal government is supreme. In 1920, the passage of the Eighteenth Amendment prohibited the manufacture, transportation, and sale of alcoholic beverages in the United States. Speakeasies became popular, and bootlegging became a profitable underground business. The ratification of the Twenty-first Amendment repealed Prohibition in 1933. Congress approved the Nineteenth Amendment, providing for women's suffrage, in 1919; the Senate had defeated women's suffrage earlier, in 1918. The states ratified the Nineteenth Amendment in time for the election of 1920.

The Legislative, Executive, and Judicial Branches

A key principle of the U.S. Constitution is separation of powers. The national government is divided into three branches—legislative, executive, and judicial—each with separate functions, but they are not entirely independent. Articles I, II, and III of the main body of the Constitution outline these functions.

The Legislative Branch

Legislative power is vested in a bicameral (two houses) Congress, which is the subject of Article I of the Constitution. The expressed or delegated powers are set forth in Section 8 and can be divided into several broad categories.

Economic powers are as follows:

1. Lay and collect taxes.

2. Borrow money.

3. Regulate foreign and interstate commerce.

4. Coin money and regulate its value.

5. Establish rules concerning bankruptcy.

Judicial powers comprise the following:

1. Establish courts inferior to the Supreme Court.

2. Provide punishment for counterfeiting.

3. Define and punish piracies and felonies committed on the high seas.

War powers of Congress include the following:

1. Declare war.

2. Raise and support armies.

3. Provide and maintain a navy.

4. Provide for organizing, arming, and calling forth the militia.

Other **general peace powers** include the following:

1. Establish uniform rules on naturalization.

2. Establish post offices and post roads.

3. Promote science and the arts by issuing patents and copyrights.

4. Exercise jurisdiction over the seat of the federal government (District of Columbia).

The Constitution also grants Congress the power to discipline federal officials through impeachment and removal from office. The House of Representatives has the power to charge officials (impeach), and the Senate has the power to conduct the trials. The first impeachment of a president was that of Andrew Johnson. Significant also is the Senate's power to confirm presidential appointments (to the cabinet, federal judiciary, and major bureaucracies) and to ratify treaties. Both houses are involved in choosing a president and vice president if there is no majority in the electoral college. The House of Representatives votes for the president from among the top three electoral candidates, with each state delegation casting one vote. The Senate votes for the vice president. The Senate has exercised this power only twice, in the disputed elections of 1800 and 1824.

The Executive Branch

Article II of the Constitution deals with the powers and duties of the president. The chief executive's constitutional responsibilities include the following:

1. Serve as commander in chief.

2. Negotiate treaties (with the approval of two-thirds of the Senate).

3. Appoint ambassadors, judges, and other high officials (with the consent of the Senate).

4. Grant pardons and reprieves for those convicted of federal crimes (except in impeachment cases).

5. Seek counsel of department heads (cabinet secretaries).

6. Recommend legislation.

7. Meet with representatives of foreign states.

8. See that federal laws are "faithfully executed."

The president's powers with respect to foreign policy are paramount. Civilian control of the military is a fundamental concept embodied in the naming of the president as commander in chief. In essence, the president is the nation's leading general. As such, the president can make battlefield decisions and shape military policy. The president also has broad powers in domestic policy. The most significant domestic policy tool is the president's budget, which the president must submit to Congress. Though Congress must approve all spending, the president has a great deal of power in budget negotiations. The president can use considerable resources in persuading Congress to enact legislation, and the president also has opportunities, such as in the annual State of the Union address, to reach out directly to the American people to convince them to support presidential policies.

The Judicial Branch

Article III of the Constitution states that "the judicial power of the United States shall be vested in one Supreme Court and in such inferior courts as the Congress may from time to time ordain and establish." The Constitution makes two references to a trial by jury in criminal cases (in Article III and in the Sixth Amendment).

The U.S. Electoral System and the Election Process

To become president, a candidate must be (1) a natural-born United States citizen, (2) a resident of the United States for at least 14 years, and (3) at least 35 years old. Each political party must select a candidate as its representative in an upcoming election. At the end of the primaries and caucuses, each party holds a national convention and finalizes its selection of its presidential nominee. Each presidential candidate chooses a vice presidential candidate.

The candidates usually begin their campaign tours once they have the nomination of their parties. In November, U.S. citizens cast their votes, but they are not actually voting directly for the presidential candidate of their choice in the general election. Instead, voters cast their votes for **electors**, who are part of the electoral college and who are supposed to vote for the candidate that their state prefers. The 55 delegates who met in Philadelphia in 1787 to draft a constitution established the electoral college originally as a compromise between electing the president by popular vote and by congressional election. At first the legislators in some states chose the electors; some states had the people elect the electors. In 1796, political parties started to operate. Each state would have the same number of electors as the state had senators and representatives. Each elector voted for two candidates. The person receiving the largest number of votes became the president, and the person receiving the second-highest number of votes became the vice president (as specified in Article II). The Twelfth Amendment to the U.S. Constitution specifies that the electors must meet in their respective states and cast their votes for president and vice president. The slates of electors pledge to vote for the candidates of the parties that the people select. Each elector must have his or her vote signed and certified. The electors send the votes to the president of the Senate for counting in front of Congress. The person having a simple majority is declared president. The House chooses the president from the top three if there is no majority. The Twentieth Amendment dictates the process that takes place if no president has qualified by the third day of January.

The president and vice president are the only two nationally elected officials. (State elections determine senators and representatives.) As discussed earlier, if no majority is achieved in the electoral college, the House of Representatives votes for the president, and the Senate votes for the vice president.

Structures and Functions of U.S. Federal, State, and Local Governments

Structures. According to the Constitution, all governmental powers ultimately stem from the people. As mentioned earlier, local governments generally handle local matters, and those issues that affect all citizens are the responsibility of the federal government. This system was a natural outgrowth of the colonial relationship between the Americans and the mother country of England.

The Tenth Amendment gives to the States those powers that the Constitution does not deny to the States and that the Constitution does not give to the federal government; if there is overlapping between the state government(s) and the federal government, the federal government is supreme.

Functions. The following powers are reserved for the federal government:

    1. Regulate foreign commerce.

    2. Regulate interstate commerce.

    3. Mint money.

    4. Regulate naturalization and immigration.

    5. Grant copyrights and patents.

6. Declare and wage war and declare peace.

7. Admit new states.

8. Fix standards for weights and measures.

9. Raise and maintain an army and a navy.

10. Govern Washington, DC.

11. Conduct relations with foreign powers.

12. Universalize bankruptcy laws.

The state governments have the following powers:

1. Conduct and monitor elections.

2. Establish voter qualifications within the guidelines established by the Constitution.

3. Provide for local governments.

4. Ratify proposed amendments to the Constitution.

5. Regulate contracts and wills.

6. Regulate intrastate commerce.

7. Provide for education for its citizens.

8. Levy direct taxes.

Social, Economic, and Political Rights in the United States

Throughout the summer and fall of 1787, the Constitutional Convention worked on the new Constitution. Of the 55 delegates, only 39 signed. George Mason of Virginia objected to the fact that the Constitution contained no bill of rights. Eventually, the Bill of Rights became the first 10 amendments to the Constitution. As time passed, Congress ratified several other amendments. Various portions of the Constitution provided for social, economic, and political rights.

Articles I, II, and III provide for the legislative, executive, and judicial powers. Article IV guarantees citizens of each state the privileges and immunities of the other states; this was to help prevent discrimination against visitors. It also ensures criminal extradition between states: If a person is convicted of a crime in one state and escapes to another state, the state in which that person is hiding must give the person up to the state from which the person escaped. In addition, Article IV provides to the states federal protection against invasion and domestic unrest.

The Bill of Rights

When the first Congress met in 1789, it had on its agenda the consideration of 12 amendments to the Constitution, written by James Madison. The states approved 10 of the 12 on December 15, 1791. Those 10 amendments make up the Bill of Rights (*Congress for Kids*):

First Amendment. Right to freedom of worship, speech, press, and assembly.

Second Amendment. Right of the people to keep and bear arms.

Third Amendment. Right against quartering of troops.

Fourth Amendment. Right against unreasonable searches and seizures.

Fifth Amendment. Rights of accused person: grand jury, due process, just compensation.

Sixth Amendment. Right to jury trial.

Seventh Amendment. Rights in suits; decisions of facts in case decided by jury; judge's role limited to questions about the law.

Eighth Amendment. Prohibition of cruel and unusual punishment.

Ninth Amendment. Rights retained by people.

Tenth Amendment. Rights retained by states.

Other Amendments to the Constitution

An amendment is either an addition to the Constitution or a change in the original text. Making additions or revisions to the Constitution is no small feat. Since 1787, more than 9,000 amendments have been proposed, but only 27 have been approved (*Congress for Kids*):

Eleventh Amendment. A citizen of one state may sue a citizen of another state only if that person has the state's permission.

Twelfth Amendment. Election of the president.

Thirteenth Amendment. Abolishment of slavery.

Fourteenth Amendment. Definition of *citizen*; protection of the citizen against states' abridging rights.

Fifteenth Amendment. Suffrage rights not denied or abridged by "race, color, or previous condition of servitude."

Sixteenth Amendment. Income tax.

Seventeenth Amendment. Senators elected by popular vote.

Eighteenth Amendment. Prohibition of intoxicating liquors.

Nineteenth Amendment. Women's suffrage.

Twentieth Amendment. Beginning and ending of terms of elected officials (members of Congress, vice president, president); presidential succession.

Twenty-first Amendment. Repeal of the Eighteenth Amendment.

Twenty-second Amendment. Limitation of president to two terms in office.

Twenty-third Amendment. District of Columbia given vote in presidential elections.

Twenty-fourth Amendment. Repeal of poll tax in federal elections.

Twenty-fifth Amendment. Appointment of vice president if vacancy in that office occurs; procedure in case of presidential disability.

Twenty-sixth Amendment. Establishment of voting age at 18.

Twenty-seventh Amendment. No change in compensation for representatives and senators can take effect until an intervening election of representatives.

The Processes of the United States Legal System

The contemporary judicial branch consists of thousands of courts and is, in essence, a dual system, with each state having its own judicial structure functioning simultaneously with a complete set of federal courts. The most significant piece of legislation with reference to establishing a federal court network was the Judiciary Act of 1789. That law organized the Supreme Court and set up the federal district courts (13) and the circuit (appeal) courts (3).

The Supreme Court today is made up of a chief justice and eight associate justices. The president, with the approval of the Senate, appoints the justices for life; the justices often come from the ranks of the federal judiciary. In recent years, the public has viewed the appointment of Supreme Court justices with intense scrutiny, and in some cases, heated political controversy has accompanied the choices for appointment. Understanding of the role of law in a democratic society results from knowledge of the nature of civil, criminal, and constitutional law and how the organization of the judicial system serves to interpret and apply such laws. Essential judicial principles include comprehension of rights, such as the right of due process, the right to a fair and speedy trial, and the right to a hearing before a jury of one's peers. Additional judicial principles include an understanding of the protections granted in the Constitution, which include protection from self-incrimination and unlawful searches and seizures. The U.S. Constitution makes two references to trials by jury (Article III and the Sixth Amendment). The accused seems to benefit by the provision because a jury consists of 12 persons; the accused cannot receive a conviction unless all 12 agree that the defendant is guilty. There is mention of a speedy trial to prevent incarceration indefinitely unless the jury finds the accused guilty and the person receives such a sentence. The public trial statement ensures that the defendant receives just treatment. In 1968, the Supreme Court ruled that jury trials in criminal courts extended to the state courts as well as the federal courts. The Sixth Amendment uses the phrase "compulsory process for obtaining witnesses." This means that it is compulsory for witnesses for the defendant to appear in court.

The Role of the United States in International Relations

The United States is not an island either geographically or politically. The United States demonstrates its leadership and participation in global interdependence economically, politically, historically, ecologically, linguistically, and culturally. The United States belonged to a group of nations (the Allied Powers) during World War II, but historian Chitwood says that when the United States ratified the treaty of the military alliance of the North Atlantic Treaty Organization (NATO) on April 4, 1949, it reached a far point in its departure from global isolation (Chitwood 867); the treaty of NATO states that each member will come to the aid of any other member that becomes a victim of outside attack. Twenty-six countries from North America and Europe entered into the treaty. NATO both safeguards and promotes the values of law, individual liberty, democracy, and the peaceful resolution of disputes; it provides a forum in which the United States, Canada, and European countries can consult about security issues and take appropriate joint action on them. The alliance considers an attack against one member as being an attack against all. NATO-led forces are helping to bring stability to Iraq, Afghanistan, Kosovo, and Darfur. NATO protects its members through military and political means (*www.nato.int/*).

The United States participates in other alliances also. For example, the United States supports the United Nations Educational, Scientific and Cultural Organization (UNESCO), a specialized United Nations agency to build peace in the minds of people, publish scientific breakthroughs, educate, build classrooms in devastated countries, encourage communication, respect diverse cultures, and promote the natural and social sciences ("United Nations Educational, Scientific, and Cultural Organization," *http://portal.unesco.org*). The United States is aware that there are common issues—like food production, human rights, use of natural resources, prejudice, poverty, and trade—that affect regions and nations worldwide. It also realizes that military and economic alliances and cartels can affect nations, regions, and the world. A country with a true sense of global interdependence realizes that its actions can affect the world. For instance, continuing to allow the use of certain sprays in a country can damage the ozone layer and affect the entire world.

ANTHROPOLOGY, SOCIOLOGY, AND PSYCHOLOGY

Anthropology is the study of human culture. Anthropologists study both modern-day and prehistoric culture. There are several types of anthropologists:

1. Archaeologists excavate and scientifically analyze the remains of extinct people to attempt reconstruction of their way of life. Richard Leakey is an archaeologist.

2. Primatologists study the group behavior of primates (nonhuman) such as gorillas, baboons, and chimpanzees. Jane Goodall is a primatologist.

3. Ethnographers gather information about culture through fieldwork done on site. Margaret Mead was an ethnographer.

4. Linguistic anthropologists study languages, particularly language in a social context.

5. Physical (or biological) anthropologists study living and fossil human beings and primates, such as chimpanzees and monkeys.

Sociology is the study of the social behavior of humans within a group. The groups studied can include families, mobs, workers in large organizations, criminals, medical groups, men, women, and so on; of particular concern is how the groups and the institutions interact. The sociologist and Nobel Prize Winner Gunnar Myrdal was a prominent sociologist; his *An American Dilemma* of 1944 dealt with the "Negro in America [which] represents nothing more and nothing less than a century-long lag of public morals" (Myrdal 24). He saw the problem as being "an integral part of, or a special phase of, the whole complex of problems in the larger civilization. It cannot be treated in isolation" (Myrdal xlix). **Psychology** is the study of human behavior—individuals and small groups of people. Educators are perhaps most familiar with psychologists Jean Piaget (a developmental psychologist who studies individuals over a lifespan) and B. F. Skinner (a behavioral or experimental psychologist). Social psychologists study the behavior of people in groups. Cognitive psychologists are interested in how people think and learn. Clinical psychologists study abnormal behavior. It is interesting, however, that some people do not classify psychology as a social studies subject.

REFERENCES

Alvarez, Lizette. "Census Director Marvels at the New Portrait of America." *New York Times*, January 1, 2001.

Cayne, Bernard S., ed. *Merit Students Encyclopedia*. Chicago: Crowell-Collier, 1969.

Chitwood, Oliver Perry, Frank Lawrence Owsley, and H. C. Nixon. *The United States: From Colony to World Power.* New York: D. Van Nostrand, 1949.

Congress for Kids. "Constitution: Amendments. *www.congressforkids.net/Constitution_amendments.htm.*

Davis, Anita Price. *North Carolina during the Great Depression: A Documentary Portrait of a Decade.* Jefferson, NC: McFarland, 2003.

Florida Smart. "Florida Population and Demographics." *www.floridasmart.com/facts/demographics.htm.*

Gordon, W. J. J. *Synectics.* New York: Harper and Row, 1961.

Halsey, William D., and Bernard Johnston, eds. *Merit Students Encyclopedia.* New York: Macmillan, 1991.

Harrington, Michael. *The Other America: Poverty in the United States.* New York: Macmillan, 1962.

Huitt, W. "Critical Thinking: An Overview." *Educational Psychology Interactive.* Valdosta, GA. 1998. *http://chiron.valdosta.edu/whuitt/col/cogsys/critthnk.html.* Last accessed July 11, 2008.

Martin, Philip L. "Immigration in the United States." Institute of European Studies, University of California, Berkeley. *http://ies.berkeley.edu/pubs/workingpapers/ay0102.html.*

Myrdal, Gunnar with the assistance of Richard Sterner and Arnold Rose. *An American Dilemma: The Negro Problem and Modern Democracy.* New York: Harper and Brothers Publishers, 1944.

NATO Official Homepage. *www.nato.int*

Schieffer, Bob. "Government Failed the People." *CBS News* (September 4, 2005).

Schug, Mark C., and R. Beery. *Teaching Social Studies in the Elementary.* Prospect Heights, IL: Waveland Press, 1987.

Schuncke, George M. *Elementary Social Studies: Knowing, Doing, Caring.* New York: Macmillan, 1988.

Smith, Adam. *An Inquiry into the Nature and Causes of the Wealth of Nations.* Dublin: Whitestone. 1776.

"United Nations Educational, Scientific, and Cultural Organization (UNESCO)," *http://portal.unesco.org.* Last accessed July 16, 2008.

U.S. Census Bureau, *Current Population Survey*, March 2003. *www.census.gov/population/socdemo/foreign/p20-534/tab0314.txt.* Last accessed July 16, 2008.

U. S. Census Bureau. "Countries of Birth of the Foreign-Born Population, 1850-2000." *Profile of the Foreign-Born Population in the United States: 2000. www.Infoplease.com/ipa/A0900547.html.* Last accessed July 11, 2008.

U.S. Census Bureau. "State and County QuickFacts: Florida." *http://quickfacts.census.gov/qfd/states/12000.html.*

Woolever, Roberta, and Kathryn P. Scott. *Active Learning in Social Studies: Promoting Cognitive and Social Growth.* Glenview, IL: Scott, Foresman, 1988.

Science

EARTH SCIENCE

Revolution of the Earth

Earth revolves around the sun. The axis of Earth is tilted at a 23.5° angle, and the axis always points toward the North Star (Polaris). The tilt and the revolution about the sun cause the seasons. **Earth's distance from the sun does not cause the seasons**. In fact, the Northern Hemisphere is closer to the sun in the winter—not in the summer. This closeness of the Earth to the sun in the winter is because of the elliptical pattern that the Earth follows as it revolves about the sun.

The Northern Hemisphere experiences **summer** when it is tilted toward the sun. Summer begins in the Northern Hemisphere on June 21, when the rays of the sun shine directly on the area. The hours of daylight are longer in the summer in the Northern Hemisphere, and the rays of the sun cover a smaller part of the surface of Earth in the summer. At that time of year, therefore, the Northern Hemisphere has hot surface temperatures and, because of the tilt of Earth, more hours of sunlight than darkness. This means that the longer direct rays of the sun last longer in the summer. When the Northern Hemisphere is tilted away from the sun, it experiences **winter**. Winter begins in the Northern Hemisphere on December 22. During this season, the days are shorter, fewer direct rays from the sun reach the Northern Hemisphere, and the hours of night are longer than in the summer. When it is summer in the Northern Hemisphere, it is winter in the Southern Hemisphere. When it is winter in the Northern Hemisphere, it is summer in the Southern Hemisphere. In the **fall** and **spring**, Earth is not tilted toward or away from the sun; it is somewhere between. The days and nights have an almost equal number of hours in the spring and fall. The Northern Hemisphere has equal days and nights at the **vernal equinox** (March 21) and at the **autumnal equinox** (September 23).

The Solar System

The solar system is the sun and its 8 orbiting planets. The sun, composed of hydrogen, has a mass 750 times that of all the planets combined. The names of the planets in order from the sun are Mercury, Venus, Earth, Mars, Jupiter, Saturn, Uranus, and Neptune. Rocky, metallic materials primarily compose the innermost planets of Mercury, Venus, Earth, and Mars; hydrogen, helium, and ices of ammonia and methane compose the outermost planets of Saturn, Uranus, and Neptune. Composed largely of hydrogen gas, Jupiter—a giant, half-formed sun—is an exception among the planets.

Earth has one satellite moon, Mars has two, and Jupiter has eight. Uranus has more than 20 moons, and Saturn has the distinguishing feature of rings. Both Earth and Venus have significant atmospheres. Jupiter has a giant red spot.

The accepted unit of measurement for expressing distances from the sun is the **astronomical unit (AU)**, with 1 AU equal to the distance from the sun to Earth. The planet closest to the sun is Mercury at 0.39 AU, and the planet farthest from the sun is Neptune at 30.1 AU.

Phases and Effects of the Moon

The moon is a satellite of Earth that orbits the Earth at the rate of one revolution every 29.5 days. Although it is the second brightest heavenly body, the moon does not give off its own light. Rather, it reflects the sun's light. The amount of lighted moon we see on Earth changes, however. Depending on where the moon is in its orbit, more or less of its lighted surface is visible from Earth. When the amount of visible lighted surface of the moon is increasing, the moon

PRAXIS Pointer

Pace yourself calmly, with your goal in sight.

is *waxing*; when the amount of visible light is decreasing, the moon is *waning*. These changes in the amount of visible lighted surface are the **phases** of the moon, which are described below:

New moon. The moon is between Earth and the sun. When the dark side of the moon is turned toward Earth, it is difficult to see the moon from Earth.

Crescent moon. As the moon continues to revolve around Earth (west to east), a crescent-shaped slice of the moon becomes visible from Earth.

Half moon (first quarter). About a week after the crescent moon, roughly one-half of the moon is visible.

Gibbous moon. Almost all the moon is visible a few days after the half moon.

Full moon. About two weeks after the new moon, Earth is between the sun and the moon. Almost all the lighted side of the moon is visible from Earth.

Half moon (last quarter). After the full-moon phase, the moon moves to another half-moon phase. The phases begin again.

When Earth blocks sunlight from reaching the moon, it creates a shadow on the moon's surface. This shadow on the moon's surface is the **lunar eclipse**. When the moon blocks sunlight from hitting Earth, the result is a **solar eclipse**. The moon exerts a **gravitational pull** on Earth. This pull causes **tides**, or periodic changes in the ocean water surfaces or sea level.

EARTH HISTORY

Geology is the study of the structure and composition of the earth. The three layers that compose the earth are the core, mantle, and crust. Solid iron and nickel make up the core, which is about 7,000 kilometers in diameter. The **mantle** is the semimolten layer

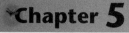

between the crust and the core. It is about 3,000 kilometers thick. The **crust** is the solid outermost layer, composed of bedrock overlaid with mineral and/or organic sediment (soil) and ranging from 5 to 40 kilometers thick.

At times, large sections of the Earth's crust move and create faults, earthquakes, volcanoes, and mountains. These moving sections of the Earth are **plates**, and the study of their movements is **plate tectonics**. **Faults** are cracks in the crust and are the results of the movements of plates. **Earthquakes** occur when plates slide past one another quickly. Volcanoes may also cause earthquakes. A seismograph measures earthquakes and uses the Richter scale. **Volcanoes** are mountains that form when two plates move away from one another to let magma reach the crust. **Magma** is molten rock beneath the Earth's crust. **Lava** is molten rock on the Earth's surface. A volcano shoots out magma, which eventually hardens into lava, and releases ash. Sometimes the erupting volcano forms rivers of lava. Volcanoes exist all over the world—for example, the Pacific Ocean, the Hawaiian Islands, and the southeastern border of Asia. The composition of volcanoes is fiery igneous rock, ash, and many layers of dirt and mud that have hardened from previous eruptions. Volcanic activity causes the crust of the Earth to buckle upward and form mountains.

Plate tectonics is a relatively new theory that has revolutionized the way geologists think about the Earth. According to the theory, large lithospheric plates form the surface of the Earth. The size and position of these plates change over time. The edges of the plates, where they move against each other, are sites of intense geologic activity such as earthquakes, volcanoes, and mountain building. Plate tectonics is a combination of two earlier ideas: continental drift and seafloor spreading. **Continental drift** is the movement of continents over the Earth's surface and their change in position relative to each other. **Seafloor spreading** is the creation of new oceanic crust at midocean ridges and movement of the crust away from the midocean ridges. The following are some of the pieces of evidence of continental drift and the underlying plate tectonics:

- The shapes of many continents are such that they look as though they are separate pieces of a jigsaw puzzle. For example, the east coasts of North America and South America and the west coasts of Africa and Europe appear to fit together.

- Many fossil comparisons along the edges of continents that look as if they fit together suggest species similarities that would make sense only if the two continents were joined at some point in the past.

- Seismic, volcanic, and geothermal activity occurs more frequently along plate boundaries than in sites far from boundaries.

- Ridges, such as the Mid-Atlantic Ridge, occur where plates are separating and lava welling up from between them as they pull apart. Likewise, mountain ranges are forming where plates are pushing against each other (for example, the Himalayas, which are still growing).

Fossil Formation

Fossils are preserved remnants of or marks made by plants and animals that were once alive. As such, fossils are one source of information about changes in the environment over time. Finding fossils of marine organisms in what is now a desert is an opportunity to discuss scientific ways of knowing, how science forms and tests hypotheses, and how theories develop to explain the reasons behind observations.

Fossils formed in several ways. In some cases, sediment covered some animals and then hardened into rock, preserving the hard parts of the animals' bodies. Other animals fell into tar pits, swamps, or quicksand, which ultimately hardened and preserved the animals' bones and teeth. Ice and mud preserved some animals in their entirety. The sticky sap from trees trapped some insects and later hardened; when oceans and sediment eventually covered the trees and sap, the sap turned to amber, in which some parts of the insects remained preserved as fossils. Some animals became petrified; others left casts of their remains. Some plants and animals left prints; for example, coal retained the prints of plants and animals pressed into it. Scientifically literate individuals understand the concepts of uncertainty in measurement and the basis of scientific theories. Such an understanding may lead the teacher in an elementary classroom to refer to fossils and rocks simply as "very old," to say that dinosaurs "lived long ago," and to preface statements of scientific theory with the observation, "Many scientists believe."

PHYSICAL SCIENCE

Matter

Matter is everything that has mass and volume. **Mass** is the amount of matter in an object; one way to measure mass is by using a lever arm balance. **Volume** is the amount of space an object occupies. Water is matter because it takes up space (that is, it has volume); light is not matter because it does not take up space.

Weight, although sometimes incorrectly interchanged with mass, is a measure of the force of gravity on an object; a spring scale can determine weight. An electronic scale may display an object's mass in grams, but the scale is dependent on gravity for its operation. An electronic scale, such as some butchers use, is accurate only when an expert (usually with the state trade agency) has adjusted the electronics for the local gravitational force. Although an object appears "weightless" as it floats inside the space shuttle, it is not; gravitational forces from both the earth and the sun keep it in orbit and affect the object. The force of gravity is proportional to the product of the masses of the two objects under consideration divided by the square of the distance between them. Earth, being larger and more massive than Mars, has proportionally stronger gravitational forces. This is the basis of the observation in H. G. Wells's *The War of the Worlds,* in which he describes the Martian invaders as "the most sluggish things I ever saw crawl" (Wells, Chapter 7, page 3).

Density is the ratio of mass to volume. An intrinsic property, density depends on the type of matter but not the amount of matter. Thus, the density of a five-ton cube of pure copper is the same as that of a small copper penny. However, the modern penny is a thin shell of copper over a zinc plug, and the density of the coin may be significantly lower than that of the older pure copper coin. Density is related to **buoyancy**. Objects sink in liquids or gases alike if they are denser than the material that surrounds them. Archimedes's principle, also related to density, states that an object is buoyed up by a force equal to the mass of the material the object displaces. Thus, a 160-pound concrete canoe will easily float in water if the volume of the submerged portion of the canoe is equal to the volume of 20 gallons of water. (The weight of water is approximately 8 pounds per gallon; therefore, 8 lbs/gal × 20 gal = 160 lbs.) Density is not the same as **viscosity**, a measure of thickness or flow ability. The strength of intermolecular forces between molecules determines, for example, that molasses will be slow in January or that hydrogen bromide is a gas in any season.

Matter can undergo chemical and physical changes. A **physical change** affects the size, form, or appearance of a material. These changes can include melting, bending, or cracking. Physical changes do not alter the molecular structure of a material. **Chemical changes** do alter the molecular structure of matter. Examples of chemical changes are burning, rusting, and digestion. Under the right conditions, compounds can break apart, combine, or recombine to form new compounds; this process is called a **chemical reaction**. Chemical equations can describe chemical reactions. For instance, sodium hydroxide and hydrochloride combine to form sodium chloride and water. The chemical equation for that reaction is

$$NaOH + HCl \rightarrow NaCl + H_2O$$

The materials to the left of the arrow are **reactants**, and materials to the right of the arrow are **products**.

Classifications of Matter

Classifications of matter also include elements, compounds, mixtures, or solutions. An **element** consists of only one type of atom. An example is iron. A symbol of one or two letters, such as Fe (iron) or C (carbon), represents an element. A **compound** is matter that comprises atoms chemically combined in definite weight proportions. An example of a compound is water, which is oxygen and hydrogen combined in the ratio of two hydrogen molecules to one oxygen molecule. A **mixture** is made up of one or more types of molecules, not chemically combined and without any definite weight proportions. For example, milk is a mixture of water and butterfat particles. Mixtures can be separated by either physical or chemical means. An example of physical means would be straining the butterfat from milk to make skim milk. **Solutions** are **homogeneous** mixtures—that is, mixtures with evenly distributed substances. An example of a solution is seawater. Separating the salt from seawater requires the process of evaporation.

PRAXIS Pointer

Relax your shoulder muscles by bringing your shoulders up toward your ears. Hold for 10 seconds—release and relax. Do this 2 to 3 times. Then try it with other muscles.

The three main **states of matter** are solids, liquids, and gases. A **solid** has a definite volume and a definite shape; an example is ice. A **liquid** has a definite volume but has no definite shape; an example is water. A **gas** has no definite volume or shape; an example is water vapor or steam.

Basic Components of the Atom

Atoms are the basic building blocks of matter. Three types of subatomic particles, which have mass and charge, make up atoms. The three components of atoms are protons, neutrons, and electrons. **Protons** and **neutrons** are in the **nucleus**, or the solid center of an atom. **Electrons** are in the outer portion of an atom.

Under most conditions, atoms are indivisible. However, atoms may split or combine to form new atoms during atomic reactions. Atomic reactions occur deep inside the sun, in nuclear power reactors, in nuclear bombs, and in radioactive decay. As mentioned earlier, a unique symbol of one or two letters, such as K (potassium) or Na (sodium), represents each element. Atoms of the same element have the same number of protons in their nuclei. An atom is the smallest particle of an element that retains the characteristics of that element. Each element has an atomic number, which is equal to the number of protons in an atom of that element. The **periodic table** is an arrangement of all the elements in order according to their atomic number; this table is a reference tool; summarizes the atomic structure, mass, and reactive tendencies of elements; and groups elements vertically according to their chemical properties. Two or more atoms may combine to form a molecule.

Energy, Temperature, and Heat

Energy is the ability of matter to move other matter or to produce a chemical change in other matter; scientists also define energy as the ability to do work. There are two main forms of energy: kinetic or potential.

Kinetic energy is the energy of motion; the energy is contained in the movement inside the object. The formula for kinetic energy is

$$KE = \tfrac{1}{2}mv^2$$

where m is the mass and v is the velocity of an object.

Potential energy is the storage of energy. An icicle hanging off the roof is an example of potential energy. The formula for potential energy is

$$PE = mgh$$

where m is mass, g is the gravitational force constant, and h is the height. The icicle's potential energy converts to kinetic energy as it falls, to sound energy as it hits the pavement, and to kinetic energy again as the fragments skitter off.

Heat is the energy of moving molecules. **Temperature** describes how hot or cold a material is. Temperature has nothing to do with the amount of heat a material has; it has to do only with the degree of "hotness" or "coldness" of the material. Temperature depends on the speed at which the molecules in a material are moving. The faster the molecules are moving, the hotter the temperature becomes. A **thermometer** measures temperature. There are several types of thermometers, but the most common are glass tubes containing mercury or a liquid, such as colored alcohol. Thermometers usually use the Fahrenheit scale or the Celsius scale.

Energy

Within the kinetic and potential forms of energy, there are seven main groups: (1) heat energy; (2) chemical energy; (3) electrical energy; (4) nuclear energy; (5) mechanical energy; (6) magnetic energy; and (7) radiant energy, a form of wave energy. **Heat energy**, as discussed above, is the energy of moving molecules. Our food stores **chemical energy** for later conversion to kinetic energy and heat in our bodies. **Electrical energy** is the energy that moving electrons produce. A stream of electrons moving through a substance is an **electric current**. Electrical energy enables us to light our homes and operate our telephones, televisions, and computers. **Nuclear energy** results when the nucleus of an atom splits in two or when the nuclei of atoms become fused together; both cases produce great amounts of energy. **Mechanical energy** is the form of energy most evident in the world. All moving bodies produce mechanical energy. The energy that machines create is mechanical energy. **Magnetic energy** is the force (pull or push) of a magnet. The poles of two magnets placed near each other will repel one another if they are alike and will attract each other if they are different. The space around a magnet can also act like a magnet; this is the magnetic field. **Radiant energy** is a form of wave energy. X-rays, infrared rays, radio waves, and ultraviolet rays are a few of the many types of radiant energy. The sun produces **solar energy**. All heat on the earth—except that from the interior of atoms—comes from the sun. The sun warms the earth, and energy from the sun enables plants to synthesize the food for their own needs and for the animals that eat them. The heat from the sun allows for evaporation. The sun is vital to survival.

THE PROCESSES OF LIFE

Comparing and Contrasting Living and Nonliving Things

Biology is the study of living things. Living things are differentiated from nonliving things by the ability to perform a specific set of life activities at some point in a normal life span. Table 5-1 describes the activities that define life. It is important to note that living things *must*, during a typical life span, be able to perform *all* these activities. It is quite common for nonliving things to perform one or more of these activities. For example, robots can move, respond, and repair, and crystals can grow: neither robots nor crystals, of course, are living things.

Table 5-1. Required Activities of Living Things

Activity	Description
Food getting	Procuring the food needed to sustain life by eating, absorption, or photosynthesis
Respiration	Exchanging of gases
Excretion	Eliminating wastes
Growth	Increasing in size over part or all of a life span
Repair	Repairing damaged tissue
Movement	Willfully moving a portion of a living thing's body, or channeling growth in a particular direction
Response	Reacting to events or things in the environment
Secretion	Producing and distributing chemicals that aid digestion, growth, metabolism, etc.
Reproduction	Making new living things similar to the parent

A **cell** is the basic structural unit of living things. In a living thing, a cell is the smallest component that can, by itself, be considered living. Plant cells and animal cells, though generally similar, are distinctly different; for example, plant cells have unique plant structures, cell walls, and vacuoles that animal cells do not have.

Distinguishing Among Microorganisms

Bacteria are single-celled living organisms. They reproduce themselves by duplicating. They do not need a host for survival. Bacteria are responsive to antibiotics.

A **virus** is smaller than one cell. It lives and multiplies within a host cell for survival; therefore, a virus is **intracellular** and not a living thing. Antibiotics, which are intended to kill living things, are not effective against viruses. The only way to treat a person with a virus is to provide supportive therapy that may help the body fight off the virus. The only way to protect a person against viruses is through vaccines. Vaccines help the body build up antibodies against viruses. Vaccines are not available for every virus, however, and do not cure viruses. Some biologists believe that a virus is a living organism; they believe that the virus can be described as a protein coat surrounding strands of nuclear material.

Protozoans are one-celled living organisms that live inside or outside a cell. Only some protozoans are susceptible to antibiotics.

Differentiating Structures and Functions of Plant and Animal Cells

As discussed earlier, a cell is the basic structural unit of living things and the smallest unit that can, by itself, be considered living. Plant cells and animal cells, though generally similar, are distinctly different. Figure 5-1 illustrates the structures of animal and plant cells.

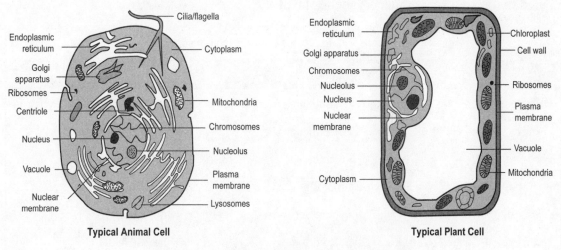

Figure 5-1. Typical Animal and Plant Cells

Cells are made of several smaller structures called **organelles**, which are surrounded by cell fluid, or cytoplasm. The functions of several cell structures are listed in Table 5-2.

Table 5-2. Cell Structures and Their Functions

Organelle	Function
Cell membrane	Controls movement of materials into and out of cells
Cell wall	Gives rigid structure to plant cells
Chloroplast	Contains chlorophyll, which enables green plants to make their own food
Cytoplasm	Jellylike substance inside a cell; comprises the cytosol and organelles but not the nucleus
Mitochondrion	Liberates energy from glucose in cells for use in cellular activities
Nucleus	Directs cell activities; holds DNA (genetic material)
Ribosome	Makes proteins from amino acids
Vacuole	Stores materials in a cell

The Plant Physiological Process

Cells perform several chemical processes to maintain essential life activities. The sum of these necessary chemical processes is called **metabolism**. Table 5-3 lists the processes related to metabolism and the organelles involved.

Table 5-3. Processes of Cell Metabolism

Process	Organelle	Life Activity
Diffusion	Cell membrane	Food getting, respiration, excretion
Osmosis	Cell membrane	Food getting, excretion
Phagocytosis	Cell membrane	Food getting
Photosynthesis	Chloroplasts	Food getting
Respiration (aerobic)	Mitochondrion	Provides energy
Fermentation	Mitochondrion	Provides energy

Cells need to move materials into their structures to get energy and to grow. The **cell membrane** allows certain small molecules to flow freely across it. This flow of chemicals from areas of high concentration to areas of low concentration is called **diffusion**. **Osmosis** is diffusion of water across a semipermeable membrane. Particles too large to pass through the cell membrane may be engulfed by the cell membrane and stored in vacuoles until they can be digested. This engulfing process is called **phagocytosis**.

All cells need energy to survive. Sunlight energy is made biologically available when plant cells convert it to chemical energy during **photosynthesis**. Photosynthesis is carried out in the **chloroplasts** of green cells. **Chlorophyll**, the pigment found in chloroplasts, catalyzes (causes or accelerates) the photosynthetic reaction that turns carbon dioxide and water into glucose (sugar) and oxygen. Sunlight and chlorophyll are needed for the reaction to occur. Because it is a catalyst, chlorophyll is not consumed in the reaction and may be used repeatedly.

The term *respiration* has two distinct meanings in the field of biology. As a life activity, respiration is the exchange of gases in living things. As a metabolic process, respiration is the release of energy from sugars for use in life activities. All living things get their energy from the digestion (respiration) of glucose (sugar). Respiration may occur with oxygen (aerobic respiration) or without oxygen (anaerobic respiration, or fermentation). Most often the term *respiration* is used to refer to aerobic respiration. Aerobic respiration occurs in most plant and animal cells. **Fermentation** occurs in yeast cells and other cells in the absence of oxygen. Fermentation by yeast produces the alcohol in alcoholic beverages and the gases that make yeast breads rise and have a light texture.

Reproduction is a process whereby living plant or animal cells or organisms produce offspring. Individual plants have growth limitations imposed by inherited characteristics and environmental conditions. If the plant grows excessively, any number of reproductive processes may be simulated. In plants, reproduction may be either sexual or asexual. **Asexual plant propagation**, also known as vegetative reproduction, is the method by which plants reproduce without the union of cells or nuclei of cells. The product of asexual plant propagation is genetically identical to the parent. Asexual propagation takes place either by **fragmentation** or by special asexual structures. An example of fragmentation is growing new plants from cuttings. **Sexual plant propagation** almost always involves seeds produced by two individuals, male and female. Most plant propagation is, in fact, from seed, including all annual and biennial plants. Seed **germination** begins when a sufficient amount of water is absorbed by the seed, precipitating biochemical changes that initiate cell division.

Water is essential for plant life. The plant needs the water to make food, among other uses. A plant usually takes in more water than it needs. To get rid of excess water, the stomata of the leaves allow the water to pass out as water vapor. This evaporation of water from the plant is **transpiration**.

Animal Physiology

Not all cells are alike. Cells that perform different functions differ in size and shape. A group of the same kind of cells is called a **tissue**. A group of the same kind of tissues working together is an **organ**. Examples of animal organs are the brain, stomach, heart, liver, and kidneys. A group of organs that work together to accomplish a special activity is a **system**. The complex organism known as the human body is made up of several organ systems.

PRAXIS Pointer

Wear a (noiseless) watch.

The **skeletal system** is composed of bones, cartilage, and ligaments. The area where two or more bones come together is called a **joint**. Bone surfaces in a joint are often covered with **cartilage**, which reduces friction in the joint. **Ligaments** are connective tissues that hold bones together. The human skeleton consists of more than 200 bones connected at joints by ligaments. Movements are effected by contractions of the skeletal muscles, to which the bones are attached by tendons. Muscular contractions are controlled by the nervous system. The **muscular system** controls movement of the skeleton and movement within organs. There are three types of muscle: striated (voluntary), smooth (involuntary), and cardiac. Tendons attach muscles to bone. Skeletal muscles work in pairs. The alternating contractions of muscles within a pair causes movement in joints. The **nervous system** has two divisions: the somatic, allowing voluntary control over skeletal muscle, and the autonomic, or involuntary, controlling cardiac and glandular functions. Voluntary movement is caused by nerve impulses arising in the brain and carried by cranial or spinal chord nerves connecting to skeletal muscles. Involuntary movement occurs in direct response to outside stimulus. Involuntary responses are called reflexes. Various nerve terminals called receptors constantly send impulses to the central nervous system. There are three types of receptors:

Exteroceptors: Pain, temperature, touch, and pressure receptors.

Interoceptors: Internal environment receptors.

Proprioceptors: Movement, position, and tension receptors.

Each receptor routes nerve impulses to specialized areas of the brain for processing.

The energy required for sustenance of the human body is supplied by food. The **digestive system** receives and processes food. The digestive system includes the mouth, esophagus, stomach, large intestine, and small intestine. The **excretory system** eliminates wastes from the body. Excretory organs include the lungs, kidneys, bladder, large intestine, rectum, and skin. The lungs excrete gaseous waste. The kidneys filter blood and excrete wastes, mostly in the form of urea. The bladder holds liquid wastes until they can be eliminated through the urethra. The large intestine absorbs water from solid food waste, and the rectum stores solid waste until it can be eliminated. The skin excretes waste through perspiration.

The **circulatory system** is responsible for internal transport in the body. It is composed of the heart, blood vessels, lymph vessels, blood, and lymph. The **immune system** is important for health and indeed life. The body defends itself against foreign proteins and infectious microorganisms by means of a complex dual system that depends on recognizing a portion of the surface pattern of the invader. Lymphocytes and antibody molecules are generated to destroy the invader molecules. The **respiratory system** performs the essential process of respiration. In humans, respiration involves the expansion and contraction of the lungs. Some animals, however, use gills and other means of respiration. The **reproductive system** is essential for the continuance of life in animals and in humans.

The Animal Physiological Processes

The essential process of **respiration** in humans is effected by the expansion and contraction of the lungs. In the lungs, oxygen enters tiny capillaries, where it combines with hemoglobin in the red blood cells and is carried to the tissues through circulation of the blood. At the same time, carbon dioxide passes through capillaries into the air contained within the lungs. Inhaling draws air into the lungs that is higher in oxygen and lower in carbon dioxide; exhaling forces air from the lungs that is high in carbon dioxide and low in oxygen.

Reproduction is the process whereby living plant or animal cells or organisms produce offspring. In almost all animal organisms, reproduction occurs during or after the period of maximum growth. Reproduction in animals can be further subdivided into asexual and sexual. **Asexual animal propagation** occurs primarily in single-celled organisms. Through a process known as **fission**, the parent organism splits into two or more daughter organisms and loses its original identity. In some instances, cell division results

воспроизведение, размножение

in the production of buds that arise from the body of the parent and then later separate to develop into new organisms identical to the parent. Reproductive processes in which only one parent gives rise to the offspring are scientifically classified as asexual reproduction. The offspring produced are identical to the parent. **Sexual animal propagation** is a result of sperm uniting with ova for fertilization. The primary means of this kind of reproduction are insemination (copulation between a male and female vertebrate) and cross-fertilization (the depositing of ova and sperm in water at some distance from each other, most commonly by fish).

Digestion is the process of receiving and processing food; food supplies the energy required for sustenance of the human body. The digestive system includes the mouth, stomach, large intestine, and small intestine. Digestion begins when food is physically broken down by mastication, or chewing, and then mixed with saliva. Food is chemically broken down in the stomach and the small intestine, where the gastric and intestinal juices, respectively, continue the process. Thereafter, the mixture of food and secretions makes its way down the alimentary canal by peristalsis, rhythmic contractions of the smooth muscle of the gastrointestinal system. The small intestine absorbs nutrients from food, and the large intestine absorbs water from solid food waste.

Circulation is the internal transportation system of the body. The circulatory system is composed of the heart, blood vessels, lymph vessels, blood, and lymph. The heart is a muscular four-chambered pump. The upper chambers are the **atria** and the lower chambers are the **ventricles.** Blood flows throughout the body. The heart pumps the blood, which first passes through the right chambers of the heart and through the lungs, where it acquires oxygen. From there, it is pumped back into the left chambers of the heart. Next, it is pumped into the main artery, the aorta, which branches into increasingly smaller arteries. Beyond that, blood passes through tiny, thin-walled structures called capillaries. In the capillaries, the blood gives up oxygen and nutrients to tissues and absorbs a metabolic waste product containing carbon dioxide. Finally, blood completes the circuit by passing through small veins, which join to form increasingly larger vessels; finally the blood reaches the largest veins that return the blood to the right side of the heart.

нечуорок

PERSONAL HEALTH; SCIENCE IN PERSONAL AND SOCIAL PERSPECTIVES

Parts and Sequences of Biogeochemical Cycles of Common Elements in the Environment

The amount of oxygen and carbon dioxide in the air remains the same as a result of the **carbon dioxide–oxygen cycle**. To make food, green plants take in carbon dioxide from the air. The waste product that plants give off in the process is oxygen. When animals breathe in oxygen to digest their food, they give off carbon dioxide as a waste product.

The amount of nitrogen in the air remains constant as a result of the **nitrogen cycle**. Nitrogen-fixing bacteria live in the soil and in the roots of legumes (for example, beans, peas, and clover). Bacteria change the nitrogen in the air (that plants cannot use) into nitrogen materials that plants can use. After animals eat plants, they give off waste materials that contain nitrogen. Bacteria in the soil act on the animals' waste materials and on dead plants and animals and break them down, making the remaining nitrogen available. **Nitrifying bacteria** return the nitrogen to the soil for plants to use. **Denitrifying bacteria** change some of the nitrogen in the materials and the dead plants and animals to free nitrogen, which returns to the air and continues the nitrogen cycle.

PRAXIS Pointer

Study the directions and format of the practice tests. Become familiar with the structure of the test, so you can save time when you begin taking the actual test. This way, you can also cut your chances of experiencing any unwanted surprises.

The air today is different in composition from what it was when the earth was formed. Large amounts of hydrogen and helium characterized the composition of air millions of years ago. As the earth cooled, water vapor, carbon dioxide, and nitrogen became components of the air. When the water vapor condensed, carbon dioxide and nitrogen remained. The plants reduced the amount of carbon dioxide in the air and increased the amount of oxygen in the air. Today pollution is changing the composition of the air.

Causes and Effects of Pollution

Pollution is any material added to an ecosystem that disrupts its normal functioning. Typical pollutants are excess fertilizer that remains in the soil or runs off into water sources, waste materials that factories and manufacturing plants dump into the water or onto the ground, and industrial emissions into the air. Pollution generates large quantities of gases and solids every day. Smokestacks, chimneys, and car exhaust pipes are some sources of air pollutants. Some pollutants are simply annoying, but others are dangerous to the health of those exposed. Continuous exposure to polluting materials discharged into the air can cause lung diseases or aggravate existing health conditions. Bomb tests (hydrogen and atom) add radioactive particles to the air, and if more testing occurs, the particles may accumulate and become increasingly dangerous.

If weather conditions prevent the distribution of polluting materials, air pollution can become increasingly severe. When cold air is next to the ground with warm air lying on top, polluting materials remain concentrated in one area. The warm air acts as a blanket, and the cold air remains stationary. This is a **temperature inversion**. A recent phenomenon (since 1950) is **acid rain**—a form of precipitation that contains high levels of sulfuric or nitric acid. Acid rain occurs when sulfur dioxide and nitrogen oxide combine with atmospheric moisture. Acid rain can pollute drinking water, damage plant and animal life, and even erode monuments and buildings. Among the primary causes of acid rain are the burning of certain fuels—including the gas used to power automobiles.

Living and Nonliving Factors That Influence Population Density

Our surroundings form a complex, interconnected system in which living organisms exist in relationship with the soil, water, and air. Because they are linked through chemical and physical processes, Earth's inhabitants are in states of continual change or dynamic equilibrium.

Ecosystem is the term for all the living and nonliving things in a given environment and how they interact. Scientifically literate individuals are aware of their surroundings, the interdependence of every aspect of those surroundings, and the impact of human activities. Mutualistic and competitive relationships also exist among the organisms in an ecosystem, determining how organisms rely on each other and how they compete and conflict with each other.

Energy transformations are the driving force within an ecosystem. Many organisms obtain energy from light. For example, light drives the process of photosynthesis in green plants. Solar energy also provides the heat that cold-blooded animals require. Another source of energy for organisms is other organisms, including other plants and animals.

When one source of energy is depleted in an ecosystem, many organisms must shift their attention to other sources of energy. For example, a bear derives energy primarily from berries, fish, or nuts, depending on the season. The **energy pyramid** for an ecosystem illustrates these relationships and identifies the organisms most dependent on the other organisms in the system. Higher-order organisms cannot survive for long without the other organisms beneath them in the energy pyramid. The availability of adequate food within an ecosystem can explain the system's functioning, the size of an animal's territory, or the effects of a single species preying too heavily on organisms above it in the food chain. Over time, ecosystems change, both from natural processes and from human activities. Scientifically literate individuals can identify how the environment changes, how those changes affect the organisms that live there, and what the differences are between long- and short-term variation. Natural succession occurs when one community replaces another. For example, colonies of fungus grow and thrive on rodent droppings under ideal conditions; then different colonies replace the ones currently thriving on the rodent droppings.

Ecology is the study of the relationship between living things and their environment. An **environment** is all the living and nonliving things surrounding an organism. A **population** is a group of similar organisms, such as a herd of deer. A **community** is a group of populations that interact with one another. A pond community, for example, is made up of all the plants and animals in the pond. An **ecosystem** is a group of populations that share a common pool of resources and a common physical or geographical area. Each population lives in a particular area and serves a special role in the community. This combination of defined role and living areas is the concept of **niche**. The niche of a pond snail, for example, is to decompose materials in ponds. The niche of a field mouse is to eat seeds in fields. When two populations try to fill the same niche, **competition** occurs. If one population replaces another in a niche, **succession** occurs. Succession is the orderly and predictable change of communities as a result of population replacement in niches.

Conservation Methods

Conservation is the practice of using natural areas without disrupting their ecosystems. This definition suggests **interdependence** among people and the world, and **practices** or actions to improve or maintain the world. These practices must recognize that there are both renewable and nonrenewable resources. **Renewable resources** are those that can endure indefinitely under wise practices; examples of renewable resources are soil, vegetation, animals, and fresh water. **Nonrenewable natural resources** can be depleted; examples of nonrenewable resources are copper, coal, oil, and metals.

Laws to manage the mining and drilling of natural resources and laws regulating the use and recycling of natural resources are among the efforts to conserve nonrenewable resources. A major component of conservation is educating people on the importance of managing nonrenewable natural resources.

Renewable resources are dependent on each other—they are **interdependent**. Crops cannot grow in the soil without water. Bees play a part in the life cycle of many plants, and animals help provide carbon dioxide for photosynthesis. Managed forests ensure a supply of wood, a steady flow of water, and protection of the soil against wind and water damage. Laws governing hunting and fishing are effective—when enforced—in ensuring that game and other animals can renew themselves and continue their role in the web of life. In the 1930s, the Civilian Conservation Corps enrolled 250,000 men aged 18 to 24 from families on relief to go to camps where they worked on flood control, soil conservation, park development, and forest projects under the direction of the federal government. Conservation is not a new concept, but it is still not as effective as it could be. Again, education is the key.

REFERENCES

Blough, Glenn O., and Julius Schwartz. *Elementary School Science and How to Teach It*. New York: Rhinehart and Winston, 1969.

Victor, Edward. *Science for the Elementary School*. New York: Macmillan, 1975.

Practice Test 1

Elementary Education: Content Knowledge (0014)

ANSWER SHEET FOR PRACTICE TEST 1

1. Ⓐ Ⓑ Ⓒ Ⓓ
2. Ⓐ Ⓑ Ⓒ Ⓓ
3. Ⓐ Ⓑ Ⓒ Ⓓ
4. Ⓐ Ⓑ Ⓒ Ⓓ
5. Ⓐ Ⓑ Ⓒ Ⓓ
6. Ⓐ Ⓑ Ⓒ Ⓓ
7. Ⓐ Ⓑ Ⓒ Ⓓ
8. Ⓐ Ⓑ Ⓒ Ⓓ
9. Ⓐ Ⓑ Ⓒ Ⓓ
10. Ⓐ Ⓑ Ⓒ Ⓓ
11. Ⓐ Ⓑ Ⓒ Ⓓ
12. Ⓐ Ⓑ Ⓒ Ⓓ
13. Ⓐ Ⓑ Ⓒ Ⓓ
14. Ⓐ Ⓑ Ⓒ Ⓓ
15. Ⓐ Ⓑ Ⓒ Ⓓ
16. Ⓐ Ⓑ Ⓒ Ⓓ
17. Ⓐ Ⓑ Ⓒ Ⓓ
18. Ⓐ Ⓑ Ⓒ Ⓓ
19. Ⓐ Ⓑ Ⓒ Ⓓ
20. Ⓐ Ⓑ Ⓒ Ⓓ
21. Ⓐ Ⓑ Ⓒ Ⓓ
22. Ⓐ Ⓑ Ⓒ Ⓓ
23. Ⓐ Ⓑ Ⓒ Ⓓ
24. Ⓐ Ⓑ Ⓒ Ⓓ
25. Ⓐ Ⓑ Ⓒ Ⓓ
26. Ⓐ Ⓑ Ⓒ Ⓓ
27. Ⓐ Ⓑ Ⓒ Ⓓ
28. Ⓐ Ⓑ Ⓒ Ⓓ
29. Ⓐ Ⓑ Ⓒ Ⓓ
30. Ⓐ Ⓑ Ⓒ Ⓓ

31. Ⓐ Ⓑ Ⓒ Ⓓ
32. Ⓐ Ⓑ Ⓒ Ⓓ
33. Ⓐ Ⓑ Ⓒ Ⓓ
34. Ⓐ Ⓑ Ⓒ Ⓓ
35. Ⓐ Ⓑ Ⓒ Ⓓ
36. Ⓐ Ⓑ Ⓒ Ⓓ
37. Ⓐ Ⓑ Ⓒ Ⓓ
38. Ⓐ Ⓑ Ⓒ Ⓓ
39. Ⓐ Ⓑ Ⓒ Ⓓ
40. Ⓐ Ⓑ Ⓒ Ⓓ
41. Ⓐ Ⓑ Ⓒ Ⓓ
42. Ⓐ Ⓑ Ⓒ Ⓓ
43. Ⓐ Ⓑ Ⓒ Ⓓ
44. Ⓐ Ⓑ Ⓒ Ⓓ
45. Ⓐ Ⓑ Ⓒ Ⓓ
46. Ⓐ Ⓑ Ⓒ Ⓓ
47. Ⓐ Ⓑ Ⓒ Ⓓ
48. Ⓐ Ⓑ Ⓒ Ⓓ
49. Ⓐ Ⓑ Ⓒ Ⓓ
50. Ⓐ Ⓑ Ⓒ Ⓓ
51. Ⓐ Ⓑ Ⓒ Ⓓ
52. Ⓐ Ⓑ Ⓒ Ⓓ
53. Ⓐ Ⓑ Ⓒ Ⓓ
54. Ⓐ Ⓑ Ⓒ Ⓓ
55. Ⓐ Ⓑ Ⓒ Ⓓ
56. Ⓐ Ⓑ Ⓒ Ⓓ
57. Ⓐ Ⓑ Ⓒ Ⓓ
58. Ⓐ Ⓑ Ⓒ Ⓓ
59. Ⓐ Ⓑ Ⓒ Ⓓ
60. Ⓐ Ⓑ Ⓒ Ⓓ

61. Ⓐ Ⓑ Ⓒ Ⓓ
62. Ⓐ Ⓑ Ⓒ Ⓓ
63. Ⓐ Ⓑ Ⓒ Ⓓ
64. Ⓐ Ⓑ Ⓒ Ⓓ
65. Ⓐ Ⓑ Ⓒ Ⓓ
66. Ⓐ Ⓑ Ⓒ Ⓓ
67. Ⓐ Ⓑ Ⓒ Ⓓ
68. Ⓐ Ⓑ Ⓒ Ⓓ
69. Ⓐ Ⓑ Ⓒ Ⓓ
70. Ⓐ Ⓑ Ⓒ Ⓓ
71. Ⓐ Ⓑ Ⓒ Ⓓ
72. Ⓐ Ⓑ Ⓒ Ⓓ
73. Ⓐ Ⓑ Ⓒ Ⓓ
74. Ⓐ Ⓑ Ⓒ Ⓓ
75. Ⓐ Ⓑ Ⓒ Ⓓ
76. Ⓐ Ⓑ Ⓒ Ⓓ
77. Ⓐ Ⓑ Ⓒ Ⓓ
78. Ⓐ Ⓑ Ⓒ Ⓓ
79. Ⓐ Ⓑ Ⓒ Ⓓ
80. Ⓐ Ⓑ Ⓒ Ⓓ
81. Ⓐ Ⓑ Ⓒ Ⓓ
82. Ⓐ Ⓑ Ⓒ Ⓓ
83. Ⓐ Ⓑ Ⓒ Ⓓ
84. Ⓐ Ⓑ Ⓒ Ⓓ
85. Ⓐ Ⓑ Ⓒ Ⓓ
86. Ⓐ Ⓑ Ⓒ Ⓓ
87. Ⓐ Ⓑ Ⓒ Ⓓ
88. Ⓐ Ⓑ Ⓒ Ⓓ
89. Ⓐ Ⓑ Ⓒ Ⓓ
90. Ⓐ Ⓑ Ⓒ Ⓓ

91. Ⓐ Ⓑ Ⓒ Ⓓ
92. Ⓐ Ⓑ Ⓒ Ⓓ
93. Ⓐ Ⓑ Ⓒ Ⓓ
94. Ⓐ Ⓑ Ⓒ Ⓓ
95. Ⓐ Ⓑ Ⓒ Ⓓ
96. Ⓐ Ⓑ Ⓒ Ⓓ
97. Ⓐ Ⓑ Ⓒ Ⓓ
98. Ⓐ Ⓑ Ⓒ Ⓓ
99. Ⓐ Ⓑ Ⓒ Ⓓ
100. Ⓐ Ⓑ Ⓒ Ⓓ
101. Ⓐ Ⓑ Ⓒ Ⓓ
102. Ⓐ Ⓑ Ⓒ Ⓓ
103. Ⓐ Ⓑ Ⓒ Ⓓ
104. Ⓐ Ⓑ Ⓒ Ⓓ
105. Ⓐ Ⓑ Ⓒ Ⓓ
106. Ⓐ Ⓑ Ⓒ Ⓓ
107. Ⓐ Ⓑ Ⓒ Ⓓ
108. Ⓐ Ⓑ Ⓒ Ⓓ
109. Ⓐ Ⓑ Ⓒ Ⓓ
110. Ⓐ Ⓑ Ⓒ Ⓓ
111. Ⓐ Ⓑ Ⓒ Ⓓ
112. Ⓐ Ⓑ Ⓒ Ⓓ
113. Ⓐ Ⓑ Ⓒ Ⓓ
114. Ⓐ Ⓑ Ⓒ Ⓓ
115. Ⓐ Ⓑ Ⓒ Ⓓ
116. Ⓐ Ⓑ Ⓒ Ⓓ
117. Ⓐ Ⓑ Ⓒ Ⓓ
118. Ⓐ Ⓑ Ⓒ Ⓓ
119. Ⓐ Ⓑ Ⓒ Ⓓ
120. Ⓐ Ⓑ Ⓒ Ⓓ

PRACTICE TEST 1

TIME: 120 minutes
       120 questions

> Four-Function or Scientific Calculator Permitted

I. LANGUAGE ARTS

1. A phrase can NEVER be

   (A) a fragment of a sentence.
   (B) a modifier.
   (C) a complete thought.
   (D) prepositional

2. The proverb "Death is a black camel, which kneels at the gates of all" is an example of

   (A) alliteration.
   (B) simile.
   (C) metaphor.
   (D) hyperbole.

3. Literacy is a person's ability to

   (A) hop and skip.
   (B) read and write.
   (C) encode and be pragmatic.
   (D) comprehend and engage.

4. In general, the entries in a table of contents are arranged according to which of the following relationships?

   (A) Alphabetical
   (B) Concrete and abstract
   (C) Linear and recursive
   (D) Order of occurrence in the book

Questions 5 and 6 refer to the following poem.

> Old Time is still a-flying;
> And this same flower that smiles today,
> Tomorrow will be dying.
> The glorious lamp of heaven, the sun,
> The higher he's a-getting,
> The sooner will his race be run,
> And nearer he's to setting.

5. Which of the following best describes the theme of the poem?

   (A) Races are to be won.
   (B) Father Time is destructive.
   (C) God is watching.
   (D) Time marches on.

6. The poet uses the examples of flowers and the sun to illustrate

   (A) love of humanity.
   (B) love of nature.
   (C) the fleeting nature of life.
   (D) the arbitrary death of natural things.

Question 7 refers to the following essay.

Creating an English garden on a mountainside in the Ouachita Mountains in central Arkansas may sound like an impossible endeavor, but after two years, this dream is becoming my reality. By digging up the rocks and re-placing them with bags of topsoil, hu-mus, and peat, the persistent gardener now has sprouts that are not all weeds. Gravel paths meander through the beds of Shasta daisies, marigolds, laven-der, valerian, iris, day lilies, Mexican heather, and other flowers. Ornamen-tal grasses, dogwood trees, and shrubs back up the flowers. Along the periodic waterway created by an underground spring, swamp hibiscus, helenium, hosta, and umbrella plants display their colorful and seasonal blooms. Large rocks dug up by a pickax outline the flowerbeds. Blistered hands are worth the effort when people stop by to view the mountainside beauty.

7. This essay can be described as being

    (A) speculative.
    (B) argumentative.
    (C) narrative.
    (D) expository.

8. "You will have 40 minutes to complete the as-signment. When your finished, give it to Ms. Fletcher or myself."

    I.   "40" should be spelled out as forty.
    II. The clauses should be joined by a semi-colon, not a period.
    III. "myself" should be "me."
    IV. "your" should be "you're."

    (A) Both I and II
    (B) Only III
    (C) Both III and IV
    (D) Only IV

9. Which of the following is the term given for the written symbols for the speech sounds?

    (A) Graphemes
    (B) Semantics
    (C) Phonemes
    (D) Phonics

10. Ms. Thompson wants to teach her students about methods of collecting data in science. This is an important skill for first graders. Which of the following describes the most ap-propriate method of teaching students about collecting data in science?

    (A) Ms. Thompson should arrange the stu-dents into groups of four. She should then have each group observe the class's pet mouse while she gently touches it with a feather. The students should record how many times out of 10 the pet mouse moves away from the feather. Then she should gently touch the class's philoden-dron 10 times with a feather. The students should record how many out of 10 times the philodendron moves away from the feather.

    (B) Ms. Thompson should arrange the stu-dents into groups of four. She should give each group five solid balls made of ma-terials that will float and five solid balls made of materials that will not float. She should have the students drop the balls into a bowl of water and record how many float and how many do not.

    (C) Ms. Thompson should show the students a video about scientific methods of gath-ering data.

    (D) Ms. Thompson should have a scientist come and talk to the class about methods of collecting data. If she cannot get a scien-tist, she should have a science teacher from the high school come and speak about sci-entific methods of data collection.

Questions 11–15 are based on the following passage.

Frederick Douglass was born Fred-erick Augustus Washington Bailey in 1817 to a white father and a slave mother.

Frederick was raised by his grandmother on a Maryland plantation until he was eight. Then he was sent to Baltimore by his owner to be a servant to the Auld family. Mrs. Auld recognized Frederick's intellectual acumen and defied the law of the state by teaching him to read and write. When Mr. Auld warned that education would make the boy unfit for slavery, Frederick sought to continue his education in the streets. When his master died, Frederick, who was only 16 years of age, was returned to the plantation to work in the fields. Later, he was hired out to work in the shipyards in Baltimore as a ship caulker. He plotted an escape, but was discovered before he could get away. It took five years before he made his way to New York City and then to New Bedford, Massachusetts. He managed to elude slave hunters by changing his name to Douglass.

At an 1841 anti-slavery meeting in Massachusetts, Douglass was invited to give a talk about his experiences under slavery. His impromptu speech was so powerful and so eloquent that it thrust him into a career as an agent for the Massachusetts Anti-Slavery Society. To counter those who doubted his authenticity as a former slave, Douglass wrote his autobiography in 1845. This work became a classic in American literature and a primary source about slavery from the point of view of a slave. Douglass went on a two-year speaking tour abroad to avoid recapture by his former owner and to win new friends for the abolition movement. He returned with funds to purchase his freedom and to start his own anti-slavery newspaper. Douglass became a consultant to Abraham Lincoln, and throughout the Reconstruction period he fought doggedly for full civil rights for freedmen; he also supported the women's rights movement.

11. According to the passage, Douglass's writing of his autobiography was motivated by

   (A) the desire to make money for the anti-slavery movement.
   (B) his desire to become a publisher.
   (C) his interest in authenticating his life as a slave.
   (D) his desire to travel and speak to slaves.

12. The central idea of the passage is that Douglass

   (A) was instrumental in changing the laws regarding the education of slaves.
   (B) was one of the most eminent human rights leaders of the nineteenth century.
   (C) was a personal friend and confidant to a president.
   (D) wrote a classic in American literature.

13. According to the author of this passage, Mrs. Auld taught Douglass to read because

   (A) Douglass wanted to go to school like the other children.
   (B) she recognized his natural ability.
   (C) she wanted to comply with the laws of the state.
   (D) he needed to be able to read so that he might work in the home.

14. The title that best expresses the ideas of this passage is

   (A) The History of the Anti-Slavery Movement in America.
   (B) The Outlaw Frederick Douglass.
   (C) Reading: A Window to the World of Abolition.
   (D) Frederick Douglass's Contributions to Freedom.

15. In the context of the passage, *impromptu* is the closest in meaning to

    (A) unprepared.
    (B) nervous.
    (C) angry.
    (D) loud.

Questions 16–18 refer to the following passage.

Gary Harris, a farmer from Conrad, Montana, has invented and patented a motorcycle helmet. It provides a brake light, which can signal traffic intentions to other drivers behind. In the United States, all cars sold are now required to carry a third, high-mounted brake light. Harris's helmet will meet this requirement for motorcyclists.

16. The passage tells about

    (A) a new invention for motorcyclists.
    (B) a brake light for motorcyclists.
    (C) Harris's helmet.
    (D) Gary Harris, inventor.

17. An implication regarding the new invention is

    (A) the new brake light requirement for cars should likewise apply to motorcycles.
    (B) the new brake light requirement for cars cannot apply to motorcycles.
    (C) If you buy a car from outside of the United States, you are exempt from the brake light requirement.
    (D) As an inventor, Gary Harris can make more money if he leaves farming.

18. Because of the new brake light requirement for cars,

    (A) drivers can readily see the traffic signals of car drivers ahead of them.
    (B) less accidents can happen on the road.

    (C) car prices will go up and will be less affordable to buy.
    (D) the additional lights on the road will become hazardous.

Questions 19 and 20 are based on the following passage.

America's national bird, the mighty bald eagle, is being threatened by a new menace. Once decimated by hunters and loss of habitat, the bald eagle is facing a new danger, suspected to be intentional poisoning by livestock ranchers. Authorities have found animal carcasses injected with restricted pesticides. These carcasses allegedly are placed to attract and kill predators such as the bald eagle in an effort to preserve young grazing animals. It appears that the eagle is being threatened again by the consummate predator, humans.

19. One can conclude from this passage that

    (A) the pesticides used are beneficial to the environment.
    (B) ranchers believe that killing the eagles will protect their ranches.
    (C) ranchers must obtain licenses to use illegal pesticides.
    (D) poisoning eagles is good for livestock.

20. The author's attitude is one of

    (A) uncaring observation.
    (B) concerned interest.
    (C) uniformed acceptance.
    (D) suspicion.

21. Which of the following is NOT synonymous with the word *mediocre*?

    (A) Original
    (B) Commonplace

(C) Passable

(D) Ordinary

22. Which author wrote: "What's in a name? That which we call a rose/ By any other name would smell as sweet"?

(A) Christopher Marlowe

(B) Ben Johnson

(C) William Shakespeare

(D) Geoffrey Chaucer

23. The meaning of *protagonist* is

(A) the landscape.

(B) a villain.

(C) the central character.

(D) a quest.

24. The literary technique of foreshadowing is often used

(A) in novels, short stories, and drama to manifest the characters' emotions by reflecting them in the natural world.

(B) in novels, short stories, and drama to hint at future developments in the plot.

(C) in lyric poetry to manifest the speaker's emotions by reflecting them in the natural world.

(D) in myths and ballads to hint at future developments in the plot.

Question 25 is based on the following passage.

Water is a most unusual substance because it exists on the surface of Earth in its three physical states: ice, water, and water vapor. Other substances exist in a solid and liquid or gaseous state at temperatures normally found at Earth's surface, but water is the only pure substance to occur in all three states on Earth.

Water is odorless, tasteless, and colorless. It is a universal solvent. Water does not corrode, rust, burn, or separate into its components easily. It is chemically indestructible. It can, however, corrode almost any metal and erode the most solid rock. A unique property of water is that, when frozen in its solid state, it expands and floats on liquid water. Water has a freezing point of 0°C and a boiling point of 100°C. Water has the capacity to absorb great quantities of heat with relatively little increase in temperature. In addition, *distilled* water is a poor conductor of electricity, but when salt is added, it is a good conductor of electricity.

25. According to the passage, what is the most unique property of water?

(A) Water is odorless, tasteless, and colorless.

(B) Water exists on the surface of the Earth in three physical states.

(C) Water is chemically indestructible.

(D) Water is a poor conductor of electricity.

Question 26 refers to the following statement.

The disparaging remarks about her performance on the job made Margaret uncomfortable.

26. The word *disparaging* is closest in meaning to

(A) congratulatory.

(B) immoral.

(C) whimsical.

(D) insulting.

27. The Japanese form of poetry called *haiku* is known for its

(A) brevity and concision.

(B) elaborate and flowery description.

(C) logic and directness of statement.

(D) humor and lifelike detail.

28. Hamlet's "To Be or Not to Be" speech, in the play by William Shakespeare, is an example of the dramatic technique known as

    (A) aside.
    (B) dialogue.
    (C) soliloquy.
    (D) comic relief.

29. Which of the following types of literature is characterized as realistic and contains a moral?

    (A) Fairy tale
    (B) Myth
    (C) Legend
    (D) Parable

II. MATHEMATICS

30. Inside a barn were lambs and people. If we counted 30 heads and 104 legs in the barn, how many lambs and how many people were in the barn?

    (A) 10 lambs and 20 people
    (B) 16 lambs and 14 people
    (C) 18 lambs and 16 people
    (D) 22 lambs and 8 people

Use the figure below and the following facts to answer Question 31.

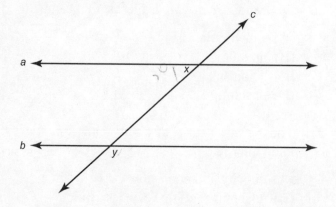

Lines a and b are parallel, c is a line, and the measure of angle x is 50°.

31. What is the measure of angle y?

    (A) 50°
    (B) 100°
    (C) 130°
    (D) 80°

32. In the given figure, assume that AD is a line. What is the measure of angle AXB?

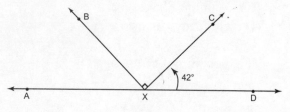

    (A) 48°
    (B) 90°
    (C) 42°
    (D) There is not enough information given to answer the question.

33. Which formula can be used to find the area of the triangle shown below?

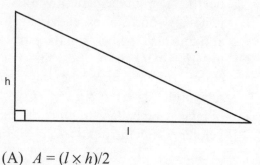

    (A) $A = (l \times h)/2$
    (B) $A = (l + h)/2$
    (C) $A = 2(l + h)$
    (D) $A = 2(l \times h)$

34. Which formula can be used to find the area of the figure below? (Assume the curve is *half* of a circle.)

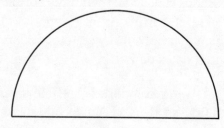

(A) $A = \pi r$

(B) $A = 2\pi r^2$

(C) $A = \pi r^2$

(D) $A = \pi r^2/2$

35. What is the greatest common divisor of 120 and 252?

(A) 2

(B) 3

(C) 6

(D) 12

36. How many odd prime numbers are there *between* 1 and 20?

(A) 7

(B) 8

(C) 9

(D) 10

37. Round the following number to the nearest hundredths place: 287.416.

(A) 300

(B) 290

(C) 287.42

(D) 287.4139

38. According to the following graph which one of the following statements is true?

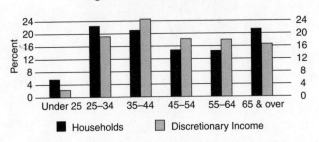

Age of Household Head

■ Households　□ Discretionary Income

Percentage Distribution of Households and Discretionary Income (Total U.S. = 100%)

(A) Middle-aged households tend to have greater discretionary income.

(B) The youngest have the most discretionary income.

(C) The oldest have the most discretionary income.

(D) The older people get, the less discretionary income they have.

39. The floor of a 99 foot × 129 foot rectangular room depicted in the diagram is to be covered in two different types of material. The total cost of covering the entire room is $136. The cost of covering the inner rectangle is $80. The cost of covering the shaded area is $56. To compute the cost of material per square foot used to cover the shaded area, which of the following pieces of information is (are) NOT necessary?

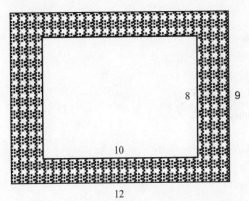

I.　The total cost of covering the entire room.

II.　The cost of covering the inner rectangle.

III.　The cost of covering the shaded area.

(A) I only

(B) II only

(C) I and II only

(D) I and III only

Use the Pythagorean theorem to answer Question 40.

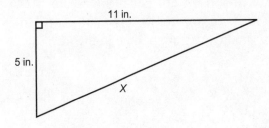

40. How many cups of water does a 7-gallon container of water hold?

    (A) 28
    (B) 56
    (C) 70
    (D) 112

41. If the two triangles, *ABC* and *DEF*, shown below, are similar, what is the length of side *DF*?

    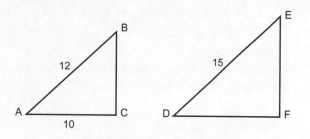

    (A) 12.5 units
    (B) 13 units
    (C) 12 units
    (D) 13.5 units

42. What is the solution to the equation $\frac{x}{3} - 9 = 15$?

    (A) 18
    (B) 8
    (C) 36
    (D) 72

43. Translate this problem into a one-variable equation and then solve the equation.

    There are ten vehicles parked in a parking lot. Each is either a car with four tires or a motorcycle with two tires. (Do not count any spare tires.) There are 26 wheels in the lot. How many cars are parked in the lot?

    (A) 8
    (B) 6
    (C) 5
    (D) 3

44. Which equation could be used to solve the following problem?

    Three consecutive odd numbers add up to 117. What are they?

    (A) $x + (x + 2) + (x + 4) = 117$
    (B) $1x + 3x + 5x = 117$
    (C) $x + x + x = 117$
    (D) $x + (x + 1) + (x + 3) = 117$

45. Use the pie chart below to answer the following question: If the total number of people voting was 600, which of the following statements are true?

    Votes for City Council

    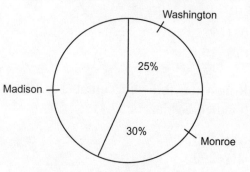

    I.   Madison received more votes than Monroe and Washington combined.
    II. Madison received 45% of the votes.
    III. Monroe received 180 votes.
    IV. Madison received 180 votes.

    (A) I and III only
    (B) I and IV only
    (C) II and III only
    (D) II and IV only

46. Which of the following scenarios could be represented by the graph shown below?

    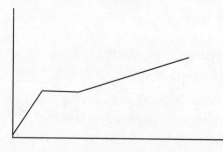

(A) Mr. Cain mowed grass at a steady rate for a while, took a short break, and then finished the job at a steady but slower rate.

(B) Mr. Cain mowed grass at a steady rate for a while, mowed at a steady but slower rate, and then took a break.

(C) Mr. Cain mowed grass at a variable rate for a while, took a short break, and then finished the job at a variable rate.

(D) Mr. Cain mowed grass at a steady rate for a while, took a short break, and then finished the job at a steady but faster pace.

47. Which one of the statements below is necessarily true according to the bar graph below?

Ms. Patton's Earnings, 1998–2002

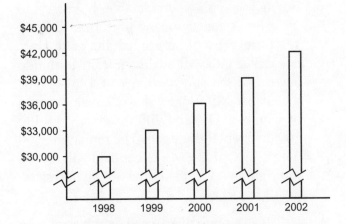

(A) The range of Ms. Patton's earnings for the years shown is $15,000.

(B) Ms. Patton's annual pay increases were consistent over the years shown.

(C) Ms. Patton earned $45,000 in 2003.

(D) Ms. Patton's average income for the years shown was $38,000.

48. Which equation could be used to solve the following problem?

Acme Taxicab Company computes fares for riders by the following formula: A passenger is charged three dollars for getting into the cab, then is charged two dollars more for every mile or fraction of a mile of the ride.

What would be the fare for a ride of 10.2 miles?

(A) $3 \times (2 \times 10.2) = y$
(B) $3 + (2 + 11) = y$
(C) $3 \times (2 + 10.2) = y$
(D) $3 + (2 \times 11) = y$

49. What does it mean that multiplication and division are *inverse operations*?

(A) Multiplication is commutative, whereas division is not. For example: 4×2 gives the same product as 2×4, but $4 \div 2$ is not the same as $2 \div 4$.

(B) Whether multiplying or dividing a value by 1, the value remains the same. For example, 9×1 equals 9; $9 \div 1$ also equals 9.

(C) When performing complex calculations involving several operations, all multiplication must be completed before completing any division, such as in $8 \div 2 \times 4 + 7 - 1$.

(D) The operations "undo" each other. For example, multiplying 11 by 3 gives 33. Dividing 33 by 3 then takes you back to 11.

50. The daily high temperatures in Frostbite, Minnesota, for one week in January were as follows:

Sunday:	−2°F
Monday:	3°F
Tuesday:	0°F
Wednesday:	−4°F
Thursday:	−5°F
Friday:	−1°F
Saturday:	2°F

What was the mean daily high temperature for that week?

(A) 7
(B) −7
(C) −1
(D) 1

51. Which of the following illustrates the distributive property?

   (A) Multiplying 23 by 16 gives the same product as multiplying 16 by 23.
   (B) The numbers 65, 70, and 12 can be added together in any order; the sum will always be the same.
   (C) The sum of 102 and 9 is the same as the sum of 9 and 102.
   (D) The product of 3 and 42 is the same as the sum of the products 3×2 and 3×40.

52. Which equation could be used to answer the following question?

   Together, a pen and a pencil cost $2.59 (ignoring tax). The pen cost $1.79 more than the pencil. What was the cost of the pencil?

   (A) $x = (2.59 - 1.79) \div 2$
   (B) $2.59 = x - 1.79$
   (C) $2.59 = x + (x + 1.79)$
   (D) $x = 2.59 - 1.79$

53. Matt has earned the following scores on his first six weekly mathematics tests: 91, 89, 82, 95, 86, and 79. He hopes for an average (mean) of 90 percent, which would just barely give him an A– in math class on his first report card. How many more total points does Matt have to earn to qualify for an A–?

   (A) 87
   (B) 3
   (C) 90
   (D) 18

54. Ms. Williams plans to buy carpeting for her living room floor. The room is a rectangle measuring 14 feet by 20 feet. She wants no carpet seams on her floor, even if that means that some carpeting will go to waste. The car-

peting she wants comes in 16-foot-wide rolls. What is the minimum amount of carpeting that will have to be wasted if Ms. Williams insists upon her no-seams requirement?

   (A) 40 square feet
   (B) 60 square feet
   (C) 80 square feet
   (D) 100 square feet

55. How many lines of symmetry do all nonsquare rectangles have?

   (A) 0
   (B) 2
   (C) 4
   (D) 8

56. Bemus School is conducting a lottery to raise funds for new band uniforms. Exactly 1,000 tickets will be printed and sold. Only one ticket stub will be drawn from a drum to determine the single winner of a big-screen television. All tickets have equal chances of winning. The first 700 tickets are sold to 700 different individuals. The remaining 300 tickets are sold to Mr. Greenfield. Given this information, which of the following statements are true?

   I.   It is impossible to tell in advance who will win.
   II. Mr. Greenfield will probably win.
   III. Someone other than Mr. Greenfield will probably win.
   IV. The likelihood that Mr. Greenfield will win is the same as the likelihood that someone else will win.

   (A) I and II only
   (B) I and III only
   (C) II and IV only
   (D) III and IV only

57. How many ten thousands are there in 1 million?

(A) 100
(B) 10
(C) 1,000
(D) 10,000

58. An owner of twin Siamese cats knows the following data:

I. the cost of a can of cat food
II. the volume of a can of cat food
III. the number of cans of cat food eaten each day by one cat
IV. the weight of the cat food in one can

Which of the data above can be used to determine the cost of cat food for seven days for the two cats?

(A) I and II only
(B) I and III only
(C) I and IV only
(D) III and IV only

59. The distance from Tami's house to Ken's house is three miles. The distance from Ken's house to The Soda Depot is two miles. Which of the following statements are true?

I. The greatest possible distance between Tami's house and The Soda Depot is five miles.
II. The greatest possible distance between Tami's house and The Soda Depot is six miles.
III. The shortest possible distance between Tami's house and The Soda Depot is one mile.
IV. The shortest possible distance between Tami's house and The Soda Depot is two miles.

(A) I and III only
(B) I and IV only
(C) II and III only
(D) II and IV only

III. SOCIAL STUDIES

60. The characteristics of fascism include all of the following EXCEPT

(A) totalitarianism.
(B) democracy.
(C) romanticism.
(D) militarism.

61. The industrial economy of the nineteenth century was based on all of the following EXCEPT

(A) the availability of raw materials.
(B) an equitable distribution of profits among those involved in production.
(C) the availability of capital.
(D) a distribution system to market finished products.

62. "Jim Crow" laws were laws that

(A) effectively prohibited blacks from voting in state and local elections.
(B) restricted American Indians to United States government reservations.
(C) restricted open-range ranching in the Great Plains.
(D) established separate segregated facilities for blacks and whites.

63. Which of the following is used to effect the release of a person from improper imprisonment?

(A) A writ of mandamus
(B) A writ of habeas corpus
(C) The Fourth Amendment requirement that police have probable cause in order to obtain a search warrant
(D) The Supreme Court's decision in *Roe v. Wade*

64. The intellectual movement that encouraged the use of reason and science and anticipated human progress was called the

(A) American system.
(B) mercantilism.
(C) Enlightenment.
(D) Age of Belief.

65. Which of the following is the correct chronological order for the events in history listed below?

I.   Puritans arrive in New England.
II. Protestant Reformation begins.
III. Columbus sets sail across the Atlantic.
IV. Magna Carta is signed in England.

(A) IV, III, II, I
(B) IV, III, I, II
(C) III, IV, II, I
(D) III, II, I, IV

66. Thomas Paine's pamphlet *Common Sense* was significant because it

(A) alerted thousands of colonists to the abuses of British rule, the oppressiveness of the monarchy, and the advantages of colonial independence.
(B) rallied American spirit during the bleak winter of 1776, when it appeared that Washington's forces, freezing and starving at Valley Forge, had no hope of surviving the winter, much less defeating the British.
(C) called for a strong central government to rule the newly independent American states and foresaw the difficulties inherent within the Articles of Confederation.
(D) asserted to its British readers that they could not beat the American colonists militarily unless they could isolate New England from the rest of the American colonies.

67. In the United States government, the function of checks and balances is meant to

(A) regulate the amount of power each branch of government has.
(B) make each branch of government independent from the others.
(C) give more power to the president.
(D) give more power to the Supreme Court.

68. The Fifteenth Amendment of the United States Constitution was ratified in 1870 to grant

(A) black women and men the right to vote.
(B) citizenship for blacks.
(C) freedom of slaves.
(D) black men the right to vote.

69. Which of the following groups did NOT play a role in the settlement of the English colonies in America?

(A) Roman Catholics
(B) Puritans
(C) Mormons
(D) Quakers

70. On the following map, which letter represents the Philippines?

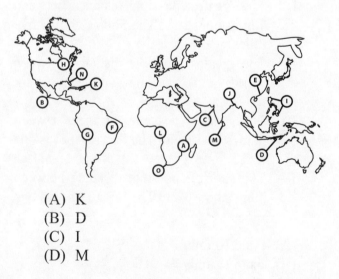

(A) K
(B) D
(C) I
(D) M

71. The Bill of Rights

   (A) listed the grievances of the colonists against the British.
   (B) forbade the federal government from encroaching on the rights of citizens.
   (C) gave all white males the right to vote.
   (D) specified the rights of slaves.

Use the bar graph to answer Questions 72 and 73.

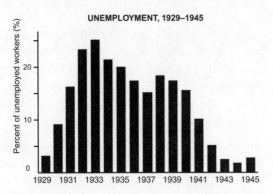

UNEMPLOYMENT, 1929–1945

72. According to the bar graph, the unemployment rate was *highest* in

   (A) 1929.
   (B) 1933.
   (C) 1938.
   (D) 1944.

73. According to the graph, the unemployment rate was *lowest* in

   (A) 1929.
   (B) 1933.
   (C) 1938.
   (D) 1944.

74. According to the following graph, which one of the following statements is true?

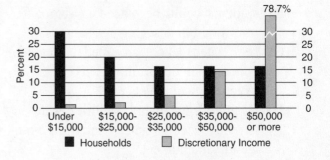

Households by Income Class

Percentage Distribution of Households and Discretionary Income (Total U.S. = 100 percent)

   (A) About 50% of households had annual incomes of less than $15,000.
   (B) Almost 75% of households had annual incomes of $50,000 or more.
   (C) About 78% of households had annual incomes of $50,000 or more.
   (D) About 20% of households had annual incomes between $15,000 and $25,000.

75. The launching of *Sputnik* by the Soviet Union in 1957 triggered increased emphasis on all of the following areas of study EXCEPT

   (A) world history.
   (B) math.
   (C) science.
   (D) foreign languages.

76. All of the following were true of education in the southern colonies EXCEPT

   (A) Private tutors were used to educate the sons of wealthy plantation owners.
   (B) The education of girls was limited to the knowledge of how to manage a household.
   (C) Slaves were taught to read so that they could study the Bible.
   (D) Teaching a slave to read or write was a criminal act.

77. The ruling of the Supreme Court in *Brown v. Board of Education of Topeka, Kansas* (1954) found that

    (A) separate educational facilities could offer equal educational opportunities to students.
    (B) students could be placed in segregated tracks within desegregated schools.
    (C) segregated schools resulted in unequal educational opportunity but caused no psychological effects.
    (D) separate educational facilities were inherently unequal and violated the Fourteenth Amendment.

78. President Lyndon B. Johnson's "War on Poverty" resulted in all of the following EXCEPT

    (A) the Peace Corps.
    (B) Head Start.
    (C) the Elementary and Secondary Education Act.
    (D) VISTA.

79. The Education for All Handicapped Children Act of 1975 mandates that schools provide free and appropriate education for all of the following EXCEPT the

    (A) mentally handicapped.
    (B) physically handicapped.
    (C) socially–emotionally handicapped.
    (D) learning disabled.

80. When a member of the House of Representatives helps a citizen from his or her district receive federal aid to which that citizen is entitled, the representative's action is referred to as

    (A) casework.
    (B) pork barrel legislation.
    (C) lobbying.
    (D) logrolling.

81. The term *Trail of Tears* refers to the

    (A) Mormon migration from Nauvoo, Illinois, to what is now Utah.
    (B) forced migration of the Cherokee tribe from the southern Appalachians to what is now Oklahoma.
    (C) westward migration along the Oregon Trail.
    (D) migration into Kentucky along the Wilderness Road.

82. The United States Constitution defines the powers of the United States Congress and the states. The United States Constitution reserves powers to the states in the Tenth Amendment, while Article I, Section 8 of the United States Constitution delegates powers to the federal government. Some powers are shared concurrently between the states and federal government. Which of the following powers are concurrent powers?

    I. Lay and collect taxes
    II. Regulate commerce
    III. Establish post offices
    IV. Borrow money

    (A) I and II only
    (B) II and III only
    (C) III and IV only
    (D) I and IV only

83. Which of the following statements best defines the role of the World Trade Organization (WTO)?

    (A) It resolves trade disputes and attempts to formulate policy to open world markets to free trade through monetary policy and regulation of corruption.
    (B) It is an advocate for human rights and democracy by regulating child labor and providing economic aid to poor countries.
    (C) It establishes alliances to regulate disputes and polices ethnic intimidation.
    (D) It regulates trade within the United States in order to eliminate monopolistic trade practices.

84. The drought of the 1930s that spanned from Texas to North Dakota was caused by

    I.   overgrazing and overuse of farmland.
    II. natural phenomena, such as below-average rainfall and wind erosion.
    III. environmental factors, such as changes in the jet stream.
    IV. the lack of government subsidies for new irrigation technology.

    (A) I and II only
    (B) II and III only
    (C) I and III only
    (D) II and IV only

85. Which of the following best describes a major difference between a state government and the federal government?

    (A) State governments have more responsibility for public education than the federal government.
    (B) State governments are more dependent on the personal income tax for revenue than the federal government.
    (C) State governments are more dependent on the system of checks and balances than the federal government.
    (D) State governments are subject to term limits, whereas federal government representatives serve unlimited terms.

86. The Battle of Waterloo is historically significant because it marked which of the following?

    (A) The defeat of William the Conqueror
    (B) The end of the French Revolution
    (C) The defeat of Napoleon
    (D) The start of the Thirty Years' War

87. The most advanced pre-Columbian civilizations of Mesoamerica were the

    (A) Aztecs and Incas.
    (B) Maya and Aztecs.
    (C) Toltecs and Pueblos.
    (D) Olmecs and the Iroquois.

IV. SCIENCE

88. To apply the concept of time zones, students need to have a clear understanding of

    (A) the International Date Line.
    (B) the Earth's yearly revolution.
    (C) the concept of meridians of longitude.
    (D) the concept of the parallels of latitude.

89. Which of the following is considered to be evidence for plate tectonics?

    (A) Continental coastline "fit"
    (B) Identical fossil evidence at "fit" locations
    (C) Intense geological activity in mountainous regions
    (D) All of the above

90. The Pacific Northwest receives the greatest annual precipitation in the United States. Which of the following statements best identifies the reason that this occurs?

    (A) The jet stream moving south from Canada is responsible for pushing storms through the region.
    (B) The region's mountains along the coast cause air masses to rise and cool, thereby reducing their moisture-carrying capacity.
    (C) Numerous storms originating in Asia build in intensity as they move across the Pacific Ocean and then dump their precipitation upon reaching land.
    (D) The ocean breezes push moisture-laden clouds and fog into the coastal region, producing humid, moist conditions that result in precipitation.

91. The probability of parents' offspring showing particular traits can be predicted by using

    (A) the Linnaean System.
    (B) DNA tests.
    (C) the Punnett Square.
    (D) none of the above.

92. A material with definite volume but no definite shape is called

    (A) titanium.
    (B) a gas.
    (C) a liquid.
    (D) a solid

93. The intensity of an earthquake is measured by a(n)

    (A) thermograph.
    (B) seismograph.
    (C) telegraph.
    (D) odometer.

94. Which of the following types of pollution or atmospheric phenomena are correctly matched with their underlying causes?

    I. Global warming—carbon dioxide and methane
    II. Acid rain—sulfur dioxide and nitrogen dioxide
    III. Ozone depletion—chlorofluorocarbons and sunlight
    IV. Aurora borealis—solar flares and magnetism

    (A) I and II only
    (B) II and III only
    (C) I and IV only
    (D) I, II, III, and IV

95. Which of the following observations best describes the "Ring of Fire"?

    (A) Similarities in rock formations and continental coastlines created the "Ring of Fire."

    (B) Earth's plates collide at convergent margins, separate at divergent margins, and move laterally at transform-fault boundaries.
    (C) Earthquakes produced waves that continue to travel through the Earth in all directions and created the "Ring of Fire."
    (D) Volcanoes form when lava accumulates and hardens.

96. _____ is defined as the ability to do work.

    (A) Force
    (B) Energy
    (C) Speed
    (D) Distance

97. The atomic number for neutral (unionized) atoms as listed in the periodic table refers to

    (A) the number of neutrons in an atom.
    (B) the number of protons in an atom.
    (C) the number of electrons in an atom.
    (D) both (B) and (C).

98. Which of the following is a phenomenon involving the physical properties of a substance?

    (A) Corrosion of iron
    (B) Burning of wood
    (C) Rocket engine ignition
    (D) Melting of ice

99. Isotopes of a given element contain

    (A) more electrons than protons with equal numbers of neutrons.
    (B) more protons than electrons with equal numbers of neutrons.
    (C) equal numbers of protons and electrons with differing numbers of neutrons.
    (D) unequal numbers of protons and electrons with differing numbers of neutrons.

100. Newton's second law of motion states "the net force acting on a body is equal to the product of its mass and its acceleration." Which of the following is a good example of the law's application?

    (A) Decreased friction between surfaces by means of lubrication
    (B) Potential energy stored in a compressed spring
    (C) A rocket lifting off at Cape Canaveral with increasing speed
    (D) Using a claw hammer to pull a nail out with multiplied force

101. Which of the following is most likely to contain the greatest thermal energy?

    (A) The Pacific Ocean with an average temperature of ~5°F
    (B) A 1 g sample of molten metal at 2,000°F
    (C) A bucket of water at 75°F
    (D) Lake Michigan at an average temperature of ~5°F

102. Which cellular component is responsible for the regulation of exchanges of substances between a cell and its environment?

    (A) The endoplasmic reticulum
    (B) The cell nucleus
    (C) The cytoplasm
    (D) The cell membrane

103. Humans have 46 chromosomes in their body cells. How many chromosomes are found in the zygote?

    (A) 2
    (B) 10
    (C) 23
    (D) 46

104. All of the following are true EXCEPT:

    (A) Heredity is the study of how traits are passed from parent to offspring.
    (B) The chemical molecule that carries an organism's genetic makeup is called DNA.
    (C) Sections of the DNA molecule that determine specific traits are called chromosomes.
    (D) The genetic makeup of an organism is altered through bioengineering.

105. Which of the following sources of energy is nonrenewable?

    (A) Hydrogen cell
    (B) Geothermal
    (C) Nuclear
    (D) Hydroelectric

106. Darwin's original theory of natural selection asserts that

    (A) all organisms have descended with modification from a common ancestor.
    (B) random genetic drift plays a major role in speciation.
    (C) species characteristics are inherited by means of genes.
    (D) speciation is usually due to the gradual accumulation of small genetic changes.

107. The lunar period is nearest in length to

    (A) 24 hours.
    (B) 30 days.
    (C) 365 days.
    (D) 1 week.

108. A supernova normally occurs when

    (A) a star first initiates fusion.
    (B) galaxies collide.
    (C) the end of a star's lifetime nears, with its nuclear fuel exhausted.
    (D) a wandering comet plunges into a star's interior.

109. The most important factor in Earth's seasonal patterns is the

(A) distance from the sun to Earth.
(B) Earth's rotation period of 24 hours.
(C) tilting of the Earth's axis.
(D) the moon and associated tides.

110. Metamorphic rocks are

(A) derived from igneous rocks.
(B) unrelated to igneous rocks.
(C) a type of sedimentary rock.
(D) a type of rock not found on this planet.

111. Seafloor spreading is characterized as

(A) plate spreading with upwelling magma forming ridges.
(B) plate collisions with associated ridge formation.
(C) plate spreading with no ridge formation.
(D) plate collisions with no ridge formation.

112. Igneous rocks are formed by

(A) magma cooling in underground cells and pockets.
(B) magma ejected aboveground as lava, which cools.
(C) layers of sediment collecting and compacting at the bottom of lakes and seas.
(D) both (A) and (B).

113. Which of the following is the name of the cell formed by the union of a male sperm and a female ovum that develops into the embryo?

(A) Haploid
(B) Zygote
(C) Diploid
(D) Cytoplasm

114. The diagram below shows a path for electric flow. As the electrically charged particle flow moves through one complete circuit, it would NOT have to go through

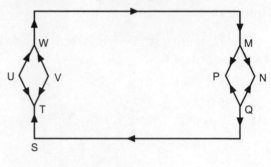

(A) V to get to W.
(B) W to get to M.
(C) Q to get to T.
(D) T to get to S.

115. A positive condition depending on the absence of cold is

(A) Fahrenheit.
(B) intense artificial cold.
(C) heat.
(D) Celsius.

116. A hot-air balloon rises when propane burners in the basket are used to heat the air inside the balloon. Which of the following statements correctly identifies the explanation for this phenomenon?

(A) Heated gas molecules move faster inside the balloon; their force striking the inside causes the balloon to rise.
(B) Hot gas molecules are themselves larger than cool gas molecules, resulting in the expansion of the gas.
(C) The amount of empty space between gas molecules increases as the temperature of the gas increases, resulting in the expansion of the gas.
(D) The combustion of propane releases product gases that are lighter than air and that are trapped in the balloon, causing it to rise.

117. A rock picked up at a bottom of a hill was found to contain tiny pieces of seashells. Which of the following is the best explanation of how this rock was formed?

    (A) It was formed on or near Earth's surface from magma or lava that flowed during a volcanic eruption.
    (B) It was formed when minerals deep inside Earth were subjected to great heat and pressure.
    (C) It was formed when sediments sank to the bottom of an ancient sea and were subjected to great pressure for long periods of time.
    (D) It was formed by seafloor spreading and erosion of the mid-ocean ridge deep in the ocean.

118. Earth's moon is

    (A) generally closer to the sun than it is to Earth.
    (B) generally closer to Earth than it is to the sun.
    (C) generally equidistant between Earth and the sun.
    (D) closer to Earth during part of the year and closer to the sun for the rest of the year.

119. Which of the following statements correctly describes each group of vertebrates?

    I.   Amphibians are cold-blooded and spend part of their life cycle in water and part on land.
    II. Reptiles are generally warm-blooded and have scales that cover their skin.
    III. Fish are cold-blooded, breathe with gills, and are covered by scales.
    IV. Mammals are warm-blooded and have milk glands and hair.

    (A) I and IV only
    (B) I, III, and IV only
    (C) IV only
    (D) I, II, III, and IV

120. Which of the following statements is NOT true?

    (A) Infectious diseases are caused by viruses, bacteria, or protists.
    (B) Cancers and hereditary diseases can be infectious.
    (C) Environmental hazards can cause disease.
    (D) The immune system protects the body from disease.

Detailed Explanations of Answers for Practice Test 1

ELEMENTARY EDUCATION: CONTENT KNOWLEDGE (0014)

1. (C)	25. (B)	49. (D)	73. (D)	97. (D)
2. (C)	26. (D)	50. (C)	74. (D)	98. (D)
3. (B)	27. (A)	51. (D)	75. (A)	99. (C)
4. (D)	28. (C)	52. (C)	76. (C)	100. (C)
5. (D)	29. (D)	53. (D)	77. (D)	101. (A)
6. (C)	30. (D)	54. (A)	78. (A)	102. (D)
7. (C)	31. (C)	55. (B)	79. (C)	103. (D)
8. (C)	32. (A)	56. (B)	80. (A)	104. (C)
9. (A)	33. (A)	57. (A)	81. (B)	105. (C)
10. (B)	34. (D)	58. (B)	82. (D)	106. (A)
11. (C)	35. (D)	59. (A)	83. (A)	107. (B)
12. (B)	36. (A)	60. (B)	84. (A)	108. (C)
13. (B)	37. (C)	61. (B)	85. (A)	109. (C)
14. (D)	38. (A)	62. (D)	86. (C)	110. (A)
15. (A)	39. (C)	63. (B)	87. (B)	111. (A)
16. (A)	40. (D)	64. (C)	88. (C)	112. (D)
17. (A)	41. (A)	65. (A)	89. (A)	113. (B)
18. (A)	42. (D)	66. (A)	90. (B)	114. (A)
19. (B)	43. (D)	67. (A)	91. (C)	115. (C)
20. (B)	44. (A)	68. (D)	92. (C)	116. (C)
21. (A)	45. (C)	69. (C)	93. (B)	117. (C)
22. (C)	46. (A)	70. (C)	94. (D)	118. (B)
23. (C)	47. (B)	71. (B)	95. (B)	119. (B)
24. (B)	48. (D)	72. (B)	96. (B)	120. (B)

PRACTICE TEST 1 PROGRESS CHART

Language Arts Content   ____/29

1	2	3	4	5	6	7	8	9	10	11

12	13	14	15	16	17	18	19	20	21	22

23	24	25	26	27	28	29

Mathematics Content   ____/30

30	31	32	33	34	35	36	37	38	39	40

41	42	43	44	45	46	47	48	49	50	51

52	53	54	55	56	57	58	59

Social Studies Content   ____/28

60	61	62	63	64	65	66	67	68	69	70

71	72	73	74	75	76	77	78	79	80	81

82	83	84	85	86	87

Science Content   ____/33

88	89	90	91	92	93	94	95	96	97	98

99	100	101	102	103	104	105	106	107	108	109

110	111	112	113	114	115	116	117	118	119	120

1.   (C)

The correct answer is (C). A phrase cannot be a complete thought. A clause, on the other hand, can be a complete thought.

2.   (C)

A metaphor is a comparison between two items without the use of *like* or *as*. In the proverb "death" is called a "black camel." A simile is a comparison that uses *like* or *as*. Alliteration is the repetition of a consonant sound, and hyperbole is an exaggeration.

3.   (B)

The most basic definition of literacy is the ability to read and write.

4.   (D)

The index of the book (A) is arranged in alphabetical order according to topic; the page number is generally given directly after the topic. The entries are not according to concrete and abstract (B) or linear and recursive (C) relationships. Answer choice (D) is the best answer; it gives the order of occurrence.

5.   (D)

Choice (D) "time marches on" is the best answer. The first line of the poem points to the theme of this poem. Answers (B) and (C) are only partially true; (B) does not reflect the gentleness of the poem; and (C) requires introducing the concept of reading into the poem, something that is not immediately present.

6.   (C)

Choice (C) is the best answer. One can interpret the poem to be an expression of love of nature (B) and humanity (A), but there is no option to choose both. (D) is not a good answer because the poem illustrates the cycle of life as opposed to the "arbitrary nature of natural things."

7.   (C)

Essays fall into four rough categories: speculative, argumentative, narrative, and expository. The purpose of this essay is narrative (C). The narrative essay may recount an incident or a series of incidents and is almost always autobiographical, in order to make a point. The informality of the storytelling makes the narrative essay less insistent than the argumentative essay but more directed than the speculative essay. But the thesis may not be as obvious or clear-cut as that in an expository or argumentative essay. This essay is not speculative (A). The speculative essay (A) is so named because, as its Latin root suggests, it looks at ideas and explores them rather than explains them. The purposes of the argumentative essay (B) are always clear: to present a point and provide evidence, which may be factual or anecdotal, and to support it. The structure is usually very formal, as in a debate, with counter positions and counterarguments. An expository essay (D) may have narrative elements, but that aspect is minor and subservient to that of explanation.

8. (C)

Both the use of "your" and "myself "is incorrect so (C) is the correct answer. While the misuse of myself is rampant in spoken English, the correct usage is only reflexive—that is, when the subject and the object of the sentence (I gave myself a raise). In all other cases, "I" or "me" should be used. Both (A) and (B) are tempting choices but neither the use of numerals instead of words nor the use of a period instead of a semicolon is grammatically incorrect.

9. (A)

The correct answer is (A). *Graphemes* are "the written symbols for the speech sounds." The word *phonemes* refers to "the speech sounds." *Phonics* refers to "the method of teaching reading that emphasizes the association between the grapheme and the phoneme." *Semantics* refers to "the study of the meaning of language."

10. (B)

A hands-on activity will best help the students learn about data collection. (B) is the only choice that employs a hands-on activity, so this is the best answer. The students would learn about direct observation by watching Ms. Thompson tickle the mouse and the philodendron (A); however, this method would not be as effective as allowing the students to conduct their own data collection. Research suggests that viewing a video (C) is an inefficient method of learning. Having a guest speaker tell the students about data collection (D) is not a good choice for first graders.

11. (C)

The passage suggests that Douglass was concerned with raising social consciousness about slavery. His interest in refuting those who doubted his claims was for the sake of authenticity.

12. (B)

Douglass was one of the eminent human rights leaders of the nineteenth century. All the other choices, while true, are irrelevant to the question and are not supported by the text.

13. (B)

The passage states, "Mrs. Auld recognized Frederick's intellectual acumen." A synonym for *acumen* is *intelligence*, *insight*, or *natural ability*. The other choices are inaccurate.

14. (D)

Choices (A), (B), and (C) are too vague or ill defined. Thus, choice (D) is correct.

15. (A)

An "impromptu" speech is one given extemporaneously, without prior preparation, or "off the cuff."

16. (A)

The best answer is (A)—it is the main idea of the passage. Choice (B) is partially correct—if it has to be specific, it should refer to the brake lights on the helmet. Choice (C) is incomplete as a key or main idea of the passage and the same could be said of choice (D).

17. (A)

It would follow that the rationale behind the new brake light requirement for cars in California is the same for all other vehicles on the road. Hence, choice (A) is the correct answer. (B) is illogical; in (C) any car driven in California, wherever it has been bought, cannot be exempt from the requirement; in (D) Harris can go on inventing while remaining a farmer—he'll make more money doing both.

18. (A)

Choice (A) is the most logical and appropriate answer. Hence, it is the correct answer. Choice (B) can be, but is not necessarily true; (C) is a logical possibility but will not drastically raise car prices beyond affordability; (D) may be true, but not as road hazards.

19. (B)

The ranchers believe that killing the eagles will protect their ranches. This is understood by the implication that "attract[ing] and kill[ing] predators . . . in an effort to preserve young grazing animals" will protect their ranches.

20. (B)

The author's use of words such as "mighty bald eagle" and "threatened by a new menace" supports concern for the topic. For the most part, the author appears objective; thus, choice (B), concerned interest, is the correct answer.

21. (A)

(A) is correct since something that is *original* is new; fresh; inventive; or novel: an original way of advertising. By definition, mediocre means that something is ordinary or of moderate quality; neither good nor bad; barely adequate. Ordinary (D) and commonplace (C) are probably closest to the meaning of mediocre. Passable, (B) suggests bare adequacy.

22. (C)

Choice (C) is the correct answer. Juliet in *Romeo and Juliet*, by William Shakespeare, speaks those lines.

23. (C)

The protagonist is the central character (C).

24. (B)

Foreshadowing is used to hint at future plot developments, not to manifest characters' or speakers' emotions. It is not used prominently in lyric poetry or in ballads.

25. (B)

The first paragraph states that this is the reason that water is a most unusual substance. Choices (A) and (C) list unusual properties of water, but they are not developed in the same manner as the property stated in choice (B). Choice (D) is not correct under any circumstances.

26. (D)

Insulting (D) is the correct definition. The other terms are either antonyms or incorrect interpretations.

27. (A)

(A) is correct. By definition, haiku poetry is too short to contain much elaborate description. The haiku form does not emphasize logic or direct statements. And while some haiku poetry is humorous and/or contains lifelike details, these qualities do not characterize all haiku poems.

28. (C)

The "To Be or Not to Be" speech is a soliloquy in which Hamlet utters his thoughts aloud at length. It is not an aside because he is not speaking briefly to the audience in the midst of other action. Because Hamlet is the only one speaking, it is not a dialogue, nor is it an example of comic relief, due to the serious tone of the speech.

29. (D)

A parable is a story that is realistic and has a moral that teaches a lesson. (D) is the correct answer. Fairy tales have the element of magic, often have a certain pattern, and may present an ideal to the reader. Myths are stories written to explain things that the teller does not understand. Legends are usually exaggerated stories about real people, places, and things.

30. (D)

Let x be the number of lambs in the barn. Then, because each person and lamb has only one head, the number of people must be $30 - x$. Because lambs have four legs, the number of lamb legs equals $4x$. Similarly, the number of human legs equals $2(30 - x)$. Thus, the equation for the total number of legs (104) is

$$4x + 2(30 - x) = 104$$

Use the distributive property, $a(b - c) = ab - ac$, to get

$$4x + 60 - 2x = 104$$

which reduces to

$$2x + 60 = 104$$

Subtract 60 from each side to get

$$2x = 44, \text{ or } x = 22.$$

So the number of lambs is 22, and the number of people is $30 - 22 = 8$.

31. (C)

When two parallel lines are crossed by another line (called a transversal), eight angles are formed. However, there are only two angle measures among the eight angles, and the sum of the two measures is 180°. All the smaller angles will have the same measure, and all the larger angles will have the same measure. In this case, the smaller angles all measure 50°, so the larger angles (including angle y) all measure 130°. To solve this problem: the smaller angle + the larger angle = 180; substitute 50 for the smaller angle: $50 + y = 180$; subtract 50 from both sides: $y = 130$.

32. (A)

One must know two things to answer the question. One is the meaning of the small square at the vertex of angle BXC. That symbol means that angle BXC is a *right angle* (one with 90°). The second is that a straight line, such as AXD, can be thought of as a *straight angle*, which measures 180°. Therefore, because the sum of the angles DXC (42°) and BXC (90°) is 132°, the remaining angle on the line must measure 48° (180° − 132°).

33. (A)

The area of any rectangle is equal to the measure of its length times the measure of its width (or, to say it differently, the measure of its base times the measure of its height). A right triangle can be seen as half of a rectangle (sliced diagonally). Answer (A) represents, in effect, half of a rectangle's area (i.e., the area divided by 2).

the 1. Then we leave off all the numbers to the right of the 1. In our problem, a 6 is in the thousandths place, so we change the 1 to a 2 to get 287.42 as our answer.

34. (D)

The formula for finding the area of any circle is $A = \pi r^2$ (about 3.14 times the length of the radius times itself). In this case, take half of πr^2; hence, answer choice (D) is correct.

35. (D)

To find the greatest common divisor (GCD), factor both numbers and look for common factors. The product of these common factors is the GCD. The GCD here is the greatest integer that divides into both 120 and 252.

$$120 = 2^3 \times 3 \times 5 \text{ and}$$
$$252 = 2^2 \times 3^2 \times 7,$$

so the GCD $= 2^2 \times 3 = 12$.

36. (A)

A prime number is an integer that is greater than 1 and that has no integer divisors other than 1 and itself. So the prime numbers between 1 and 20 (not including 1 and 20) are: 2, 3, 5, 7, 11, 13, 17, and 19. But 2 is not an odd number, so the odd primes between 1 and 20 are: 3, 5, 7, 11, 13, 17, and 19. Hence, there are seven odd primes between 1 and 20.

37. (C)

Place values are as follows: 1,000s, 100s, 10s, 1s, decimal point, 10ths, 100ths, 1,000ths. The 1 is in the hundredths place. If the number to the immediate right of the 1 (i.e., the number in the thousandths place) is greater than or equal to 5, we increase 1 to 2; otherwise, we do not change

38. (A)

Graph reading and interpretation is the primary focus of this question. Choice (B) is obviously wrong because the youngest have the least discretionary income. The oldest group has less discretionary income than those between the ages of 25 and 65; therefore, item (C) is wrong. The discretionary income for all ages over 25 is more than for those under 25; (D) is incorrect.

39. (C)

To find the cost per square foot of material to cover the shaded area, divide the total cost of covering the shaded area (III) by the square footage of the shaded area. Only option III is necessary; I and II are *not* necessary. The answer is therefore (C). The problem would be solved as follows: The total area of the larger rectangle is the base times the height, 12 ft × 9 ft, which equals 108 sq. ft. Therefore, the area of the shaded portion surrounding the inner rectangle is

$$108 \text{ sq ft} - 80 \text{ sq ft} = 28 \text{ sq ft}$$

If the total cost of material is $56 to cover the shaded area of 28 square feet, the cost per square foot is $56/28 sq ft = $2/sq ft.

40. (D)

The best way solve this problem is to see it as unit analysis. Keep in mind that you want your answer in cups, so write the measurements as fractions with denominators of 1. You will need the conversion factor and, therefore, you need to know how many quarts are in a gallon, etc.

$$\frac{7 \text{ gal}}{1} \times \frac{4 \text{ qt}}{1 \text{ gal}} \times \frac{2 \text{ pt}}{1 \text{ qt}} \times \frac{2 \text{ c}}{1 \text{ pt}}$$

Just like numbers in a fraction, the measurements (e.g. gal, qt) cancel each other out leaving you with the numbers:

$$7 \times 4 \times 2 \times 2 = 112,$$

so the answer is (D) 112 cups.

41. (A)

If two triangles are similar, they have the exact same shape (although not necessarily the same size). This means that the corresponding angles of the two triangles have the same measure and the corresponding sides are proportional. To find the missing side (side DF), set up the proportion:

$$AB/AC = DE/DF$$

or, by substituting the given values,

$$12/10 = 15/x$$

where x is the length of side DF. This can be read as "12 is to 10 as 15 is to x." The problem can be solved by using cross multiplication. Thus, $12x = 150$, or $x = 12.5$.

42. (D)

Using the rules for solving one-variable equations, the original equation is transformed as follows:

$$x/3 - 9 = 15$$

Adding 9 to each side of the equation gives

$$x/3 = 24$$

Multiplying both sides by 3 gives

$$x = 72$$

43. (D)

One way to solve the problem is by writing a one-variable equation that matches the information given:

$$4x + 2(10 - x) = 26$$

The $4x$ represents four tires for each car. Use x for the number of cars because you do not know this number at first. Then $(10 - x)$ represents the number of motorcycles in the lot. (If there are 10 vehicles total, and x of them are cars, subtract x from 10 to get the number of "leftover" motorcycles.) Then $2(10 - x)$ stands for the number of motorcycle tires in the lot. The sum of the values $4x$ and $2(10 - x)$ is 26, which gives the equation above. Using the standard rules for solving a one-variable equation, x (the number of cars in the lot) equals 3. Another approach to answering a multiple-choice question is to try substituting each choice for the unknown variable in the problem to see which one makes sense.

44. (A)

The correct equation must show three consecutive odd numbers being added to give 117. Odd numbers (just like even numbers) are each two units apart. Only the three values $(x, x + 2, x + 4)$ given in choice (A) are each two units apart. Because the numbers being sought are odd, one might be tempted to choose (D). However, the second value in choice (D), $(x + 1)$, is not two units apart from the first value (x); it is different by only one.

45. (C)

Washington and Monroe together received 55 percent of the votes. Everyone else voted for Madison; Madison must have received 45 percent of the votes. (All of the candidates' percentages must add up to 100 percent.) Statement I cannot be true, and statement II must be true. Monroe received 30 percent of the 600 votes; 0.30 times 600 is 180, so statement III is true. Madison received 45 percent of the vote, and 45 percent of 600 is 270, so statement IV is false. Therefore, only II and III are true, and the correct answer is (C).

46. (A)

The somewhat steep straight line to the left tells you that Mr. Cain worked at a steady rate for a while. The completely flat line in the middle tells you he stopped for a while—the line does not go up because Mr. Cain did not cut grass then. Finally, the line continues upward (after his break) less steeply (therefore more flatly), indicating that he was working at a slower rate.

47. (B)

Because Ms. Patton's increases were constant ($3,000 annually), and because the directions tell you that only one statement is true, choice (B) must be the correct answer. To be more confident, however, you can examine the other statements. The range of Ms. Patton's earnings is $12,000 (the jump from $30,000 to $42,000), not $15,000, so choice (A) cannot be correct. Although Ms. Patton may have earned $45,000 in 2003, you do not know that because the graph goes only to 2002; choice (C) cannot be correct. Choice (D) gives the incorrect earnings average; it was $36,000, not $38,000.

48. (D)

All riders must pay at least $3, so 3 will be added to something else in the correct equation. Only choices (B) and (D) meet that requirement. The additional fare of $2 "for every mile or fraction of a mile" tells you that you will need to multiply the number of miles driven (use 11 because of the extra fraction of a mile) by 2, leading to the correct answer of (D).

49. (D)

It is true that multiplication is commutative and division is not (A), but that is not relevant to their being inverse operations. Choice (B) also contains a true statement, but again the statement is not about inverse operations. Choice (C) gives a false statement; in the example shown, the order of operations tells you to compute $8 \div 2$ before any multiplication. As noted in choice (D), two operations being inverse indeed depends on their ability to undo each other.

50. (C)

To find the average (mean) of a set of values, first add them together. In this case, the negative and the positive integers should be added together separately. Those two sums are -12 and 5. (The zero can be ignored; it does not affect either sum.) Then -12 and 5 should be added together for a sum of -7. To complete the work, the sum of -7 must be divided by the number of values (7), giving -1.

51. (D)

In simple notation form, the distributive property is as follows:
$$a(b + c) = (a \times b) + (a \times c)$$
This means that, when multiplying, you may have some computational options. Consider answer choice (D). The distributive property allows us to break 42 down into the convenient addends 2 and 40. You can then multiply each addend separately by 3. Thus, 3×2 equals 6, and 3×40 equals 120. Then, courtesy of the distributive property, we can add those products together to get 126. Only answer choice (D) is illustrative of the distributive property.

52. (C)

The total price of the two items in the original problem is given as $2.59, hinting that equation (B) or (C) may be correct. (In both cases, $2.59 is shown as the sum of two values.)

Examine the right side of equation (C): Note that one value is $1.79 higher than the other. That is, in equation (C), *x* could stand for the price of the pencil, and (*x* + 1.79) could stand for the price of the more expensive pen. Hence, equation (C) is the right one. None of the others fit the information given.

53. (D)

It is helpful to compute Matt's current average. Adding his scores, you get 522. Dividing that by 6 (the number of scores), you find that his average is 87%. Similarly, you can multiply 90 by 6 to compute the number of total points it would take to have an average of 90 (90 × 6 = 540). Matt earned only 522 points, so he was 18 shy of the A–.

54. (A)

The only way carpet from a 16-foot-wide roll will cover Ms. Williams' floor without seams is if she buys 20 feet of it. She can then trim the 16-foot width to 14 feet so that it fits her floor. Buying 20 feet of a 16-foot-wide roll means that she will have to buy 320 square feet. Her living room has an area of only 280 square feet (14 feet × 20 feet), so she'll be wasting 40 square feet (320 – 280), but no more.

55. (B)

If you can fold a two-dimensional figure so that one side exactly matches or folds onto the other side, the fold line is a line of symmetry. The figure below is a nonsquare rectangle with its two lines of symmetry shown.

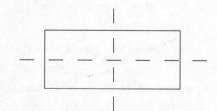

One might think that lines drawn from opposite corners are lines of symmetry, but they're not. The two halves would be the same size and shape, but wouldn't fold onto each other. Note that the question asked about nonsquare rectangles. Squares (which are rectangles) have four lines of symmetry.

56. (B)

Statement I is true because the winner could be Mr. Greenfield and it could be someone else. Statement II is not true, even though Mr. Greenfield bought many more tickets than any other individual. He still has a block of only 300; 700 ticket stubs in the drum aren't his. This tells us that statement III is true. Finally, statement IV is false. Don't confuse the true statement "all tickets have an equal chance of winning" with the false statement that "all persons have an equal chance of winning."

57. (A)

You know that 10,000 contains 4 zeros, or 10^4 in place value. The number 1,000,000 contains 10^6, or 6 zeros. Thus, 10^6 divided by 10^4 is 10^2, or 100. You may divide 10,000 into 1,000,000, but that is the laborious way to solve this. Choice (A) is correct.

58. (B)

You are challenged to analyze which data you would need to calculate the cost of feeding two cats for seven days. If you calculate the cost for one cat for seven days, then double the answer, you will have an approximate cost for two cats. The total cost for one cat is the cost of a can of food times the number of cans of food eaten each day by one cat, times seven days. Double this figure to find the answer for both cats.

59. (A)

Drawing a sketch with dots marking the possible locations of the two houses and The Soda Depot is a good idea. You can start with dots for the two houses, using inches for miles:

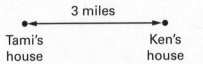

3 miles

Tami's house   Ken's house

If you then draw a dot representing The Soda Depot two miles (inches) to the right of Ken's house, as in the figure that follows, you see that the greatest possible distance between Tami's house and The Soda Depot is five miles:

3 miles   2 miles

Tami's house   Ken's house   Soda Depot

If you draw The Soda Depot dot to the left of Ken's house, as in the figure below, you see that The Soda Depot could be as close as one mile to Tami's house, but no closer. Only statements I and III, then, are true.

1 miles   2 miles

Tami's house   Soda Depot   Ken's house

60. (B)

"Democracy" is the correct response because it is the antithesis of the authoritarianism of fascism. Indeed, the totalitarian, romantic, militaristic, and nationalistic characteristics were, in large part, a reaction against the perceived inadequacies of democracy.

61. (B)

The industrial economy of the nineteenth century was not based on an equitable distribution of profits among all those who were involved in production. Marxists and other critics of capitalism condemned the creed of capitalists and the abhorrent conditions of the industrial proletariat. Raw materials, a constant labor supply, capital, and an expanding marketplace were critical elements in the development of the industrial economy.

62. (D)

In the 1880s and 1890s, the United States Supreme Court struck down desegregation laws and upheld the doctrine of segregated "separate but equal" facilities for blacks and whites. These laws became known as "Jim Crow" laws. Their impact was to allow racist governments in the South to set up "separate but unequal" facilities in which blacks were forced to sit in the rear of streetcars and buses and to eat in the back rooms of restaurants, were excluded completely from white businesses, and had to use separate and usually inferior public restroom facilities. These laws allowed white supremacists to "put blacks in their place" and effectively kept blacks from achieving anything near equal status. It wasn't until the 1950s and 1960s that new Supreme Court decisions finally forced the repeal of these laws.

63. (B)

A writ of habeas corpus (B) is a court order that directs an official who is detaining someone to produce the person before the court so that the legality of the detention may be determined. The primary function of the writ is to gain the release of someone who has been imprisoned without due process of law. For example, if the police detained a suspect for an unreasonable time without officially charging the person with a crime, the person could seek relief from a court in the form of a writ of habeas corpus. (A) is incorrect because a writ of mandamus is a court order commanding an official to perform a legal duty of his or her office. It is not used to prevent persons from being improperly imprisoned. The Fourth Amendment requirement that police have probable cause in order to obtain a search warrant regulates police procedure. It is not itself a mechanism for gaining the release of a person for improper imprisonment, so (C) is incorrect. Answer (D) is incorrect because the decision in *Roe v. Wade* dealt with a woman's right to have an abortion; it had nothing to do with improper imprisonment.

64. (C)

The American system (A), as conceived by Henry Clay, referred to the nationalist policy of uniting the three economic sections of the United States in the time following the War of 1812. Mercantilism (B) was an economic theory whose principal doctrine was the belief that the wealth of nations was based on the possession of gold. The Age of Belief (D) is tied to tradition and emotion. The Enlightenment (C) is the best possible answer.

65. (A)

The Magna Carta was signed in 1215. Columbus's voyages began in the fifteenth century. The Protestant Reformation occurred in the sixteenth century. The Puritans came to America in the seventeenth century. Therefore, the best choice is (A).

66. (A)

Thomas Paine wrote several pamphlets before and during the American Revolution. *Common Sense* was the most significant because it carefully documented abuses of the British parliamentary system of government, particularly in its treatment of the American colonies. Paine portrayed a brutish monarchy interested only in itself and pointedly argued how independence would improve the

colonies' long-term situation. His argument was directed at the common man, and it struck a chord unlike anything previously written in the colonies. Its publication in 1774 was perfect in reaching the public at just the moment that their questions and concerns regarding British rule were peaking. The answers provided in Paine's essays were pivotal in the subsequent behavior of many colonists who, until that time, had been unsure of what they believed regarding independence and British rule. Answer (B) is incorrect. Paine wrote another essay called *American Crisis* during the winter of 1776. This essay, not *Common Sense*, helped rally American spirits during that long, demoralizing winter. Answers (C) and (D) are also incorrect. Paine wrote to an American, not a British, audience. He also wrote *Common Sense* well before American independence was achieved.

67. (A)

Choice (A) is correct; checks and balances provide each of the branches with the ability to limit the actions of the other branches. (B) is incorrect; branches of the federal government do not achieve independence from each other because of checks and balances. Choices (C) and (D) are also incorrect because they deal with only one branch, whereas the system of checks and balances involves the manner in which the three branches are interrelated.

68. (D)

The best choice is (D). The Fifteenth Amendment granted black males the right to vote. (A) is incorrect because the voting right was given to black males only, not women of any race. (B) is incorrect because the Fourteenth Amendment granted citizenship to former slaves. (C) is incorrect because the Thirteenth Amendment granted freedom to slaves.

69. (C)

Choices (A), (B), and (D) all played a role in the early settlements of the English colonies in America. The correct response is answer choice (C); Mormonism was founded at Fayette, New York, in 1830, by Joseph Smith. The Book of Mormon was published in 1830; it describes the establishment of an American colony from the Tower of Babel.

70. (C)

The letter *K* represents Cuba, the letter *D* represents Indonesia, and the letter *M* represents Sri Lanka. The correct answer is (C) because the letter *I* represents the Philippine Islands.

71. (B)

The Bill of Rights clearly states that Congress may not make laws abridging citizens' rights and liberties. Choices (C) and (D) are incorrect because the Bill of Rights does not talk about voting rights or slaves. A list of grievances (A) is contained in the Declaration of Independence.

72. (B)

The 1933 bar is highest, and the graph measures the percentage of unemployment by the height of the bars. The bars for 1929 (A), 1938 (C), and 1944 (D) are all lower than the bar for 1933, the year in which unemployment was the highest.

73. (D)

The bar for the year 1944 (the bar between 1943 and 1945) is the lowest bar on the graph. As previously mentioned, the graph measures the percentage of unemployment on the length of the bars.

The bars for 1929 (A), 1933 (B), and 1938 (C) are all higher than the bar for 1944.

74. (D)

Choice (A) is wrong because about 30 percent, not 50 percent, of households had under $15,000. Choices (B) and (C) are also incorrect because slightly more than 15 percent fell into this category.

75. (A)

The United States was shocked when the Soviet Union launched *Sputnik* in 1957. Comparisons between Soviet education and the education available in United States public schools indicated a need to emphasize math (B), science (C), and foreign languages (D) for the United States to compete with other countries and to remain a world power.

76. (C)

The general public believed that the slaves would be more submissive if they remained illiterate; therefore, most slaves were never taught to read or write. Teaching a slave to read or write was, in fact, a criminal act.

77. (D)

In handing down its decision in *Brown v. Board of Education of Topeka, Kansas* in 1954, the Supreme Court stated that "Separate but equal has no place . . . Separate educational facilities are inherently unequal and violate the equal protection clause of the Fourteenth Amendment."

78. (A)

The Peace Corps (A) was established by President John F. Kennedy. Johnson's VISTA (D) was modeled after the Peace Corps. Head Start (B) and the Elementary and Secondary Education Act (C) were also put into effect as part of President Johnson's "War on Poverty."

79. (C)

The Education for All Handicapped Children Act of 1975 provides for mentally (A) and physically (B) handicapped as well as learning disabled children (D). It does not include socially-emotionally handicapped youngsters.

80. (A)

The term *casework* (A) is used by political scientists to describe the activities of members of Congress on behalf of individual constituents. These activities might include helping an elderly person secure social security benefits or helping a veteran obtain medical services. Most casework is actually done by congressional staff and may take as much as a third of the staff's time. Representatives supply this type of assistance for the good public relations it provides. Pork barrel legislation (B) is rarely, if ever, intended to help individual citizens. Pork barrel legislation authorizes federal spending for special projects, such as airports, roads, or dams, in the home state or district of the representative. It is meant to help the entire district or state. Also, there is no legal entitlement on the part of a citizen to a pork barrel project, such as exists with social security benefits. Choice (C) is not the answer because lobbying is an activity directed toward the representative, not one done by the member of Congress. A lobbyist attempts to get members of Congress to support legislation that will benefit the group that the lobbyist represents. Logrolling (D) is incorrect because it does not refer to a congressional service for constituents. It refers instead to the congressional practice of trading votes on different bills. Representative X will vote for Representative Z's pork barrel project, and in return representative Z will vote for representative X's pork barrel project.

81. (B)

The term *Trail of Tears* is used to describe the forced relocation of the Cherokee tribe from the southern Appalachians to what is now Oklahoma (B). The migration of Mormons from Nauvoo, Illinois, to the Great Salt Lake in Utah (A), and the westward movements along the Oregon Trail (C) and, much earlier, the Wilderness Road (D) all took place and could at times be as unpleasant as the Cherokees' trek. They were voluntary, however, compared to the Cherokee migration and therefore did not earn such sad titles as the "Trail of Tears."

82. (D)

Both state and federal governments have the power to lay and collect taxes and to borrow money. Article I, Section 8 of the Constitution establishes the powers of Congress, whereas the Tenth Amendment to the Constitution (the last amendment within the Bill of Rights) sets forth the principle of reserved powers to state governments. State constitutions give states the power to lay and collect taxes.

83. (A)

The main purposes of the WTO are to open world markets to all countries and thus promote economic development, and to regulate the economic affairs between member states

84. (A)

Overgrazing, overuse of farmland, and a lack of rainfall caused the drought of the 1930s.

85. (A)

The responsibility for public education belongs to the state governments. The federal government has often passed legislation to regulate and provide funds for public education, but the main responsibility for establishing and regulating education resides with the state governments.

86. (C)

French-ruled peoples viewed Napoleon as a tyrant who repressed and exploited them for the glory and advantage of France. The Battle of Waterloo is historically significant because it marked the defeat of Napoleon in 1815.

87. (B)

The Maya and the Aztecs occupied the area of Central America and Southern Mexico called Mesoamerica. Both groups were accomplished builder, astronomers, and mathematicians. Choice (A) is incorrect because the Inca civilization was not a Mesoamerican group. They developed an advanced civilization in South America, in present-day Peru and Ecuador. Choice (C) is incorrect because only the Toltecs were from Mesoamerica; the Pueblo Indians were from present-day New Mexico in North America. Choice (D) is incorrect because only the Olmecs were Mesoamerican. The Iroquois civilizations developed in North America.

88. (C)

The best choice is (C); the Earth is divided into 24 zones based on the meridians of longitude, which are determined using the rotation of the Earth and its exposure to sunlight. This rotation creates day and night, and consequently the concept of time. Choice (A) is incorrect because the International Date Line is only one of 24 meridians of the Earth. Choice (B) is incorrect because the term revolution describes the movement of the Earth around the sun, which affects the seasons but not necessarily the time zones. Choice (D) is incorrect because the parallels of latitude do not affect the time zones.

89. (D)

The east coast of South America and the west coast of Africa fit together like pieces of a jigsaw puzzle. Fossil remains in locations where "fit" is observed are too well matched to be coincidental. Earthquakes and volcanism are more prevalent in mountainous regions, where plates collided, than in other regions. Thus, all support the theory of plate tectonics.

90. (B)

The region's mountain ranges are the main reason for the high precipitation.

91. (C)

All known living things are grouped in categories according to shared physical traits. The process of grouping organisms is called classification. Carl Linné, also known as Linnaeus, devised the classification system used in biology today. In the Linnaean system (A), all organisms are given a two-word name (binomial). The name consists of a genus (e.g., *Canis*) and a species (e.g., *lupus*) designation. The DNA holds the genetic materials of a cell, so (B) could not be the correct answer. (D) is not a correct choice since both (A) and (B) are incorrect. When the genetic type of parents is known, the probability of the offspring showing particular traits can be predicted by using the Punnett Square (C). A Punnett Square is a large square divided into four small boxes. The genetic symbol of each parent for a particular trait is written alongside the square, for one parent along the top and for the other parent along the left side, as shown in the figure.

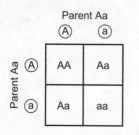

Each gene symbol is written in the boxes below or to the right of it. This results in each box having two gene symbols in it. The genetic symbols in the boxes are all the possible genetic combinations for a particular trait of the offspring of these parents. Each box has a 25 percent probability of being the actual genetic representation for a given child.

92. (C)

A liquid has a definite volume, but it molds to the shape of the container holding it. Titanium (A) is a solid (D), and solids have a definite shape and volume, so (A) and (D) are not the best answers. A gas will expand to fit the container in both volume and shape, so (B) is not the correct answer.

93. (B)

The instrument for measuring the intensity of an earthquake is a seismograph. A thermograph (A) measures temperature; a telegraph (C) is a communication device; and an odometer (D) measures distance traveled, so (A), (C), and (D) are not correct.

94. (D)

All are correctly matched.

95. (B)

Expansion occurring on the ocean floor creates pressure around the edges of the Pacific Plate and produces geologic instability where the Pacific Plate collides with the continental plates on all sides. Neither earthquakes (C), hardened lava (D), nor rock similarities (A) alone are sufficient to account for the "Ring of Fire."

96. (B)

Energy is defined as the ability to do work. Work occurs when a force (push or pull) is applied to an object, resulting in movement. Work = force × distance. The greater the force (A) applied, or the longer the distance traveled (D), or the greater the interval between two points, the greater the work done, but they are not the ability to do the work. Speed is rate of movement, so (C) is not the best answer.

97. (D)

Atoms are neutral, so the net charge must be zero, requiring that the number of negative particles (electrons) equals the number of positive particles (protons).

98. (D)

(A), (B), and (C) all involve chemical changes in which iron, wood, and rocket fuel, respectively, react with other substances to produce a reactant product with different chemical properties. Melted ice in the form of water still has the same chemical formula, so the correct answer is (D).

99. (C)

Isotopes are atoms with the same number of protons and electrons but different number of neutrons. Isotopes for a given element all have the same chemical properties, differing only in their atomic weight, or number of neutrons.

100. (C)

Newton's second law states that an unbalanced force acting on a mass causes the mass to accelerate. In equation form, $F = ma$, where F is force, m is mass, and a is acceleration. Only (C) involves a mass that is being accelerated by an unbalanced force.

101. (A)

Thermal energy is the total amount of internal energy of a given body, whereas temperature is a measure of the vibrational activity of atoms or molecules within the material. Therefore, thermal energy involves both the mass and temperature of a given body. Thus, (A) is the most likely answer because its mass far exceeds 1 g, a bucket of water, and Lake Michigan. (B) is ruled out because, even though its temperature is very high, its mass is extremely small.

102. (D)

The cell membrane (D) is a selectively permeable barrier that permits some substances to pass through while forming a barrier for others. None of the other choices have this property.

103. (D)

A zygote is the cell formed by the union of a male sperm and a female ovum. The zygote develops into the embryo following the instruction of its DNA. (D) is correct because the zygote of a human is a cell derived from a sperm containing 23 chromosomes and an egg containing 23 chromosomes. A haploid has only one copy of each chromosome and therefore half the number of chromosomes found in other cells of the body. A diploid has two copies of each chromosome. (A) cannot be the correct answer because it represents too few chromosomes for either a haploid sex cell or a diploid body cell. (B) cannot be the correct answer because it also represents too few chromosomes for either a haploid sex cell or a diploid body cell. (C) cannot be the correct answer because it represents the number of chromosomes in a sperm or an egg.

104. (C)

Genes are the sections of the DNA molecule that determine specific traits.

105. (C)

Nuclear energy (C) is nonrenewable. Nuclear energy has potential advantages in providing large quantities of energy from a small amount of source material, but the process of radioactive decay is nonreversible.

106. (A)

Choices (B), (C), and (D) are ruled out because Darwin was unaware of the genetic work that was later done by Mendel. Darwin and most other nineteenth-century biologists never knew of Mendel and his research. It was not until the beginning of the twentieth century that Mendel's pioneering research on genetic inheritance was rediscovered.

107. (B)

The lunar period is about 30 days, or one month, which is the time it takes for the moon to orbit Earth one time.

108. (C)

A star "going nova" is presumed to be at the end of its life. As hydrogen (or sometimes helium) is depleted, the fusion reaction becomes incapable of sustaining the pressures required to push the star's mass outward against the pull of gravity. The star then collapses, resulting in a gigantic explosion known as a supernova. Choice (A) is neither observed nor possible; (B) is not observed; and (D), although occasionally observed, does not trigger nova-sized explosions.

109. (C)

The tilting of Earth's axis causes the Northern Hemisphere to point more sunward in the summer months and away from the sun in the winter months (with the reverse being true for the Southern Hemisphere), so (C) is the correct answer. (B) is ruled out because the rotation period is the same from season to season. (A) is ruled out because Earth is actually somewhat closer to the sun in December through January than it is in June through July, which is winter for the Southern Hemisphere. (D) is ruled out because this is a daily, not a seasonal, phenomenon.

110. (A)

Igneous rocks are transformed, or "metamorphosed," into metamorphic rocks. Thus, they are related to igneous, not sedimentary, rocks and are found on this planet.

111. (A)

According to the theory of plate tectonics, plate spreading is associated with magma upwelling to fill the vacated space, which forms ridges at these locations. This is true also under the oceans.

112. (D)

The raw material for igneous rock formation is magma, which—when cooled either above or below ground—becomes igneous rock.

113. (B)

The correct answer is (B). A zygote is the cell formed by the union of a male sperm and a female ovum. The zygote develops into the embryo following the instruction of its DNA. A haploid has only one copy of each chromosome and therefore half the number of chromosomes found in other cells of the body. A diploid has two copies of each chromosome. Cytoplasm is the contents of a cell, outside the nucleus.

114. (A)

Note that the particle flow divides at two points, T and M. At these points, the flow has two paths to reach either point W or point Q. Thus, the correct choice is (A). Particle flow can reach point W by going through point U, rather than V. It would have to flow through all other points listed in order to make a complete circuit or total clockwise path.

115. (C)

Because heat is a positive condition depending on the absence of cold, (C) is the correct answer. Fahrenheit and Celsius are measures of temperature, not conditions; therefore, (A) and (D) are incorrect choices. Heat is the opposite of intense artificial cold; (B) is not acceptable.

116. (C)

The gas molecules themselves do not expand in size when heated, but the spaces between them increases as the molecules move faster. The expanding hot air leaves the balloon body through the opening at the bottom. With less air in the balloon casing, the balloon is lighter. The combustion products of propane are carbon dioxide (molar mass 44 g/mol), which is heavier than air, and water (molar mass 18 g/mol), which is lighter.

117. (C)

The correct answer is (C). The question asks you to apply your knowledge of rock formation and the processes of Earth's history to a single sample, a rock containing tiny pieces of seashells. The presence of seashells in a rock on a hillside indicates that the hillside was under water many years ago. When the ancient sea existed, shells, which are "houses" of sea creatures, would have fallen to the seabed when the animals died. The pressure of the

water over very long periods of time would have compacted and cemented the sediment and the shells into rocks that were later exposed when the sea dried up. Hence, the answer (C).

118. (B)

The moon is much closer to Earth than it is to any other celestial body or to the sun.

119. (B)

Reptiles are not generally warm-blooded; all other statements are correct.

120. (B)

Cancers and hereditary diseases (B) are *not* infectious. Diseases caused by viruses, bacteria, or protists (A) that invade the body are called infectious diseases. These disease-causing organisms are collectively referred to as germs. Despite the fact that the immune system protects the body from disease (D), environmental hazards can still cause disease (C). (B) is the only answer that is false and therefore is the answer to this question.

Practice Test 2

Elementary Education:
Content Knowledge (0014)

ANSWER SHEET FOR PRACTICE TEST 2

1. (A) (B) (C) (D)
2. (A) (B) (C) (D)
3. (A) (B) (C) (D)
4. (A) (B) (C) (D)
5. (A) (B) (C) (D)
6. (A) (B) (C) (D)
7. (A) (B) (C) (D)
8. (A) (B) (C) (D)
9. (A) (B) (C) (D)
10. (A) (B) (C) (D)
11. (A) (B) (C) (D)
12. (A) (B) (C) (D)
13. (A) (B) (C) (D)
14. (A) (B) (C) (D)
15. (A) (B) (C) (D)
16. (A) (B) (C) (D)
17. (A) (B) (C) (D)
18. (A) (B) (C) (D)
19. (A) (B) (C) (D)
20. (A) (B) (C) (D)
21. (A) (B) (C) (D)
22. (A) (B) (C) (D)
23. (A) (B) (C) (D)
24. (A) (B) (C) (D)
25. (A) (B) (C) (D)
26. (A) (B) (C) (D)
27. (A) (B) (C) (D)
28. (A) (B) (C) (D)
29. (A) (B) (C) (D)
30. (A) (B) (C) (D)

31. (A) (B) (C) (D)
32. (A) (B) (C) (D)
33. (A) (B) (C) (D)
34. (A) (B) (C) (D)
35. (A) (B) (C) (D)
36. (A) (B) (C) (D)
37. (A) (B) (C) (D)
38. (A) (B) (C) (D)
39. (A) (B) (C) (D)
40. (A) (B) (C) (D)
41. (A) (B) (C) (D)
42. (A) (B) (C) (D)
43. (A) (B) (C) (D)
44. (A) (B) (C) (D)
45. (A) (B) (C) (D)
46. (A) (B) (C) (D)
47. (A) (B) (C) (D)
48. (A) (B) (C) (D)
49. (A) (B) (C) (D)
50. (A) (B) (C) (D)
51. (A) (B) (C) (D)
52. (A) (B) (C) (D)
53. (A) (B) (C) (D)
54. (A) (B) (C) (D)
55. (A) (B) (C) (D)
56. (A) (B) (C) (D)
57. (A) (B) (C) (D)
58. (A) (B) (C) (D)
59. (A) (B) (C) (D)
60. (A) (B) (C) (D)

61. (A) (B) (C) (D)
62. (A) (B) (C) (D)
63. (A) (B) (C) (D)
64. (A) (B) (C) (D)
65. (A) (B) (C) (D)
66. (A) (B) (C) (D)
67. (A) (B) (C) (D)
68. (A) (B) (C) (D)
69. (A) (B) (C) (D)
70. (A) (B) (C) (D)
71. (A) (B) (C) (D)
72. (A) (B) (C) (D)
73. (A) (B) (C) (D)
74. (A) (B) (C) (D)
75. (A) (B) (C) (D)
76. (A) (B) (C) (D)
77. (A) (B) (C) (D)
78. (A) (B) (C) (D)
79. (A) (B) (C) (D)
80. (A) (B) (C) (D)
81. (A) (B) (C) (D)
82. (A) (B) (C) (D)
83. (A) (B) (C) (D)
84. (A) (B) (C) (D)
85. (A) (B) (C) (D)
86. (A) (B) (C) (D)
87. (A) (B) (C) (D)
88. (A) (B) (C) (D)
89. (A) (B) (C) (D)
90. (A) (B) (C) (D)

91. (A) (B) (C) (D)
92. (A) (B) (C) (D)
93. (A) (B) (C) (D)
94. (A) (B) (C) (D)
95. (A) (B) (C) (D)
96. (A) (B) (C) (D)
97. (A) (B) (C) (D)
98. (A) (B) (C) (D)
99. (A) (B) (C) (D)
100. (A) (B) (C) (D)
101. (A) (B) (C) (D)
102. (A) (B) (C) (D)
103. (A) (B) (C) (D)
104. (A) (B) (C) (D)
105. (A) (B) (C) (D)
106. (A) (B) (C) (D)
107. (A) (B) (C) (D)
108. (A) (B) (C) (D)
109. (A) (B) (C) (D)
110. (A) (B) (C) (D)
111. (A) (B) (C) (D)
112. (A) (B) (C) (D)
113. (A) (B) (C) (D)
114. (A) (B) (C) (D)
115. (A) (B) (C) (D)
116. (A) (B) (C) (D)
117. (A) (B) (C) (D)
118. (A) (B) (C) (D)
119. (A) (B) (C) (D)
120. (A) (B) (C) (D)

TIME: 120 minutes
120 questions

┌───┐
│ **Four-Function or Scientific Calculator Permitted** │
└───┘

I. LANGUAGE ARTS

Questions 1 and 2 refer to the following paragraph:

(1) One potential hideaway that until now has been completely ignored is De Witt Isle, off the coast of Australia. (2) Its assets are 4,000 acres of jagged rocks, tangled undergrowth, and trees twisted and bent by battering winds. (3) Settlers will have avoided it like the plague, but bandicoots (rat like marsupials native to Australia), wallabies, eagles, and penguins think De Witt is just fine. (4) Why De Witt? (5) So does Jane Cooper, 18, a pert Melbourne High School graduate, who emigrated there with three goats, several chickens, and a number of cats brought along to stand guard against the bandicoots. (6) "I was frightened at the way life is lived today in our cities," says Jane. (7) "I wanted to be alone, to have some time to think and find out about myself."

1. Which of these changes is grammatically correct?

   (A) Sentence 1—Change "has been" to "have been."
   (B) Sentence 7—Delete "to have."
   (C) Sentence 3—Change "will have" to "have."
   (D) Sentence 4—Change "emigrated" to "immigrated."

2. Which one of these changes would make the passage flow more logically?

   (A) Put Sentence 5 before Sentence 4.
   (B) Begin the passage with Sentence 4.
   (C) In Sentence 1, delete "off the coast of Australia."
   (D) Begin the passage with Sentence 2.

Questions 3 and 4 are based on the following:

In a unit on ecology for a fifth-grade class, the teacher presents the following poem:

The days be hot, the nights be cold,
But cross we must, we rush for gold.

The plants be short, the roots spread wide,
Me leg she hurts, thorn's in me side.

I fall, I crawl, I scream, I rave,
Tiz me life that I must save.

How can it be, I've come undone,
Here 'neath this blazin' eternal sun?

The days be hot, the nights be cold,
Me lonely bones alone grow old.

3. What physical setting is the poem describing?

    (A) A forest
    (B) A tundra
    (C) A swamp
    (D) A desert

4. The type of writing in the poem can best be described as

    (A) colloquial.
    (B) narrative.
    (C) metaphoric.
    (D) factual.

5. Mrs. Nemetski is preparing a unit on literary genres. She presents the class with the following story:

    > A fisherman was trying to lure fish to rise so that he could hook them. He took his bagpipes to the banks of the river and played them. No fish rose out of the water. Next he cast his net into the river and when he brought it back, the net was filled with fish. Then he took his bagpipes again and as he played, the fish leaped up in the net.
    >
    > "Ah, now you dance when I play," he said to an old fish.
    >
    > "Yes," said the old one, "when you are in a person's power you must do as he commands."

    To which genre does this story belong?

    (A) Narrative
    (B) Character analysis
    (C) Editorial
    (D) Fable

Questions 6–8 refer to the following:
A flea and a fly in a flue
Were caught, so what could they do?
Said the fly, "Let us flee."

"Let us fly," said the flea.
So they flew through a flaw in the flue.

—Anonymous

6. What form of poetry did the teacher present to her class?

    (A) An elegy
    (B) A ballad
    (C) A limerick
    (D) A haiku

7. The repetition of the *fl-* in *flea*, *fly*, and *flue* is called

    (A) alliteration.
    (B) onomatopoeia.
    (C) imagery.
    (D) symbolism.

8. A follow-up assignment might include:

    I.   having students illustrate the poem.
    II. asking students to write their own poem in this form.
    III. having students clap their hands to practice the rhythm of the poem.

    (A) I only
    (B) I and II only
    (C) I and III only
    (D) I, II, and III

"If turnips are not blue, then the sky is falling."

9. Given that the previous sentence is true, which one of the following sentences MUST also be true?

    (A) If turnips are blue, then the sky is not falling.
    (B) If the sky is falling, then turnips are not blue.
    (C) If the sky is not falling, then turnips are blue.
    (D) If the sky is not falling, then turnips are not blue.

10. Sequential language acquisition occurs when students

    (A) learn a second language after mastery of the first.
    (B) learn a second language at the same time as the first.
    (C) learn two languages in part.
    (D) develop language skills.

11. Mr. Chan is teaching his class how to recognize propaganda. He presents his class with the slogan "Buy a brand-new Whizzer bike like the ones all your friends have." Which propaganda device is he illustrating?

    (A) Bandwagon
    (B) Testimonial
    (C) Card-stacking
    (D) Glittering generality

12. What do the following sentences illustrate?

    Laura tried to do her best.

    The judge tried the case harshly.

    (A) Grammatical errors
    (B) Synonyms and antonyms
    (C) Rules of spelling
    (D) Words with multiple meanings

Question 13 is based on the following poem:

Richard Cory
By Edwin Arlington Robinson

Whenever Richard Cory went down town,
We people on the pavement looked at him:
He was a gentleman from sole to crown,
Clean favored, and imperially slim.

And he was always quietly arrayed,
And he was always human when he talked;
But still he fluttered pulses when he said,
"Good-morning," and he glittered when he
    walked.

And he was rich—yes, richer than a king—
And admirably schooled in every grace;
In fine we thought that he was everything
To make us wish that we were in his place.

So on we worked, and waited for the light,
And went without the meat, and cursed the
    bread;
And Richard Cory, one calm summer night,
Went home and put a bullet through his head.

13. Richard Cory represents the

    (A) wisdom of age.
    (B) happiness of love.
    (C) deception of appearance.
    (D) contentment of youth.

14. A teacher presents the following sentences to her class. Which one is correct?

    (A) I don't like hiking as much as I like cross-country skiing.
    (B) I don't like to hike as much as I like cross-country skiing.
    (C) I don't like hiking as much as I like to ski cross-country.
    (D) I don't like to hike as much as I like going cross-country skiing.

Read the passage below, and then answer Questions 15–18.

The issue of adult literacy has finally received recognition as a major social problem. Unfortunately, the issue is usually presented in the media as a "women's interest issue." Numerous governors' wives and even Laura Bush have publicly expressed concern about literacy. As well-meaning as the politicians' wives may be, it is more important that the politicians themselves recognize the seriousness of the problem and support increased funding for literacy programs.

Literacy education programs need to be directed at two different groups of people with very different needs. The first group is composed of people who have very limited reading and writing skills. These people are complete illiterates. A second group is composed of people who can read and write but whose skills are not sufficient to meet their needs. This second group is called functionally illiterate. Successful literacy programs must meet the needs of both groups.

Instructors in literacy programs have three main responsibilities. First, the educational needs of the illiterates and functional illiterates must be met. Second, the instructors must approach the participants in the program with empathy, not sympathy. Third, all participants must experience success in the program and must perceive their efforts as worthwhile.

15. What is the difference between illiteracy and functional illiteracy?

(A) There is no difference.
(B) A functional illiterate is enrolled in a literacy education program but an illiterate is not.
(C) An illiterate cannot read or write; a functional illiterate can read and write but not at a very high skill level.
(D) There are more illiterates than functional illiterates in the United States today.

16. What does "women's interest issue" mean in the passage?

(A) The issue is interesting to women only.
(B) Many politicians' wives have expressed concern over the issue.
(C) Women illiterates outnumber male illiterates.

(D) Politicians interested in illiteracy often have their wives give speeches on the topic.

17. According to the passage, which of the following is NOT a characteristic of successful literacy programs?

(A) Participants should receive free transportation.
(B) Participants should experience success in the program.
(C) Instructors must have empathy, not sympathy.
(D) Programs must meet the educational needs of illiterates.

18. What is the author's opinion of the funding for literacy programs?

(A) Too much
(B) Too little
(C) About right
(D) Too much for illiterates and not enough for functional illiterates

Read the passage below, and then answer Questions 19–22.

Language not only expresses an individual's ideology, it also sets perimeters while it persuades and influences the discourse in the community that hears and interprets its meaning. Therefore, the language of failure should not be present in the learning environment (i.e., the classroom) because it will have a prohibitive impact on the students' desire to learn as well as a negative influence on the students' self-esteem. The *Oxford English Dictionary* defines *failure* as "a fault, a shortcoming, a lack of success, a person who turns out unsuccessfully, becoming insolvent, etc." We as educators might well ask ourselves if this is the sort of doctrine that we want to permeate our classrooms. Perhaps our own university axiom, *mens agitat molem* ("the mind can move mountains") will help us discover if, indeed, the concepts of failure are really the types of influences we wish to introduce to impressionable new students. Is the mind capable of moving a mountain when it is already convinced it cannot? One must remain aware that individuals acquire knowledge at independent rates of speed. Certainly no one would suggest that one infant "failed" the art of learning to walk because she acquired the skill two months after her infant counterpart. Would anyone suggest that infant number one failed walking? Of course not. What would a mentor project to either toddler were he to suggest that a slower acquisition of walking skills implied failure? Yet we as educators feel the need to suggest student A failed due to the slower procurement of abstract concepts than student B. It is absolutely essential to shift the learning focus from failure to success.

19. Which of the following statements best conveys the meaning of the passage?

    (A) Learning is something that happens at different speeds and is, therefore, natural.
    (B) Instructors need to be sensitive to students' individual needs.
    (C) Instructors need to shift the educational focus from failure to success in learning environments.
    (D) Failure is a potential hazard in the classroom and should be avoided at all costs.

20. As stated in the context of the passage, what does "university axiom" mean?

    (A) University Latin

    (B) University motto
    (C) University rhetoric
    (D) University sophomore

21. According to the passage, what will have a negative effect on students' self-esteem?

    (A) The rhetoric of diction
    (B) The slower procurement of abstract concepts
    (C) The learning focus from failure to success
    (D) The language of failure

22. According to the passage, what does language do besides aid individual expression?

    (A) It establishes individual thought and tells of individual philosophies.
    (B) It paints visual images and articulates individual declaration.
    (C) It suggests individual axioms and community philosophy.
    (D) It persuades and influences the discourse in the community that hears and interprets its meaning.

23. To explain and clarify ideas is the purpose of which of the following types of writing?

    (A) Expository
    (B) Persuasive
    (C) Descriptive
    (D) Narrative

24. *Hiss* is an example of

    (A) metaphor
    (B) personification
    (C) simile
    (D) onomatopoeia

Read the passage below, and then answer Questions 25–27.

The early decades of the fifteenth century were a period in our history when English took a "great (linguistic) vowel shift" by redistributing the vowel pronunciation and configuration. Each vowel changed its sound quality, but the distinction between one vowel and the next was maintained. There was a restructuring of the sounds and patterns of communication. One has to conclude that a concurrent stress and exhilaration was also occurring within the perimeters of the literate society. Musicians, artists, poets, and authors all must have relished the new freedom and experimentation that was now possible with the newfound linguistic shifts.

25. The passage tells about

(A) a shift in vowel pronunciation and configuration.
(B) a fifteenth-century renaissance for musicians, artists, poets, and authors.
(C) a new-found linguistic freedom from conventional sound and linguistic structure.
(D) various vowel stresses and their effect on artistic expression.

26. What is the meaning of the word *linguistic* as used in the passage?

(A) Artistic freedom
(B) Verbal or rhetorical
(C) Social or expressive
(D) Vowel configuration

27. Because "each vowel changed its sound quality,"

(A) there was a restructuring of the sounds and patterns of communication.
(B) language could never be spoken in the same way again.
(C) artists had to develop new means of expression.

(D) communication went through a divergent change of status and culture.

Read the passage below, and then answer Questions 28–30.

The teaching apprentice initiated the discussion in a clear and well-prepared manner. To _____ the lecture topic, the teaching apprentice utilized overhead transparencies of both lexicon and abstract representation to better _____ the theories behind various pedagogical concepts. The class culminated whereby students established enthymemes extrapolated from the class discussion. The class maintained integrity and continuity.

28. Which of these grouped words, if inserted in order into the passage's blank lines, would address the logical sequencing of the narrative?

(A) refute; criticize
(B) conflate; discern
(C) undermine; explain
(D) support; illustrate

29. The definition of the term *pedagogical* as used in the passage means

(A) "academic."
(B) "abstract."
(C) "meaningless."
(D) "obtuse."

30. The passage suggests that the author's classroom experience was

(A) a needless waste of time and energy.
(B) intelligible and pragmatic.
(C) haphazard and disorderly.
(D) too advanced and complicated.

31. Which of the following is NOT a type or form of poetry?

    (A) Limerick
    (B) Couplet
    (C) Free verse
    (D) Metaphor

II. MATHEMATICS

32. The following data represent the ages of 17 people enrolled in an adult education class:

    32, 33, 34, 35, 36, 42, 42, 42, 43, 50, 51, 61, 61, 62, 63, 68, 79

    Adina organized the data as follows:
    3   2, 3, 4, 5, 6
    4   2, 2, 2, 3
    5   0, 1
    6   1, 1, 2, 3, 8
    7   9

    The display Adina used is called which one of the following?

    (A) Box-and-whisker plot
    (B) Stem-and-leaf plot
    (C) Cumulative histogram
    (D) Pictograph

33. The Ungerville cafeteria offers a choice for lunch on its Mexican Day special. You can choose either a taco or a burrito. You can choose a filling of chicken, beef, or beans, and you have a choice of six different beverages. To determine the total number of possible different lunches consisting of a taco or burrito, one filling, and one beverage, which mathematical process would be most useful?

    (A) Factor tree
    (B) Conditional probability

    (C) Factorials
    (D) Counting principle

34. The spinner shown below is divided into equal sections.

    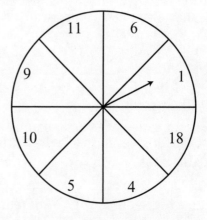

    What is the probability of landing on a section with a number that is a multiple of 3?

    (A) $\dfrac{5}{8}$

    (B) $\dfrac{5}{6}$

    (C) $\dfrac{3}{8}$

    (D) $\dfrac{3}{10}$

35. The average speed of a plane is 600 kilometers per hour. How long does it take the plane to travel 120 kilometers?

    (A) 0.2 hour
    (B) 0.5 hour
    (C) 0.7 hour
    (D) 5 hours

36. Nathan stayed up all night studying for his exams. He began his studies at 9:45 P.M. and ended at 6:22 A.M. How long did he study?

    (A) 7 hr 23 min
    (B) 7 hr 37 min

(C) 8 hr 37 min

(D) 8 hr 23 min

37. The price of a sweater was reduced by 50 percent during a clearance sale. To sell the sweater at the original price, by what percentage must the new price be increased?

(A) 200 percent

(B) 50 percent

(C) 75 percent

(D) 100 percent

38. A recipe for spinach pasta uses the following ingredients:

Ingredient	Amount
Oranges	2
Scallions	¾ bunch
Cream	1 cup
Angel-hair pasta	12 oz.
Baby spinach	3 bags

This recipe serves 4 people and takes 17 minutes to prepare. To serve 10 people, how many ounces of angel-hair pasta are required?

(A) 15

(B) 20

(C) 25

(D) 30

39. Given the following numerical computation, which operation should be performed first?

$$\frac{5 + 3(4 - 2)^2}{4}$$

(A) Addition

(B) Subtraction

(C) Division

(D) Powering

40. Jose conducted a survey of 20 classmates to determine their favorite breakfast drink. The results are shown in the following table:

Beverage	Number of Classmates
Orange juice	6
Milk	4
Tea	2
Soda	2
Other	6

To create a pie chart for this data, how many degrees should be used for the sector representing milk?

(A) 40°

(B) 72°

(C) 86°

(D) 90°

41. Joshua's tie has three colors. One-half of the tie is blue, one-fifth is brown, and the rest is burgundy. What fraction of the tie is burgundy?

(A) $\frac{5}{7}$

(B) $\frac{2}{10}$

(C) $\frac{3}{10}$

(D) $\frac{7}{10}$

42. Dawn draws a picture of a parallelogram on the board. All of the following are properties of a parallelogram EXCEPT:

(A) Opposite sides are equal.

(B) Opposite angles are equal.

(C) Diagonals are equal.

(D) Diagonals bisect each other.

43.

> A number diminished by 5 is
> 3 more than 7 times the number.

If we let *n* represent the number referred to above, which one of the following best represents the statement shown above?

(A) $n + 5 > 7n + 3$
(B) $n - 5 > 7n + 3$
(C) $n - 5 > 7(n + 3)$
(D) $n - 5 = 7n + 3$

44. Which of the following is the equivalent of 6^6?

(A) 36
(B) 66
(C) 46,656
(D) 7,776

45. Which types of graphs or charts would be appropriate for displaying the following information?

**Favorite lunch foods of
40 surveyed sixth graders:**

Pizza	18
Chicken Nuggets	12
Macaroni and Cheese	4
Tacos	4
Hamburgers	2

I. Bar graph
II. Circle (pie) chart
III. Scatter plot
IV. Broken-line graph

(A) I and II only
(B) III and IV only
(C) I and III only
(D) II and IV only

46. Dividing 6.2 by 0.05 yields

(A) 124.
(B) 1.24.
(C) 12.4.
(D) 0.124.

47. Use the figure that follows to answer the question.

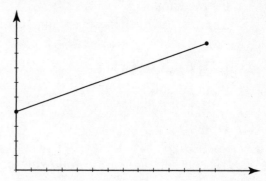

Which of the following situations might the graph illustrate?

I. The varying speed of an experienced runner over the course of a 26-mile race.
II. The number of households a census taker still has to visit over the course of a week.
III. The value of a savings account over time, assuming steady growth.
IV. The changing height of a sunflower over several months.

(A) I and II only
(B) III and IV only
(C) II, III, and IV only
(D) I, III, and IV only

48. The following graph shows the distribution of test scores in Ms. Alvarez's class.

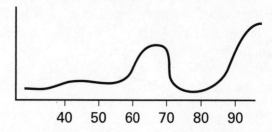

Which of the following statements do you know to be true?

I. The majority of students scored higher than 60.

II. The test was a fair measure of ability.

III. The mean score is probably higher than the median.

IV. The test divided the class into distinct groups.

(A) I and II only

(B) I and IV only

(C) I, III, and IV only

(D) IV only

49. What is the solution to the following equation?

$$\frac{x}{3} - 9 = 15$$

(A) 18

(B) 8

(C) 36

(D) 72

50. What are the solutions to the following equation?

$$3x - 11 = 1$$

(A) 2 and –2

(B) 3 and –3

(C) 4 and –4

(D) 1 and –1

51. Three small circles, all the same size, lie inside a large circle as shown below. The diameter AB of the large circle passes through the centers of the three small circles. If each of the smaller circles has area 9π, what is the circumference of the large circle?

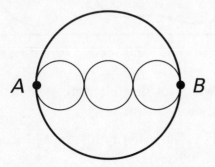

(A) 9

(B) 18

(C) 18π

(D) 27π

52. One day, 31 students were absent from Pierce Middle School. If that represents about 5.5 percent of the students, what is the population of the school?

(A) 177

(B) 517

(C) 564

(D) 171

53. Which of the following are equivalent to 0.5 percent?

I. One-half of one percent

II. 5 percent

III. $\frac{1}{200}$

IV. 0.05

(A) I and III only

(B) I and IV only

(C) II and III only

(D) II and IV only

54. Which point represents the y-intercept of the equation $2x = 3y - 12$?

(A) (4, 0)

(B) (0, –6)

(C) (–6, 0)

(D) (0, 4)

55. The slope m passes through points (–6, 0) and (0, 4) on the coordinate plane. Using the formula $m = \frac{y_2 - y_1}{x_2 - x_1}$ $(x_1 \neq x_2)$, which of the following statements are true?

I. The slope of the line is negative.

II. The slope of the line is positive.

III. The y-intercept of the line is –6.

IV. The y-intercept of the line is 4.

(A) I and III only
(B) I and IV only
(C) II and III only
(D) II and IV only

56. Use the graph below to answer the following question: Which inequality describes the graph?

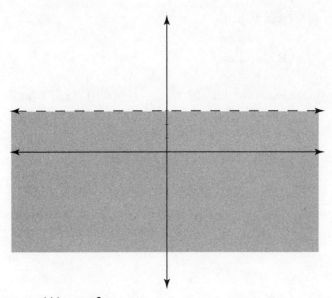

(A) $y < 3$
(B) $x < 3$
(C) $y > 3$
(D) $x > 3$

57. Which of the following comes closest to the actual length of side x in the triangle below?

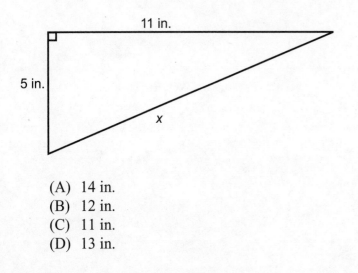

11 in.

5 in.

x

(A) 14 in.
(B) 12 in.
(C) 11 in.
(D) 13 in.

58. Use the figure below to answer the question that follows.

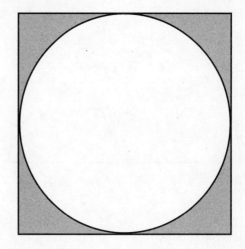

What is the approximate area of the shaded region, given that the radius of the circle is 6 units and the square inscribes the circle?

(A) 106 square units
(B) 31 square units
(C) 77 square units
(D) 125 square units

59. Use the figure below to answer the question that follows.

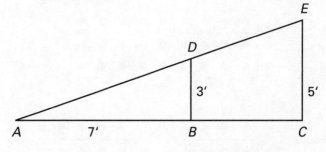

The figure is a sketch of a ramp. Given that the two ramp supports (DB and EC) are perpendicular to the ground, and the dimensions of the various parts are as noted, what is the approximate distance from point B to point C?

(A) 4.7 feet
(B) 4.5 feet
(C) 4.3 feet
(D) 4.1 feet

60. The needle on the dial points most nearly to which reading?

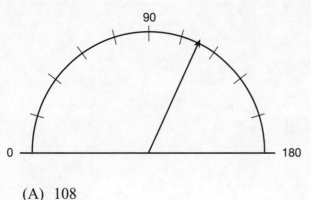

(A) 108
(B) 128
(C) 114
(D) 117

61. The diagram below could be used to model which one of the following?

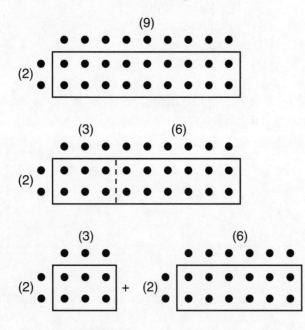

(A) Distributive property
(B) Associative property of addition
(C) Commutative property of multiplication
(D) Associative property of multiplication

62. What is the approximate volume of the following cylinder?

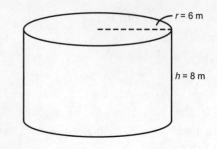

(A) 904 cm³
(B) 301 cm³
(C) 151 cm³
(D) 452 cm³

63. Given the numbers –2, –1, –½, 0, 1, 3, which Venn diagram expresses the characteristics of the numbers correctly by type?

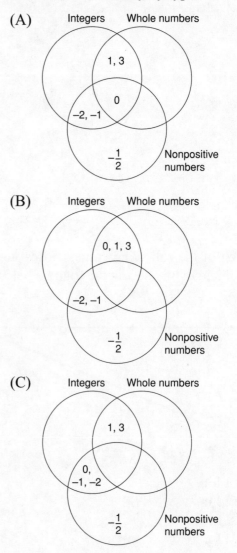

(D)

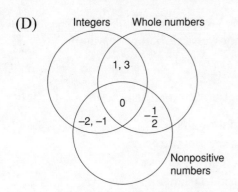

64. The diagram below displays a factor tree for the number x. What is the value of x?

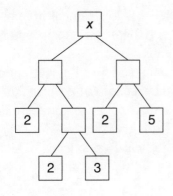

(A) 14
(B) 80
(C) 100
(D) 120

65. Assume that one pig eats 4 pounds of food each week. There are 52 weeks in a year. How much food do 10 pigs eat in a week?

(A) 40 lb.
(B) 520 lb.
(C) 208 lb.
(D) 20 lb.

III. SOCIAL STUDIES

66. A topographical map is one that shows the

(A) population distribution of a region.

(B) climate of a region.
(C) landscape and water of a region.
(D) political boundaries of a region.

67. The culture of a people consists of its

I. religion.
II. language.
III. social organization.

(A) I only
(B) I and II only
(C) II and III only
(D) I, II, and III

68. The monotheism of the ancient Hebrews spread throughout the ancient world and led to the formation of Christianity and Islam. This is an example of

(A) cultural diffusion.
(B) religious homogeneity.
(C) global interdependence.
(D) demographic data.

69. A nomadic lifestyle would most likely be found in the

(A) English countryside.
(B) Scandinavian fjords.
(C) Sahara Desert.
(D) Canadian Rockies.

70. Which of the following are research tools?

I. The library
II. The Internet
III. Interviews

(A) I only
(B) I and II only
(C) I and III only
(D) I, II, and III

71. The term *colonialism* can be used to describe

(A) Spanish conquests in the sixteenth century.
(B) the medieval system of guilds.

(C) Haitian independence from France in 1804.

(D) the sale of indulgences by the Catholic Church.

72. Mr. DeVito's class is studying immigration to the United States. Which concept would be appropriate to introduce?

(A) Divestment

(B) Assimilation

(C) Feudalism

(D) Nationalism

73. Ms. Rodriguez is teaching social studies and outlining skills. What would be the most appropriate heading for the following outline list?

I. _____

A. More government regulation

B. Reform of corrupt political practices

C. Concern for the problems of workers

(A) Reconstruction

(B) The Progressive Era

(C) The Cold War Era

(D) The New Frontier

74. The widespread use of computers has led to national concern over

(A) increased environmental pollution.

(B) guarding the right to privacy.

(C) protection of the right to petition.

(D) a decrease in television viewing.

75. Economic resources include all of the following EXCEPT

(A) land.

(B) labor.

(C) capital.

(D) values.

76. In teaching social studies, a teacher puts these two quotations on the board:

By uniting we stand, by dividing we fall.

—John Dickinson, 1768

Yes, we must all hang together or most assuredly we shall hang separately.

—Benjamin Franklin, 1776

These quotations illustrate the concept of

(A) nationalism.

(B) confederacy.

(C) equality.

(D) totalitarianism.

77. Mr. Galili is teaching about the Civil War and its aftermath in social studies. He explains that the Jim Crow laws were attempts by the

(A) federal government to improve the status of African Americans and Native Americans.

(B) state and local governments to restrict the freedom of African Americans.

(C) states to ban organizations such as the Ku Klux Klan.

(D) Radical Republicans in Congress to carry out reconstruction plans.

78. In announcing the Emancipation Proclamation, Lincoln's immediate purpose was to

(A) free black slaves in all of the slave states.

(B) free black slaves in only the border slave states that had remained loyal to the Union.

(C) let the Southern states know that whether or not they chose to secede from the Union, slavery would not be tolerated by his administration once he took office.

(D) rally Northern morale by giving the war a higher moral purpose than just preserving the Union.

79. Which of the following was NOT associated with the Civil War era?

(A) Morrill Land Grant

(B) Emancipation Proclamation

(C) Manifest Destiny

(D) The Homestead Act

80. Which of the following was NOT a main motivating factor for European explorers?

    (A) Protecting royalty
    (B) Fame and fortune
    (C) Control of trade routes
    (D) Spreading Christianity

81. The United States has a two-party system, while several European governments have a multiparty system. Which of the following statements is true about political parties in the United States but not true about political parties in multiparty European governments?

    (A) Political parties form coalitions in order to advance their policy initiatives through Congress.
    (B) Single-member district voting patterns clearly identify candidates for seats in political offices.
    (C) Parties provide candidates for office and organize campaigns to get the candidate elected.
    (D) Political parties are linked to religious, regional, or social class groupings.

82. In what year did the Salem Witch Trials take place?

    (A) 1492
    (B) 1692
    (C) 1792
    (D) 1592

83. Which of the following best describes the western Pacific region of Canada, comprising British Columbia and the Yukon?

    (A) The area contains many uninhabitable areas, including a mix of arid desert like terrain and rugged mountain ranges that hinder rail and car transportation, resulting in minimal population settlement.

    (B) The area contains arid deserts and vast grasslands that are ideal for cattle farming and oil production.
    (C) The area contains the vast majority of Canada's natural resources and the majority of Canada's population.
    (D) The area contains 50 percent of Canada's population, resulting in 70 percent of Canada's manufacturing.

84. The concept of the division of power between the state governments and the federal government is known as

    (A) separation of church and state.
    (B) socialism.
    (C) federalism.
    (D) feudalism.

85. The New Deal legislation developed to alleviate the strain of the Great Depression on the nation's economy was under which president?

    (A) Franklin D. Roosevelt
    (B) Herbert Hoover
    (C) Theodore Roosevelt
    (D) Harry S. Truman

86. Which of the following would be considered a primary source in researching the factors that influenced U.S. involvement in the Korean War?

    I. The personal correspondence of a military man stationed with the 5th Regimental Combat Team (RCT) in Korea.
    II. A biography of Harry S. Truman by David McCullough, published in 1993.
    III. A journal article about the beginning of the Korean War by a noted scholar.
    IV. An interview with Secretary of Defense George Marshall.

    (A) I and II only
    (B) II and IV only
    (C) II and III only
    (D) I and IV only

87. Which of the following were major causes of the Great Depression?

   I.   Hoarding money greatly reduced the money supply, resulting in higher prices for consumer goods.
   II. The gold standard limited the amount of the money supply, reducing money circulation and causing a drop in prices and wages.
   III. The Smoot-Hawley Tariff Act increased tariffs, which resulted in increased prices for consumer goods.
   IV. The stock market crash reduced the value of companies, causing them to raise prices of consumer goods.

   (A) I and II only
   (B) II and III only
   (C) III and IV only
   (D) I, II, and III

88. Which Revolutionary War battle is considered the turning point in the war because it led to direct French assistance for the Americans?

   (A) Trenton
   (B) Bunker Hill
   (C) Yorktown
   (D) Saratoga

89. Which of the following is NOT one of the five themes of geography?

   (A) Location
   (B) Economic growth
   (C) Human-environmental interaction
   (D) Regions, patterns, and processes

90. According to the feudal system, serfs were

   (A) peasants.
   (B) lords.
   (C) property owners.
   (D) clergy.

91. Martin Luther is associated with which of the following?

   (A) *The Last Supper*
   (B) *Institutes of the Christian Religion*
   (C) *The Prince*
   (D) *95 Theses*

92. Which of the following is the study of the social behavior of humans within a group?

   (A) Sociology
   (B) Anthropology
   (C) Physiology
   (D) Psychology

93. Supply and demand refers to

   (A) resources owned by individuals.
   (B) resources owned collectively by society.
   (C) when society produces the types and quantities of goods that most satisfy its people.
   (D) the availability of resources based on consumer consumption.

94. "The shot heard 'round the world" is associated with which of the following events?

   (A) The settlement of Jamestown
   (B) The Civil War
   (C) The Boston Tea Party
   (D) The Revolutionary War

95. December 7, 1941, is the date of what major event in history?

   (A) The United States drops the atomic bomb on Hiroshima.
   (B) Castro overthrows the Cuban government.
   (C) The Japanese attack Pearl Harbor.
   (D) Rosa Parks refuses to give up her seat.

96. The war powers of Congress include which of the following?

I. Declare war
II. Raise and support armies
III. Provide and maintain a navy
IV. Provide for organizing, arming, and calling forth the militia

(A) I and II only
(B) III only
(C) I, II, III, and IV
(D) II and III only

97. The main purpose of the Monroe Doctrine was to

(A) end European colonial interference in Latin America.
(B) increase U.S. colonial efforts in Asia.
(C) assist Spain in maintaining its Latin American empire.
(D) monitor the 13 colonies.

98. The central banking system of the United States that issues bank notes and lends money to member banks is known as which of the following?

(A) The stock market
(B) The stock exchange
(C) The Federal Reserve
(D) The Bank of the United States

IV. SCIENCE

99. The atmospheres of the moon and other celestial bodies were studied by using telescopes and spectrophotometers long before the deployment of interplanetary space probes. In these studies, scientists used the spectral patterns of sunlight that passed through the atmosphere of distant objects to learn what elements make up those atmospheres. Which of the following explains the source of the black-line spectral patterns?

(A) When an element is excited, it gives off light in a characteristic spectral pattern.
(B) When light strikes an object, some wavelengths of light are absorbed by the surface and others are reflected to give the object its color.
(C) When light passes through a gas, light is absorbed at wavelengths characteristic of the elements in the gas.
(D) The black lines are the spectra of ultraviolet light, which is called black light because it cannot be seen with the human eye.

100. Ms. Rosenberg writes these words on the chalkboard:

Igneous
Sedimentary
Metamorphic

She is going to teach a lesson on
(A) geography.
(B) biology.
(C) chemistry.
(D) geology.

101. A teacher takes a beaker of colored water and pours it from a long, slim vessel into a short, wide vessel. The teacher is illustrating the principle of

(A) natural selection.
(B) deduction.
(C) conservation.
(D) accommodation.

102. The creation of wildlife refuges and the enforcement of game hunting laws are measures of

(A) conservation.
(B) exploitation.
(C) conservatism.
(D) population control.

103. Diagrams, tables, and graphs are used by scientists mainly to

   (A) design a research plan for an experiment.
   (B) test a hypothesis.
   (C) organize data.
   (D) predict an independent variable.

104. Mrs. Korenge is teaching a unit on ecology. She tells her class, "A new type of fuel gives off excessive amounts of smoke. Before this type of fuel is used, an ecologist would most likely want to know

   (A) what effect the smoke will have on the environment."
   (B) how much it will cost to produce the fuel."
   (C) how long it will take to produce the fuel."
   (D) if the fuel will be widely accepted by the consumer."

105. The data table below shows average daily air temperature, wind speed, and relative humidity for four days at a single location.

Day	Air Temperature (°c)	Wind Speed (Mph)	Humidity (%)
Monday	40	15	60
Tuesday	65	10	75
Wednesday	80	20	30
Thursday	85	0	95

On which day was the air closest to being saturated with water vapor?

   (A) Monday
   (B) Tuesday
   (C) Wednesday
   (D) Thursday

106. Ms. Posner is doing a unit on plants with her class. She took three seeds and put them in three different locations. Each seedling was grown in the same soil and each received the same amount of water. At the end of six days, the results were put in this table:

Data Table

Location	Height (cm)	Leaf Color
Sunny windowsill	7	Green
Indirect sunlight	9	Green
Closed closet	11	Whitish yellow

What hypothesis was most likely being tested here?

   (A) A plant grown in the dark will not be green.
   (B) The type of soil a plant is grown in influences how tall it will be.
   (C) Plants need water to grow.
   (D) Plants grown in red light are taller than plants grown in green light.

107. Which of the following is a cone-shaped formation one might find on the floor of a cave?

   (A) Stalactite
   (B) Stalagmite
   (C) Graphite
   (D) None of the above

108. We may be told to "gargle with saltwater" when we suffer from a sore throat. Which of the following phenomena would be used to explain this advice?

   (A) Lowering of vapor pressure
   (B) Increasing osmotic pressure
   (C) Increasing boiling point
   (D) Decreasing freezing point

109. Which of the following is not the direct result of volcanic activity?

    (A) Sedimentary rock
    (B) Igneous rock
    (C) Magma
    (D) Lava

110. Each population lives in a particular area and serves a special role in the community, which is known as its *niche*. For example, the niche of a hawk is to eat mice in fields. Sometimes one population replaces another in a *niche*. This occurrence is known as which of the following?

    (A) Natural selection
    (B) Adaptation
    (C) Conservation
    (D) Succession

111. Which of the following characteristics of a sound wave is associated with its pitch?

    (A) Amplitude
    (B) Frequency
    (C) Wavelength
    (D) Speed

112. The flowchart below shows part of the water cycle. The question marks indicate the part of the flowchart that has been deliberately left blank.

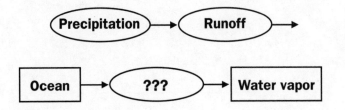

Which process should be shown in place of the question marks to best complete the flowchart?

    (A) Condensation
    (B) Deposition
    (C) Evaporation
    (D) Infiltration

113. Producing and distributing chemicals that aid digestion, growth, and metabolism is known as

    (A) excretion.
    (B) secretion.
    (C) reproduction.
    (D) respiration.

114. The smallest possible uncharged unit of ordinary matter identifiable as an element is

    (A) compound.
    (B) molecule.
    (C) cytoplasm.
    (D) atom.

115. Which of the following directs cell activities and holds DNA?

    (A) Ribosome
    (B) Cell membrane
    (C) Nucleus
    (D) Cell wall

116. A cycling of materials is represented in the diagram below.

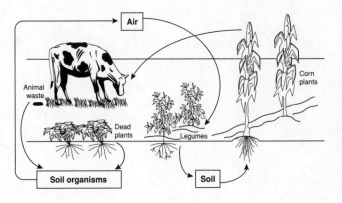

Which of the following statements is supported by the events shown in the diagram?

    (A) Materials are cycled among living organisms only.
    (B) Materials are cycled among heterotrophic organisms only.

(C) Materials are cycled between the living and nonliving components of the environment.

(D) Materials are cycled among the physical factors of the environment by the processes of condensation and evaporation.

117. Over time, mutations within individuals give them differing abilities to adapt and survive to changing environments and habitats. The survival of some individuals who are better able to adapt to change is known as which of the following?

(A) Natural selection
(B) Evolution
(C) Overpopulation
(D) Adaptation

118. To move a heavy book across a tabletop at a constant speed, a person must continually exert a force on the book. This force is primarily used to overcome which of the following forces?

(A) The force of gravity
(B) The force of air resistance
(C) The force of friction
(D) The weight of the book

119. Human body temperature regulation via the skin involves

(A) respiration.
(B) transpiration.
(C) perspiration.
(D) sensation.

120. Photosynthesis ($CO_2 + H_2O \Rightarrow$ glucose + oxygen) is a

(A) reduction process in which oxygen is reduced by a coenzyme.
(B) reduction process in which hydrogen is oxidized by a coenzyme.
(C) reduction process in which hydrogen is reduced by a coenzyme.
(D) reduction process in which oxygen is oxidized by a coenzyme.

Detailed Explanations of Answers for Practice Test 2

ELEMENTARY EDUCATION: CONTENT KNOWLEDGE (0014)

1. (C)	25. (A)	49. (D)	73. (B)	97. (A)
2. (A)	26. (B)	50. (A)	74. (B)	98. (C)
3. (D)	27. (A)	51. (C)	75. (D)	99. (C)
4. (A)	28. (D)	52. (C)	76. (A)	100. (D)
5. (D)	29. (A)	53. (A)	77. (B)	101. (C)
6. (C)	30. (B)	54. (D)	78. (D)	102. (A)
7. (A)	31. (D)	55. (D)	79. (C)	103. (C)
8. (D)	32. (B)	56. (A)	80. (A)	104. (A)
9. (C)	33. (D)	57. (B)	81. (B)	105. (D)
10. (A)	34. (C)	58. (B)	82. (B)	106. (A)
11. (A)	35. (A)	59. (A)	83. (C)	107. (B)
12. (D)	36. (C)	60. (D)	84. (C)	108. (B)
13. (C)	37. (D)	61. (A)	85. (A)	109. (A)
14. (A)	38. (D)	62. (A)	86. (D)	110. (D)
15. (C)	39. (B)	63. (A)	87. (A)	111. (C)
16. (B)	40. (B)	64. (D)	88. (D)	112. (C)
17. (A)	41. (C)	65. (A)	89. (B)	113. (B)
18. (B)	42. (C)	66. (C)	90. (A)	114. (D)
19. (C)	43. (D)	67. (D)	91. (D)	115. (C)
20. (B)	44. (C)	68. (A)	92. (A)	116. (C)
21. (D)	45. (A)	69. (C)	93. (D)	117. (A)
22. (D)	46. (A)	70. (D)	94. (D)	118. (C)
23. (A)	47. (B)	71. (A)	95. (C)	119. (C)
24. (D)	48. (B)	72. (B)	96. (C)	120. (C)

PRACTICE TEST 2 PROGRESS CHART

Language Arts Content   ____/31

1	2	3	4	5	6	7	8	9	10	11

12	13	14	15	16	17	18	19	20	21	22

23	24	25	26	27	28	29	30	31

Mathematics Content   ____/34

32	33	34	35	36	37	38	39	40	41	42	43

44	45	46	47	48	49	50	51	52	53	54	55

56	55	56	57	58	59	60	61	62	63	64	65

Social Studies Content   ____/33

66	67	68	69	70	71	72	73	74	75	76	77

78	79	80	81	82	83	84	85	86	87	88	90

91	92	93	94	95	96	97	98

Science Content   ____/22

99	100	101	102	103	104	105	106	107	108	109

110	111	112	113	114	115	116	117	118	119	120

1. (C)

The verb phrase "will have avoided" implies that an action will occur in the future. However, it is clear that the author is describing what has already happened; therefore, "have avoided" is the correct verb usage.

2. (A)

Sentence 3 ends by describing all of the animals who have made De Witt Isle their home. The best transition to sentence 4 introduces Jane Cooper and then explains why she chose this particular place.

3. (D)

The poem describes a blazing hot environment with cold nights. Plants are small with wide roots, and no mention is made of rain; therefore, it would be a desert. The plants are not the type to be found in a forest, where there would be natural covering from the sun. A swamp would be rainy, and a tundra is a cold, icy environment.

4. (A)

Colloquial language is informal or conversational. The author's use of "The days be hot, the nights be cold" and "Tiz me life that I must save" is nonstandard English; thus, it is considered colloquial. A narrative is a long story, while factual writing, as the name implies, gives readers facts. Metaphors are comparisons without the use of the words *like* or *as*.

5. (D)

A fable is a story that teaches a lesson; therefore, the passage can be classified as a fable. A narrative is generally a long, fictional piece. A character analysis scrutinizes one or more characters that are presented. An editorial gives an opinion on a specific subject.

6. (C)

A limerick is a humorous poem in the rhythm a-a-b-b-a. The first two lines rhyme; the second two lines rhyme; and the last line rhymes with the first two lines. An elegy is a mournful poem. A ballad is a long poem that tells a story. Haiku is a form of poetry with a 17-syllable verse, divided into three units of 5, 7, and 5 syllables.

7. (A)

Alliteration is the repetition of consonant sounds. Onomatopoeia occurs when a word actually sounds like the sound it makes. Imagery is a way to portray something by comparison. Symbolism occurs when a word or phrase represents something else.

8. (D)

Illustrating the poem would allow younger children to visualize its humor, while clapping their hands as the poem is read reinforces its rhythm.

Older children could write their own poems in this style.

"attempted"; in the second sentence, it means "judged."

9. (C)

In an if/then statement, the phrase following the *if* is called the hypothesis and the phrase following the *then* is called the conclusion. Given an original statement, only the contrapositive is guaranteed to have the same truth-value. The contrapositive is obtained by swapping the hypothesis and conclusion phrases and also negating them. *Note:* The negative of "turnips are not blue" is "turnips are blue."

10. (A)

Students speaking two languages learn one of two ways: sequentially, in which one language is mastered before the study of the second language has begun, or simultaneously, in which both languages are learned concurrently (B). Sequential language acquisition does not mean a student learns two languages in parts (C) or develops language skills (D).

11. (A)

The statement tries to influence readers by telling them that all of their friends own this particular item. This device is known as bandwagon. A testimonial is a quote by someone, whether by name or anonymously, that vouches for the product. Card-stacking is the intentional organization and arrangement of material to make one position look good and another position look bad. A glittering generality is the use of an emotionally appealing word or concept to gain approval without thinking.

12. (D)

The two sentences show two meanings for the verb *try*. In the first sentence, the word means

13. (C)

Robinson shows the reader that, although Richard Cory seems to have everything—riches, grace, and the respect of others—he was inwardly very unhappy and committed suicide.

14. (A)

These sentences illustrate the grammatical rule of parallelism. The phrase before the "like" or "as" have to match, or be parallel to the phrase after the "like" or "as." Choice (B) states: "to hike" and "skiing." Choice (C) states: "hiking" and "to ski." Choice (D) gives us "to hike" and "going cross-country skiing." Only choice (A) shows parallelism in its use of "hiking" and "skiing." Therefore, choice (A) is correct.

15. (C)

Choice (C) is correct because these are the definitions of *illiterate* and *functional illiterate* stated in paragraph 2.

16. (B)

Choice (B) is correct because the passage begins by stating that many politicians' wives have expressed interest in literacy.

17. (A)

This question must be answered using the process of elimination. You are asked to select a statement that names a possible program component that is not characteristic of successful literacy programs. Choice (A) is correct because the other choices are specifically mentioned in the passage.

18. (B)

Choice (B) is correct because the author specifically states that politicians should support increased funding for literacy programs.

19. (C)

The passage suggests that education is at present based primarily on failure and negative reinforcement and that, in order to create a more productive and positive learning environment, the emphasis must shift to success.

20. (B)

Axiom in this case is another word for "motto." It can also mean "an accepted truism or principle," which would also apply here. Answers (A), (C), and (D) are erroneous definitions; therefore, (B), university motto, is the correct answer.

21. (D)

The passage states that "the language of failure . . . will have a prohibitive impact on the students' . . . self-esteem," so (D) is the correct answer.

22. (D)

The first paragraph of the passage tells the reader that, in addition to personal expression, language also has the power to persuade and influence.

23. (A)

The purpose of expository writing is to explain and clarify ideas. The purpose of persuasive writing is to convince the reader of something. The purpose of descriptive writing is to provide information about a person, place, or thing. A narrative is a story or an account of an incident or a series of incidents.

24. (D)

A metaphor is a comparison between two items without the use of *like* or *as*. Personification is attributing human characteristics to an inanimate object. A simile is a comparison that uses *like* or *as*. Onomatopoeia is the use of a word that connotes or produces the sound it is meant to convey. The correct answer, onomatopoeia, is (D).

25. (A)

The passage tells of the "great (linguistic) vowel shift" of the early fifteenth century. While the passage speaks of (B), an artistic renaissance; (C), new linguistic freedoms; and (D), effects on artistic expression, these are all results of the shift and not the shift itself. The shift is what the passage is about.

26. (B)

In this case, *linguistic* refers to speaking, talking, verbiage, and/or the act of oration. Choice (B), verbal or rhetorical, is the correct answer.

27. (A)

Answers (B), (C), and (D) are generalized answers resulting from the vowel shift. Choice (A) is a direct result of the shift and is quoted directly from the passage.

28. (D)

A teaching apprentice would be expected to lay the foundation for her lecture and then present greater detail by way of example, or as the passage puts it, "illustration." Someone in this position, having set this task for herself, would not be prone to refuting her own lecture notes; attempting to cause confusion; or, perhaps least of all, working to subvert the lecture topic she herself had elected to teach.

29. (A)

The definition of the term *pedagogical* is "academic." Answers (B), "abstract"; (C), "meaningless"; and (D), "obtuse," are incorrect.

30. (B)

The author's classroom experience was answer (B), intelligible (understandable) and pragmatic (practical or utilitarian). The passage gives credence to this by the author's use of such words as "clear and well-prepared."

31. (D)

A metaphor is not a type or form of poetry, so (D) is the correct answer. Metaphors are figures of speech that help create imagery in poems or other forms of writing. Limericks, couplets, and free verse are all types or forms of poetry.

32. (B)

A stem-and-leaf plot shows the data in numerically increasing order. The leaf is the last digit to the right, and the stem is the remaining digit or digits disregarding the leaf. For example, given the number 27, 7 is the leaf, 2 is the stem.

Stem	Leaf
2	7

33. (D)

The counting principle states the following:

If there are m different ways to choose a first event and n different ways to choose a second event, then there are $m \times n$ different ways of choosing the first event followed by the second event.

There are three stages in this example:

Stage 1   taco or burrito   2 choices

Stage 2   filling   3 choices

Stage 3   beverage   6 choices

Total possible different outcomes: $2 \times 3 \times 6 = 36$.

34. (C)

Successful events are multiples of 3. This includes 6, 9, and 18. There are three successful events. The total number of possible outcomes is 8.

The probability of landing on a multiple of $3 = \frac{3}{8}$.

35. (A)

The plane travels 600 kilometers in 1 hour. To travel 120 kilometers, you need $\frac{1}{5}$ of an hour, or 0.2 hour. 120 is what part of 600? Write it as a fraction:

120/600, which reduces to $\frac{1}{5}$. Change to a decimal by dividing 1.00 by 5 = 0.2.

36. (C)

Nathan studied for 8 hours and 37 minutes. Answer (C) is correct. One way to calculate elapsed time is to start with the hours: 8 hours elapse from 9:45 P.M. to 5:45 A.M.; 15 minutes elapse from 5:45 to 6:00 A.M.; 22 minutes elapse from 6:00 to 6:22 A.M. Add the 15 minutes to the 22 minutes for a total of 37 minutes. Add this to the 8 hours for the total time spent studying.

37. (D)

The sweater's price was cut by half. Therefore, it needs to be doubled to sell at the original price. For example,

Original price: $20.00

50 percent sale: $10.00

To go back to the original price, you must double the sale price, which is the same as increasing it by 100 percent.

38. (D)

We establish a proportion relating the number of people to the ounces of angel-hair pasta. The proportion would be $\frac{4}{10} = \frac{12}{x}$. Then cross multiply and divide by 4.

39. (B)

The order of operations requires us to do all operations within grouping symbols first. A parenthesis is a grouping symbol. The first operation to be performed is $4 - 2$.

40. (B)

Four of the twenty people chose milk. That is, $\frac{4}{20}$, or $\frac{1}{5}$, of the people chose milk. Consequently, $\frac{1}{5}$ of the 360° pie chart should be associated with milk.

41. (C)

The blue and the brown comprise $\frac{1}{2} + \frac{1}{5}$ of the tie. Use 10 as the lowest common denominator. Thus, the blue and brown make up $\frac{7}{10}$ of the tie. The balance $\left(1 - \frac{7}{10}\right) = \frac{3}{10}$ belongs to the burgundy.

42. (C)

Properties of a parallelogram include:

- The sum of its angles equals 360°.
- Opposite sides are equal.
- Opposite sides are parallel.
- Opposite angles are equal.
- Adjacent angles are supplementary (add to 180°).
- Diagonals bisect each other.

Diagonals are equal only if the parallelogram is a rectangle.

43. (D)

Diminished means "made smaller." This implies subtraction; therefore, a number n diminished by 5 means $n - 5$. Three more than 7 times the number n is $7n + 3$, and finally, *is* means "equals." Putting it all together, $n - 5 = 7n + 3$.

44. (C)

6 to the 6th power is $6 \times 6 \times 6 \times 6 \times 6 \times 6$, or 46,656. It is not 36, which would be only 6×6, or 6^2. Choice (B), or 66, represents placing the 6 beside another 6; that is not the correct answer. The answer 7,776 represents 6 only to the 5th power.

45. (A)

A bar graph works well here. The height of each of the five bars is determined by the number of votes for each lunch food. A circle or pie chart could also be used. The 18 votes for pizza give the fraction $\frac{18}{40}$, so pizza would be assigned 45% of the area of a circle chart, or 162°. The same approach would tell us the appropriate size of each lunch food's slice of the pie chart. A scatter plot illustrates the relationship between sets of data. A broken-line graph generally illustrates change over time. Neither is appropriate for illustrating the given data.

46. (A)

The correct answer is 124. After moving the decimal, a whole number answer is needed.

47. (B)

One way to approach the problem is to examine each scenario for reasonableness. Even though a runner's mile-by-mile pace in a marathon varies up and down, the runner continually increases the distance covered, and the graph will always move upward, so situation I doesn't go with the graph. The number of households a census taker has left to visit decreases with each visit, so situation II doesn't fit either. Both situations III and IV are examples of steady growth, so both match the graph.

48. (B)

Just from looking at the graph, it's clear that most of the space under the curve is past the 60 mark on the x-axis, so answer (D) is eliminated because it doesn't include statement I. Statement II can't be answered by what the graph shows. It appears possible that certain questions were too hard for many in the class and that there weren't enough questions to differentiate B students from C students, but perhaps the class performed exactly as it should have, given the students' ability and Ms. Alvarez's teaching. The distribution can give a teacher many clues about the test and the students, and even herself, but by itself, it tells us nothing about the fairness of the test. Thus, answer (A) can be eliminated. Statement III is also false; in left-skewed distributions such as this one, the median is higher than the mean. This is true because the mean is lowered by the lowest scores, while the median is relatively unaffected by them. Statement IV is true: one fairly large group has scored in the high 80s and 90s and another discernible group in the low to mid-60s, whereas few students fall outside these two groups. Thus, the answer has to be (B).

49. (D)

Using the rules for solving one-variable equations, the original equation is transformed as follows:

$$\frac{x}{3} - 9 = 15$$

Adding 9 to each side of the equation gives $\frac{x}{3} = 24$.

Multiplying both sides by 3 gives $x = 72$.

50. (A)

Again, using the rules for solving one-variable equations produces these transformations:

$$3x - 11 = 1$$

Adding 11 to each side of the equation gives

$$3x^2 = 12$$

Dividing both sides by 3 gives

$$x^2 = 4$$

Next, find the square roots of 4: 2 and –2.

The solutions can be checked by substituting them (one at a time) into the original equation to see if they work. In this case, both 2 and –2 work.

51. (C)

Let r be the length of the radius of each of the small circles and let R be the length of the radius of the large circle. Then, $R = 3r$. The area of each of the small circles is $\pi r^2 = 9\pi$. Now divide both sides of the equation by π:

$$r^2 = 9, r = 3.$$

Then,

$$R = 3r = 3 \times 3 = 9.$$

Therefore, the circumference of the large circle is

$$C = 2\pi R = 2\pi \times 9 = 18\pi.$$

52. (C)

One way to arrive at the answer is to set up a proportion, with one corner labeled x:

$$\frac{31}{x} = \frac{5.5}{100}$$

To complete the proportion (and to find the answer), cross-multiply 31 and 100, giving 3,100, then divide by 5.5, giving approximately 564.

53. (A)

The value 0.5 is equivalent to $\frac{5}{10}$ or $\frac{1}{2}$. That means that 0.5 percent (which is one way to read the original numeral) is the same as one-half of 1 percent, so answer I is correct.

One-half of 1 percent is not the same as 5 percent, so answer II cannot be correct.

$\frac{1}{200}$ is equivalent to 0.5 percent. Here's why: 1 percent is equivalent to $\frac{1}{100}$. Half of 1 percent (0.5 percent, as noted above) is $\frac{.5}{100}$; therefore, answer III is correct. Choice IV is not correct because 0.05 is equivalent to 5 percent, which is not the same as .5 percent. Therefore, only I and III [choice (A)] are correct.

54. (D)

The y-intercept of a linear equation is the point at which its graph passes through, or intercepts, the vertical y-axis. One way to determine the y-intercept is by rewriting the equation in y-intercept form:

$$y = mx + b$$

If a linear equation is in that form, b tells you where the graph of the line intercepts the y-axis. In this case, you rewrite (or transform) the equation following these steps:

$$2x = 3y - 12$$

Switch around to	$3y - 12 = 2x$
Add 12 to both sides	$3y - 12 + 12 = 2x + 12$
Simplify	$3y = 2x + 12$
Divide by 3	$y = \frac{2}{3}x + 4$

That final version of the equation is indeed in y-intercept form. The 4 tells you that the graph of the equation intercepts the y-axis at point (0, 4).

$$c^2 = 146$$
$$c = \sqrt{146} \approx 12$$

55. (D)

It is helpful to make a sketch of the line on the coordinate plane. (To do that you need to know how to plot individual points.) The line "travels" from the lower left to the upper right, meaning that it has a positive slope. Statement II is therefore true. The y-intercept of a line is the spot at which the line crosses, or intercepts, the vertical axis. In this case, that's at point (0, 4). (You can simply say that the y-intercept is 4, without mentioning the 0.) Statement IV is therefore true as well. A second way to determine slope is to use the slope formula, which would give you $\frac{4-0}{0-(-6)} = \frac{4}{6} = \frac{2}{3}$ which is positive.

56. (A)

Consider various random points in the shaded area: (5, –2), (–1, 2), (12, 2.5), and (–9, 1). Notice that all points in the shaded area have a y-coordinate value less than 3. The inequality that states this fact is the one in (A) ("y is less than 3").

57. (B)

Use the Pythagorean theorem to compute the length of any side of any right triangle, as long as you know the lengths of the other two sides. Here is the theorem: For any right triangle with side lengths of a, b, and c, and where c is the length of the hypotenuse (the longest side, and the one opposite the right angle), $c^2 = a^2 + b^2$.

$$c^2 = 11^2 + 5^2$$

or

58. (B)

First, it is helpful to view the shaded area as the area of the square minus the area of the circle. With that in mind, you simply need to find the area of each simple figure, and then subtract one from the other.

You know that the radius of the circle is 6 units in length. That tells you that the diameter of the circle is 12 units. Because the circle is inscribed in the square (meaning that the circle fits inside the square touching in as many places as possible), you see that the sides of the square are each 12 units in length. Knowing that, you compute the area of the square as 144 square units (12 × 12).

Using the formula for finding the area of a circle (πr^2), and using 3.14 for π, you get approximately 113 square units (3.14 × 6 × 6). Then, you subtract 113 (the area of the circle) from 144 (the area of the square) for the answer of 31.

59. (A)

To answer the question, you must recognize that triangles ADB and AEC are similar triangles, meaning that they have the same shape. That also means that the corresponding angles of the two triangles are the same, or congruent, and that corresponding sides of the two triangles are proportional. Given that, you can set up the following proportion, where x is the distance from point A to point C:

$$\frac{3}{7} = \frac{5}{x}$$

Solving the proportion by cross multiplication, you see that the length of segment AC is about 11.7. Knowing that the length of segment AB is 7 feet, you subtract to find the length of BC (11.7 – 7 = 4.7).

60. (D)

You should first count the number of spaces on the dial: There are 10. Five spaces equals 90 units, and 90 divided by 5 is 18 units. Each space is worth 18 units. The needle points to about halfway between marks 6 and 7. Thus, one-half of 18, plus 6 times 18, is 117. Choice (D) is the correct reading.

61. (A)

The distributive property (of multiplication over addition) can be demonstrated algebraically as

$$a(b + c) = ab + bc$$

The diagrams in the example display as follows:

$$2(9) = 18$$

$$2(3 + 6) = 18$$

$$2(3) + 2(6) = 18$$

62. (A)

The formula for finding the volume of a cylinder is:

$$V = \pi r^2 h$$

This means that the volume is equal to π (about 3.14) times the measure of the radius squared, times the height of the cylinder. In this case, that's

$$3.14 \times 6^2 \times 8$$

or

$$3.14 \times 36 \times 8$$

or about 904 cm. (Note that the final answer is given in cubic centimeters.)

63. (A)

Venn diagrams are overlapping circles that display elements of different sets. They show ele-

ments common to more than one set as well as elements unique to only one set.

$$-2, -1, 0, 1, 3 \text{ are integers}$$

$$-2, -1, -\tfrac{1}{2}, 0 \text{ are nonpositive numbers (Note:}$$
Zero is neither positive nor negative.)

$$0, 1, 3 \text{ are whole numbers}$$

64. (D)

A factor tree decomposes an integer into its prime factors by continuously factoring a given number into two factors until there are no further factors other than 1 and the number. For example, the factor tree for 12 appears as follows:

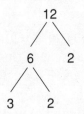

To work a factor tree backward (from the bottom up), multiply the factors to obtain the composite number they come from.

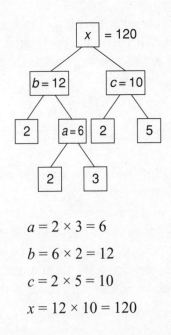

$$a = 2 \times 3 = 6$$

$$b = 6 \times 2 = 12$$

$$c = 2 \times 5 = 10$$

$$x = 12 \times 10 = 120$$

65. (A)

Here one must use only needed information. Do not be distracted by superfluous data. Simple multiplication will do. If one pig eats four pounds of food per week, how much will 10 pigs eat in one week? $10 \times 4 = 40$ pounds. The problem intentionally contains superfluous data (52 weeks), which should not distract the reader from its easy solution. Ratio and proportion will also work here:

$$\frac{1}{10} = \frac{4}{x},$$

$x = 40$ pounds per week

66. (C)

The topography of a region is specifically the nature of its landscape—mountains, deserts, plateaus, oceans, and lakes. Population distribution would be shown on a demographic map. Climate and political boundaries are separate entities.

67. (D)

The culture of a people is the way in which the people live. It encompasses their religion, language, social organization, customs, traditions, and economic organization.

68. (A)

Cultural diffusion refers to the extending of an aspect of culture from one area to another and its inclusion in the culture(s) of other people. Religious homogeneity is the similitude of religion, not its spread. Global interdependence refers to the importance of one country to another, usually in terms of economics. Demographics is the study of population trends.

69. (C)

A nomadic lifestyle is one in which people do not settle in one area; instead, they roam from place to place and set up temporary living arrangements in each place. The desert is an area of nomadic lifestyle because it generally does not support agriculture and does not have sufficient water for people to settle in one place permanently.

70. (D)

The library offers the student books, articles, journals, and so on, with which to do research. The Internet is a very useful tool because of its convenience and its access to hundreds of sites. Interviews with relevant people can offer an important glimpse into the personal stories or issues of a topic.

71. (A)

Colonialism is the extension of a nation's rule beyond its borders by the establishment of settlements in which indigenous populations are directly ruled or displaced. Colonizers generally dominate the resources, labor, and markets of the colonial territory. In the sixteenth century, Spain extended its rule to parts of North America, South America, and the Caribbean. Guilds were the forerunners of modern trade unions, a system in which people who practiced similar crafts joined together. Haiti's independence from France removed the colonialism that France had imposed upon this island. Indulgences were practices of the Catholic Church in medieval times in which Catholics bought pardons from the church.

72. (B)

Assimilation is the process in which a minority racial, cultural, religious, or national group becomes part of the dominant cultural group. Divestment occurs when a country removes itself, whether it is economically, militarily, or socially, from something in which it had previously invested. Feudalism was a system in which people were protected by lords in exchange for their labor. Nationalism, or patriotism, is the feeling of pride and belonging that people have for their country.

73. (B)

The Progressive Era in the early twentieth century can be described as one in which government concerned itself with reform. The progressives, as they called themselves, worked to make American society a better and safer place in which to live. They tried to make big business more responsible through regulations of various kinds. They worked to clean up corrupt city governments, to improve working conditions in factories, and to improve living conditions for those who lived in slum areas, a large number of who were recent immigrants.

74. (B)

A great concern of educators, parents, and the general public is privacy in using computers. The Internet is a vast worldwide network, and users worry that what is sent over the Internet may not be secure.

75. (D)

Economic resources are those that provide goods and services to people. Economic resources are considered to be scarce, while wants are unlimited. Therefore, land, labor, and capital are considered resources, while values are not goods or services that are limited.

76. (A)

Both speakers are referring to the colonies that were later to become the United States of America. This feeling of togetherness and pride for one's country is called nationalism. Confederacy occurs when one group joins in opposition to another. Totalitarianism is the rule by a dictator—the antithesis of these quotes; while equality denotes equal rights.

77. (B)

The Jim Crow laws were in existence from the 1880s (post–Civil War) to the 1960s. A majority of American states enforced segregation using these laws. States and cities could impose legal punishment on people for a variety of "infractions" dealing with African Americans. Intermarriage between the races was forbidden, and in both the public and private sectors, blacks and whites were separated.

78. (D)

Lincoln's immediate purpose in announcing the Emancipation Proclamation was to rally flagging Northern morale. Lincoln waited until after a major Union victory, at Antietam in 1862, so he couldn't be charged with making the announcement as an act of desperation. He recognized that the costs of the war had reached a point where preserving the Union would not be a powerful enough reason to motivate many Northerners to continue the war. Framing the war as a war against slavery would mobilize powerful abolitionist forces in the North and perhaps create an atmosphere of a holy crusade rather than one of using war to resolve a political conflict. While the Emancipation Proclamation had the announced purpose of freeing the slaves, Lincoln himself indirectly stated that freeing the slaves was a means to a greater end, preserving the Union.

79. (C)

The Morrill Land Grant, Emancipation Proclamation, and The Homestead Act were all parts of the post–Civil War Reconstruction efforts. Manifest Destiny refers to the belief in the expansion of the American nation to the Pacific Ocean and beyond.

80. (A)

Exploration was based on many motivating factors. Some sought fame and fortune, others wanted control of the trade routes, and others sought adventure. Many explorers had religion as their main incentive, either the desire to spread the word or to find freedom from persecution. While royal figures sponsored and encouraged voyages, protecting royalty was not a central motivating factor for exploration. (A) is the correct answer.

81. (B)

Multiparty systems use an electoral system based on proportional representation. Therefore, each party gets legislative seats in proportion to the votes it receives. In the United States, the candidate who receives a plurality of the votes is declared the winner.

82. (B)

In Salem, Massachusetts, a group of young girls accused servants from West India and older white members of the community, mostly women, of exercising powers that Satan had given to them. Other towns also experienced turmoil and charged residents with witchcraft. In Salem alone, the juries pronounced 19 people guilty; in 1692, after the execution of all 19 victims, the girls admitted their stories were not true.

83. (C)

The western or Pacific Coast of Canada is known as the Cordillera region. It receives an exceptional amount of rain and includes some of the tallest and oldest trees in Canada, similar to northern California. The area is full of rugged mountains with high plateaus and desert-like areas.

84. (C)

Separation of church and state refers to the idea that church administration and public administration should be under different authorities. Socialism is an economic system in which the basic means of production are primarily owned and controlled collectively. Feudalism is a concept of land management in which lords pledge service to the king in order to maintain title to their lands. Division of power between the state governments and the federal government is known as federalism. This is the constitutional framework in which all power not given to the federal government is reserved for the states.

85. (A)

In his inaugural address, Roosevelt assured the nation that "the only thing we have to fear is fear itself." He called a special session of Congress from March 9 to June 16, 1933, which passed a great body of legislation that has left a lasting mark on the nation. Historians have divided Roosevelt's legislation into the First New Deal (1933–1935) and a new wave of programs beginning in 1935 called the Second New Deal.

86. (D)

Both the personal correspondence of a military man stationed with the 5th RCT in Korea and an interview with Secretary of Defense George Marshall are primary sources because they involve correspondence or testimony from individuals who were actually involved in the Korean War.

87. (A)

A limited money supply and rising prices were major causes of the Great Depression. The money supply was most affected by the gold standard, and the Smoot-Hawley Tariff Act further affected consumer prices.

88. (D)

The battle at Saratoga marked the end to a British three-pronged campaign to split New England from the other colonies. With the surrender of Burgoyne's army, the Americans had won a major victory and captured an entire British army. This victory gave the French the evidence they needed that the Americans could actually win the war, and gave them a chance to avenge their loss to the British in the Seven Years' War. The French now recognized the American government and declared war on England.

89. (B)

The five themes of geography are (1) place; (2) location; (3) human-environmental interaction; (4) movement and connections; and (5) regions, patterns and processes.

90. (A)

According to the feudal system, serfs or peasants served the landlords who owned the land they worked.

91. (D)

Martin Luther authored the *95 Theses*. Leonardo da Vinci painted *The Last Supper*. John Calvin wrote *Institutes of the Christian Religion. The Prince* was written by Machiavelli.

92. (A)

Sociology is the study of the social behaviors of human beings in group settings.

93. (D)

The economic principle of supply and demand refers to the availability of resources based on consumer consumption.

94. (D)

In Lexington, Mass., 77 local minutemen (trained militiamen who would respond at a moment's notice) and others, having been alerted by Paul Revere's ride and other communications, awaited the British on the village green. A shot was fired; it is unknown which side fired first, but this became "the shot heard 'round the world."

95. (C)

December 7, 1941, marks the attack on Pearl Harbor. The United States dropped the atomic bomb on Hiroshima on August 6, 1945. Fidel Castro overthrew the dictator-led government in Cuba in January 1959. On December 11, 1955, Rosa Parks refused to give up her seat on the bus to protest discriminatory laws.

96. (C)

The war powers of Congress include the right to declare war; raise and support armies; provide and maintain a navy; and provide for organizing, arming, and calling forth the militia.

97. (A)

The main purpose of the Monroe Doctrine was to stop European colonial interference in Latin America. In December 1823, President Monroe included in his annual message to Congress a statement that the peoples of the American hemisphere were "henceforth not to be considered as subjects for future colonization by any European powers."

98. (C)

The Federal Reserve issues bank notes, lends money to member banks, maintains reserves, supervises member banks, and helps set the national monetary policy. The stock market is the mechanism that enables the trading of company stocks. It is different from the stock exchange, which is a corporation in the business of bringing together stock buyers and sellers. The Bank of the United States was proposed by Alexander Hamilton to standardize currency and manage the debt created by the Revolutionary War.

99. (C)

All of the choices are true, but only choice (C) addresses the exercise. Black line spectra are formed when the continuous spectra of the sun passes through the atmosphere. The elements in the atmosphere absorb wavelengths of light characteristic of their spectra (these are the same wavelengths given off when the element is excited—for example, the red color of a neon light). By examining the line spectral gaps, scientists can deduce the elements that make up the distant atmosphere. Choice (A) is true, but it explains the source of a line spectrum. Choice (B) is true, and it explains why a blue shirt is blue when placed under a white or blue light source. Recall that a blue shirt under a red light source will appear black because there are no blue wavelengths to be reflected. Choice (D) is partially true because black lights do give off ultraviolet light that the human eye cannot see.

100. (D)

Igneous, *sedimentary*, and *metamorphic* are terms that describe varieties of rocks; therefore, they would be taught in a lesson on geology, which is the study of the earth's history.

101. (C)

The law of conservation states that a material will have the same volume regardless of the shape of the container in which it is placed. Accommodation and its sister concept, assimilation, is the way in which one incorporates new information into one's way of thinking. Piaget is the Swiss psychologist who did experimental work on these concepts. Natural selection is a Darwinian concept stating that a species will naturally evolve to retain useful adaptive characteristics. Deduction is a method of reasoning.

102. (A)

Wildlife refuges are places specifically created so that animals can have a safe haven. Similarly, game hunting laws prevent hunters from killing animals indiscriminately. Exploitation is the opposite: It means using a resource for our own ends, regardless of the effects on the resource. Conservatism is a political point of view that espouses keeping the status quo in society.

103. (C)

Diagrams, tables, and graphs are different ways to display information. These would be most useful in organizing that information. They would not assist in making predictions, testing a hypothesis, or designing a research plan, but they could be helpful in any of these endeavors.

104. (A)

An ecologist is concerned about environmental issues; therefore, he or she would be most interested in the effect of the fuel's smoke emissions. Cost and time factors do not concern the environmentalist. Similarly, consumer acceptance is not the domain of the environmentalist.

105. (D)

Relative humidity measures the percentage of water vapor in the air. The higher the humidity, the more water vapor exists in the air. Thursday had the highest relative humidity (95%), so (D) is the correct answer.

106. (A)

The variable in this experiment is light. The three plants were given different amounts of light, so choice (A) is the correct answer. The plants were grown in the same soil and given the same amount of water. The experiment does not deal with red light.

107. (B)

A stalagmite is a cone-shaped deposit form on the floor of the cave; (B) is the correct answer. A stalactite is an icicle-shaped lime deposit hanging from the roof or sides of a cave. Graphite is the material found in a pencil.

108. (B)

Salt is a strong electrolyte that completely dissociates in solution. When this solution is in contact with a semipermeable membrane, like the inflamed cells in the throat, water moves across the membrane from the side with the lowest solute concentration to the side of higher solute concentration. In the case of the sore throat, water from inside the inflamed cells moves out toward the higher concentration salt water, and the throat cells shrink due to the loss of water. All the items listed are colligative properties that, like osmotic pressure, are a function of the number, but not the nature, of particles in solution.

109. (A)

Sedimentary rock may be formed by pressure over a period of time; it is not always the direct result of volcanic activity. (A) is the correct answer. Igneous rock is formed from heat and can be the result of volcanic activity. Magma is molten rock within the earth; it may pour forth during a volcanic eruption. Lava is a product of a volcanic eruption.

110. (D)

Natural selection occurs when the stronger or more advantageous traits of a species are continued through reproduction. An adaptation is a structure or behavior that increases a living thing's ability to survive and reproduce. Conservation is the practice of using natural areas without disrupting their ecosystems. The correct answer is (D). Succession is the orderly and predictable change of communities as a result of population replacement in niches.

111. (C)

The frequency of a wave is associated with pitch. Middle C has a frequency of 440 cycles per second. However, wavelength and frequency are directly related by the relationship $v = c / \lambda$, where v (nu) is the frequency, c is the speed of sound, and λ (lambda) is wavelength.

112. (C)

To turn water (a liquid) into water vapor (a gas) the process of evaporation must occur. Condensation is the reverse—turning a gas into a liquid. Deposition occurs when something is deposited in an area, and infiltration is the process by which one item permeates another item.

113. (B)

Secretion is the process of producing and distributing chemicals that aid digestion, growth, and metabolism. Excretion is the elimination of wastes. Reproduction is the process of making new living things. Respiration is the process of exchanging gases.

114. (D)

The atom is the smallest possible uncharged unit of ordinary matter, so (D) is the answer. While a molecule (B) is also fundamental to matter, it is larger than an atom. A compound (A) is a combination of two or more elements, which cannot be smaller than an atom. A cytoplasm (C) is the jelly-like substance inside a cell.

115. (C)

The nucleus directs cell activities and holds the DNA. A ribosome makes protein from amino acids. The cell membrane controls movement of materials in and out of the cell. The cell wall gives rigid structure to plant cells.

116. (C)

The diagram shows cycling among air, legumes, soil organisms, dead plants, live plants, and animals. This means that the cycling occurs between the living and nonliving parts of the environment.

117. (A)

The survival of some individuals who are better able to adapt to change is known as natural selection. This concept is also explained as "survival of the fittest."

118. (C)

The force of friction between the book and the table is the primary force that must be overcome to move the book. An experiment to study these frictional forces could keep all other variables (size and weight of the book, speed of travel) constant while measuring the force needed to move the book using a spring scale. Different experiments could change the surface of the book by covering the book with wax paper, construction paper, or sandpaper.

119. (C)

The body regulated water and heat through perspiration. Transpiration describes a process not involving humans. Thus, (B) is not correct. Respiration (A) is breathing in humans and will cause some water loss. However, the question asks how the body regulated substances through the skin. (D), sensation, is the ability to process or perceive. The skin does have nerve endings that can sense, but this does not involve temperature or water regulation.

120. (C)

The answer is (C) because by definition photosynthesis is the chemical reaction that results in a reduction.

Index

PRAXIS 0014